PLANNING FROM BELOW

PLANNING *from* BELOW

A Decentralized Participatory Planning Proposal
VOLUMES I AND II

Marta Harnecker and José Bartolomé
with the collaboration of Noel López

Translated by FEDERICO FUENTES

MONTHLY REVIEW PRESS
New York

Library of Congress Cataloging-in-Publication Data available from the publisher

ISBN 978-1-58367-755-1 paperback
ISBN 978-1-58367-756-8 cloth

Originally published by Centro de Investigaciones "Memoria Popular Latinoamericana"
Havana, Cuba, February 2018.
Series: Socialismo del siglo XXI
Sub-series: Planificando desde abajo No. 2

Marta Harnecker and José Bartolomé
Planning from Below: A guide for decentralized participatory planning
Volumes I: Theoretical Aspects; Volume II: Methodological Aspects

MONTHLY REVIEW PRESS, NEW YORK, NEW YORK

monthlyreview.org

TABLE OF CONTENTS

VOLUME I. PLANNING FROM BELOW. A PROPOSAL OF DECENTRALIZED PARTICIPATORY PLANNING. THEORETICAL ASPECTS

VOLUME II. PLANNING FROM BELOW: A PROPOSAL OF DECENTRALIZED PARTICIPATORY PLANNING. METHODOLOGICAL ASPECTS

FOREWORD

Democratic decentralisation and popular participation in the development process were important elements of the agenda of the first communist government elected after the formation of the new state of Kerala, India in 1957. However, comprehensive legislation for empowering local governments was abandoned after the communist government was dismissed by the Centre Cabinet following violent anti communist agitations by right wing forces. Kerala had to wait four decades until the victory of the Left Democratic Front (LDF}in the 1996 state elections for this dream to become a reality.

By then the national parliament had amended the Indian Constitution making the local governments as a mandatory and uniform third tier of governance below the Central and the State governments. The Left in Kerala utilised this opportunity for large scale mass mobilisation for initiating decentralised planning and to empower the local government structure. More than a third of the state plan budget for new projects and schemes were devolved to the local governments. But they had to prepare comprehensive local plans before they could claim the allotted funds. Procedures were laid down to ensure that the process to develop these plans was inclusive, participatory and scientific. Thus, a hitherto technical planning process was turned into a tool for social mobilisation at several levels, all the way to the grassroots. This movement was called Peoples Plan Campaign (PPC).

As the then Kerala Planning Board Member in charge of the PPC, I was totally engrossed in this process. But at that point I had not yet read about the international experiences of participatory planning. The PPC was a home grown project and the experience that we were relying on was our own. Firstly, the numerous micro development experiments that were blossoming in the region, particularly initiated by Peoples Science Movement. The second source of inspiration was the studies of the academics and researchers in institutions such as Centre for Development Studies (CDS) in Kerala. Finally, the political debates within the Communist Movement, and the aggressive stand of veteran communist leaders like EMS Namboodiripad in favour of decentralisation, provided the political vision. It was therefore a surprise for me to know that similar experiments were successfully carried out in Latin America, and that it was in fact an important component of Left political parties inthe reg10n.

Later, there were opportunities to exchange ideas about the experiences elsewhere. For instance, I heard of the experiments in Porto Alegre through my participation at a conference in Wisconsin, USA. Subsequently my book on participatory planning experiences of Kerala was translated and published in Spanish and Portuguese.I had known of Marta as an advisor to the Government of Hug·o Chavez in Venezuela and had a great interest in meeting her. I had an invitation to attend the Conference of Intellectuals, Artists and Social Movements in Defence of Humanity held in Venezuela in 2004, but was unable to travel there. Finally, I met Marta when she travelled to India in March 2014, which is also when I came to know about her books and videos on participatory planning.

During that visit, she travelled across Kerala to understand the process that had taken place here. She interacted with local government representatives, academics, visited cooperatives and we had long discussions and debates on the vision for 21st century socialism. Marta has this student-like curiosity to understand intimately how things were done so that beyond the broad framework, she is able to relate with the experience of a process she seeks to understand. But what struck me most was that she was not working on a theoretical monograph, but on a more practical manual on how best to democratise political processes on the ground.

For socialism to succeed, in the future, it will need a high level of popular participation. It is fulfilling that from mere objects, people can become active agents of their political and social life. There is a lesson in the fact that where the Left is strong, this democratisation agenda is present; this democratisation does not have to wait for socialism to be a reality, rather it can be a powerful instrument in the struggle for socialism. We know how to utilise parliamentary democracy and constitutional rights to mobilise and organise people.pre

Participatory planning deepens the democratic content of our struggles and therefore has the potential to strengthen mobilisation for progressive transformation.

Thus the design of the decentralisation process is very important, along with adequate tools that can be readily understood and used. Building on systematic learning from experiences in different countries, this book offers exactly that.

Such a process of progressive transformation is in constant need to reinvent itself to avoid routinisation and bureaucratic capture and to ensure that one is addressing a ground situation that is always in flux. I cannot emphasise enough, the relevance to have such a perceptive scrutiny of the Kerala experience, as well as provide a comparative analysis of similar experiences.

Finally, it is commendable that despite being faced with immense challenges on the health front, Marta remains consistently involved in our common and collective struggle for progressive transformation towards socialism.

This book is a testimony to her resolve for a just and better world.

—DR. T. M. THOMAS ISSAC
Finance Minister of Kerala State, India
March 2018

PREFACE

1. This book is aimed at those who want to build a humanist and solidarity-based society. A society based on the greatest possible participation of the people. A society built on a model of sustainable development that is directed towards satisfying people's genuine needs equitably, and not the artificial wants created by capitalism in its irrational drive to obtain more profits. A

society that does all this while ensuring that humanity's future is not put at risk. A society in which the organized people decide what and how to produce.

2. The issue therefore, is how to achieve complete and active protagonism?[1] How can we guarantee, as much as possible, that all citizens, and not just activists or leftists, take an interest in participation? How can we achieve the participation of middle class sectors alongside popular sectors? How can we ensure that solidarity prevails over selfish interests? How can we respond to the concerns of the most disadvantaged and neglected people?

3. The authors of this book are convinced that it is through what we have called "decentralized participatory planning" that we can achieve these objectives. We have reached this conclusion not on the basis of books or academic debates, but largely through studying first-hand a range of practical experiences in participatory budgets and participatory planning.

4. We were attracted to the experience of participatory budgeting undertaken by the regional Workers' Party government in Porto Alegre, Brazil, because we saw it as a new, non-corrupt, transparent way of governing that delegated meaningful power to the people.

5. In Venezuela, we got a strong sense of how individuals and the collective subject flourished as a result of former president Hugo Chavez's initiative to promote the creation of communal councils — small community governments— and grant them resources for small projects. This was not done in a populist manner, with the state coming in and resolving a community's problem for them; rather it was the result of a process of participatory planning, whereby citizens in the community carried out what Chavez called "the communal cycle." This involved a diagnosis of the situation in the community, the development of a plan and budget, the implementation of a project, and the monitoring, evaluation and control over the carrying out of the project. And all this in small geographical spaces made up of no more than 2 thousand inhabitants.

6. Without a doubt, I was also taught some vital lessons from the practical experiences I was directly involved in during my stay in Venezuela, both in Libertador municipality in the state of Carabobo, and Torres municipality in Lara. To this list I should also add the knowledge obtained from participating in: "Planning in the Commune" workshops held with a group of spokespeople from the Union Noreste commune in San Jacinto, Barquisimento, Lara (October 2008); La Azulita commune, Merida (December 2008); and "Planning in the Community" workshops held for facilitators in Falcon municipality, in the state of Falcon (21-22 March 2009) and Rio Caribe, Arismendi municipality, Sucre (16-17 October 2009).

---

1. The term "protagonism" is a new word that has become widely used on the Latin American left to emphasize that the people should be the principal actors in building democracy. The English word "protagonist" has begun to be employed by the left in the same way. The idea is that ordinary people participate in and become masters of their own communities and their own development. In North American progressive circles, the term "empowered deliberative democracy" is sometimes used in a generally parallel sense

7. Further, our analysis was greatly enhanced by what we learnt from one of the first large-scale experiences in the world of "decentralized participatory planning", which was undertaken in the Indian state of Kerala. There, an elected communist government decided in 1996 to carry out an important process of decentralization, involving not only monetary resources, but also material and human resources, to aid in the implementation of local development plans and facilitate the active participation of the people. This has led to greater participatory and economic development in Kerala when compared to the rest of India, and a growth in the self-esteem and self-confidence of the people. This type of decentralization allowed for greater local government autonomy when it came to planning their development, which enabled much more effective participatory planning. That is why we have titled our work: decentralized participatory planning (DPP).

8. Such a process can ensure that the people as a whole, and not only an elite, manage the wealth of society and begin to put that wealth at the service of society. That is why we believe that DPP is an essential feature of the new humanist and solidarity based society we want to build.

9. DPP has no political biases because all citizens are invited to participate in the creation and implementation of the development plan, in contributing their criteria and ideas, and in collaborating in the diversity of tasks involved in this process. All of this can help provide a space for coming together for people from across a wide political spectrum, including those that have never been members of a party or reject parties and politicians due to their often deserved reputations for corruption and favoritism.

10. This form of planning is more than just an ideal instrument for achieving substantial citizens' participation in the management of public affairs, because when people become involved in the planning process, they no longer feel like beggars demanding solutions from the state. They become the creators of their own destiny, and the destiny of their communities. This makes them grow as human beings; it gives them dignity, it increases their self-esteem and broadens their knowledge on political, cultural, social, economic and environmental issues.

11. In this activity, as in all human activity, there is a joint product.[2] The first is the plan itself, which is an objective material product that has been developed in a participatory manner and is tangible in the sense that it is there for all to see. The second is a subjective human product that is much less tangible and can only be seen through discerning eyes. It is the transformation of the people, their growth as human beings, which occurs as a result of their involvement in this process, as noted above.

12. This is an educational process in which those that participate learn to inquire about the causes of things, to respect the opinion of others, to understand that the problems they face are not exclusive to their street or neighborhood but are related to the overall situation of the economy, the national social situation, and even the international situation. They learn that everyone's problems and every community's problems should be examined within the context of the reality that other people and other communities face, which may be much more difficult and urgent than theirs. Through this, new relations of solidarity and complementarity are created that place an emphasis on the collective rather than the individual.

13. All this means that those who participate in this process are politicized, in the broadest sense of the term, and develop an independent mind that can no longer be manipulated by a media that remains overwhelmingly in the hand of the opposition.

---

2. This idea that in all human activity there are two results, two joint products, comes from Michael A. Lebowitz.

14. This book is an attempt to develop a simple guide, written in easily accessible language, which could help local governments facilitate a process of participatory planning (PP)[3].

15. The original text has been revised several times. The Venezuelan economist Noel Lopez, with whom I published the e-book *Planificación participativa en la comunidad* (*Participatory Planning in the community*), played a big role in some of the earlier drafts. In more recent drafts, I relied on the collaboration of the Spanish economist José Bartolome who became a co-author of this book. I have also received vital input from Ximena de la Barra (Chile). I have also been able to rely on useful suggestions from Tomás Villasante (Spain), Rafael Enciso (Colombia/Venezuela), Francisco Cañizales (Venezuela), Evaristo Marcano (Venezuela), Álvaro Sáenz (Ecuador) and Carlos García Pleyán (Spain). I want to thank all of them for having accompanied me during the process of writing this text. I would like to also thank Federico Fuentes, the translator of this text and Dr. JoAnne Engelbert of the U.S. for her helpful suggestions on the translation. A very special role was played by Richard Franke (U.S.) who, motivated by his pedagogical vocation, has done a meticulous job in editing the English text, pointing out repetitions, suggesting clarifications and re-ordering some ideas. I would like to thank all of them for having accompanied us in the writing of this book.

16. This book consists of two volumes. In the first volume, we provide a general overview of the decentralized planning process. The second volume looks at our methodological proposal for how to carry out this process in communities, territorial areas and municipalities. Both the first and second volumes include an arsenal of instances and documents that will be required for all types of communities. We have paid particular attention to ensure they are useful for all contexts. This is not to say, however, that all municipalities and communities, particularly the smallest and poorest ones, should carry out all the tasks proposed here, as in these cases this may be out of their reach. The complexity of the process will depend on the level of decentralized achieved.

17. This first, more theoretical, volume contains two parts. The first part deals with conceptual aspects (planning, decentralized participatory planning, its political importance, necessary conditions for carrying out the process, the role of organized communities and the different phases and steps that need to be undertaken). The second part covers the different actors and instances involved in the process. This first volume has five Appendixes: the first outlines the three levels of decentralization and the responsibilities each level must assume; the second deals with the electoral process to use for forming the different representative bodies in the participatory planning process; the third offers a proposal for how to distribute financial resources to territorial areas in such a way as to ensure that the less well off benefit the most; the fourth provides an example timeline for the process, and the fifth deals with the issue of how to consolidate community organization once the planning process is over.

18. The detailed index we have provided helps give our readers a clearer vision of its content.

19. Of course, you may decide that our ideas are useful and take them up, or you may decide otherwise. Importantly, these ideas are always subject to revision in light of new experiences and lessons learned along the way.

---

3 . We have re-worked sections from two previous books published in Spanish: Planificando desde abajo. Una propuesta de planificación participativa descentralizada (El Viejo Topo, España, 2015) and *Planificando para construir organización comunitaria* (El Viejo Topo, España, 2016). Those that have read these books with not find a lot of new material here besides an improved explanation of certain concepts and the order of presentation. There is also the clear advantage of having all this information on municipal decentralized participatory planning in one single text.

20. Although an ideal scenario would involve the central state deciding to decentralize an important part of the nation's resources earmarked for development, there is no doubt that a majority of countries are a long way from finding themselves in such a situation. Nevertheless, we believe that this should not stop local authorities who want to kick-start decentralized participatory planning processes in their local area from doing so and, in doing so, to contribute to the process of building the capacities of the citizens through their own concrete experiences and practice, and help them become protagonists of the new society we want to build, one in which peoples' participation is a central feature.

21. Both authors would be extremely happy if our proposal was put into practice somewhere as part of a pilot project of local governments willing to promote participation, starting from the geographical smallest spaces that here we define as communities, and that afterwards, participants could pass on their suggestions for how to correct or adjust our proposal, based on the lived experience of trying to implement it.

—Marta Harnecker
December 7th, 2017

VOLUME I
Theoretical Aspects

PART I. CONCEPTUAL ASPECTS

CHAPTER I. WHAT WE MEAN BY DECENTRALIZED PARTICIPATORY PLANNING

1) SEEKING THE GREATEST PROTAGONISM POSSIBLE

22. In this book, we will take as our starting point the fact that we want to build a society that is radically democratic, solidarity-based and respectful of nature. This will be a society consciously built by the people, where the people, and not an elite, decide how they want to live and how to share the social wealth produced within that society so that everyone can live a full and meaningful life (Sumak Kawsay[4]). Such a life will be based on equity, solidarity, efficiency and efficacy. To accomplish these several goals, we have to create spaces and methods that allow us to achieve these objectives.

23. We need geographic spaces where people have the opportunity to become informed, state their positions and make decisions (community level, workplace, schools, universities, interest groups).

24. We also need **methods** that can facilitate the greatest possible participation of the people, where they become informed, discuss and vote, where their decisions become a reality. With properly defined units and appropriate methods, they can actively participate in the construction of that more just and solidarity-based society we all want to live in. We believe that the best method for achieving these objectives is locally based participatory planning.

2) WHAT WE MEAN BY PLANNING

25. Before turning to the issue of participatory planning, we would first like to explain what we mean by planning.[5]

26. One can govern in a good or bad manner. Sometimes we are not sufficiently clear about the goals we want to reach or we base them on an incorrect reading of the reality we are trying to change, and therefore make mistakes that drag us away, rather than bring us closer to those goals. It is also possible that, even having clearly set out our intentions and correctly chosen our actions, we underestimate the resources we need to carry them out or are not capable of visualizing sufficiently in advance certain obstacles that could prevent us from reaching our goals.

27. What distinguishes a good government from one that isn't good? Why do some achieve their aims while others get shipwrecked along the way?

---

4. A quechua word.

5. Paragraphs 8 to 13 are taken from Flavio Carucci T, *Agendas sociales. Construyendo acuerdos para el desarrollo local* (Caracas: GTZ, Escuela de gerencia social, ILDIS, 2009), 14.

28. A good government does not improvise; instead it reflects before moving into action and makes decisions based on appropriate information that allows it to achieve the results it is looking for.

29. Decisions based on concrete facts, something that should accompany all government actions, are part of what we understand planning to be.

30. Planning therefore requires thinking before moving into action. The opposite of planning is improvisation; that is, making decisions without thinking about or having prior knowledge of the possible consequences of our intentions. Of course everyone in government has to plan to some extent given that, in one way or another, they have to think before moving into action. Sometimes however, they think things through so little or base their thoughts on such flimsy information, that their actions come across as if they were improvising.

31. This process covers different elements that are closely linked to the tasks that any government must carry out. The planning process includes:
- have a goal to strive towards;
- closely study the reality you are seeking to change;
- clearly define the sought after changes;
- explore the different actions that could be taken to achieve these changes, and the material, human and financial costs required to implement them;
- select the most efficient and viable actions;
- carry out the selected actions; and
- evaluate the final results in order to make any necessary adjustments.

32. A society may decide to plan its development because it believes that in order to achieve the objectives it has set out, this process cannot be left to chance or to the whims of the market. Conscious collective actions are required to overcome injustices and redesign economic policies and practices so as to improve people's wellbeing.

33. Achieving these objectives in their totality takes years and involves actions that go beyond simply improving services and public infrastructure, as important as these are. Development requires actions that will impact on society as a whole: eliminating or reducing inequality; creating jobs; using available resources in a sustainable manner that protects the environment; developing cooperatives and other initiatives that go in the direction of eliminating exploitation; and reducing dependency on foreign markets, among others.

34. Lastly, we should not forget that development occurs in a defined geographical area that has particular characteristics: watersheds, mountains, coastlines, rivers and lakes, land that is more or less fertile, tourist regions, land that is suitable for building houses, high-risk zones, urban areas, etc. Every area will also go through a particular process of demographic change that, in one way or another, is inter-related to what happens in neighboring communities and in the country as a whole. That is why it is also important to take demographic information into account.

3) TOWARD DECENTRALIZED PARTICIPATORY PLANNING

35. Now, there is no single formula for planning. It can be carried out behind closed doors by a technical team or involve different levels of people's participation, from a simple consultation to direct involvement in decision making.

36. The type of planning we advocate is the antithesis of the centralized planning implemented in the former Soviet Union. There it was thought that to coordinate all efforts towards building a new society, a central authority had to decide objectives and means. It was a process in which decisions were always made from above, on many occasions without taking into consideration the

fact that down below was where people best understood their problems and possible solutions.

37. On the other hand, processes that claim to be participatory budget processes often limited themselves to being processes of consultation only. Rather than promoting a process of decision making by citizens, those in power restricted participation to only consulting them in regards to public works and services that need to be implemented. A willingness to listen to people represents a step forward, but it is very limited. In such cases people in local areas are called upon to participate in working groups where they are asked to point out their main priorities for public works and services for their respective communities. A technical team collects these priorities. Here it **is the technicians and not the people** who then decide which projects to implement.[6].

a) The need for planning to be participatory

38. We advocate a more empowered participation process, in which the people genuinely discuss and decide their priorities, as much as possible design their own projects and implement them if they are capable of doing so without having to depend on higher levels (although the door is always left open to ask for specialized technical assistance if required).

39. If the project is too big, or is technically very complex, or its impact will affect a more extensive area, then the capacity to execute it should be assumed by a higher up level. We are therefore talking about a planning process that seeks to involve the citizenry in as many aspects of the process of planning as possible; that is why we call it **participatory planning.**

b) The need for planning to be decentralized

40. If the state decides everything, there is no room for local initiatives. Therefore, in order to ensure the full participation of people, we must take the plans of small localities as our starting point – where the potential of people's participation is greatest – and apply the principle that everything that can be done at a lower level should be decentralized to that level. Only those tasks that cannot be carried out at the lower levels should be assigned to the higher levels of administration and technical proficiency. This approach is referred to in much of the development literature as the "principle of subsidiarity." In addition to providing a logic for decentralization, this principle allows for a back-and-forth planning process as the different levels communicate their needs and their competencies (responsibilities) to each other. We describe this principle in more detail, with reference to Kerala, in paragraph 132.

41. Of course, we are not talking about anarchic decentralization. The ideal scenario would involve a national system of participatory planning that would bring together community plans, the plans developed by territorial areas or communes, and those of municipalities or cantons, as well as the plans of any other level of government.

42. While recognizing the need for a national plan, the type of planning we are proposing allows local institutions to play a fundamental role not only in contributing to the design and implementation of the national plan but also by having the autonomy to plan within their own territory and carry out an important part of the national plan. The national plan has a real existence in the degree to which it expresses itself in the lowest, most local levels of decentralization: the reality of the nation emerges from the neighborhoods and villages.

---

6. In November 2004, at a meeting of 800 high-level cadres from the government of President Chavez, it was recommended to put participatory planning into practice across the country. However, despite this clear directive from the president, this method was implemented by very few mayoralties and in many cases it was limited to a merely participatory consultation.

43. Of course, we are referring here to a relative autonomy, as the general guidelines of the national plan have to be respected. What we are talking about is adjusting it to the specific social, cultural and economic realities of each geographical area.

44. Moreover, we envisage a decentralization that is infused with a spirit of solidarity, which favors the most disadvantaged localities and social sectors. One of the important roles of the state and local governments is to redistribute resources in order to protect the weakest and help them develop.

45. In order to emphasize the fact that decentralization is a crucial element in the type of planning we are proposing, we have called the process **decentralized participatory planning**.

46. Just as we were initially influenced by the emphasis President Chavez placed on planning at the level of the communal councils, a topic we will return to later on, our current understanding of planning has been further influenced – as we mentioned in the introduction – by the experience of decentralized participatory planning which they have developed over more than a decade, and with much success, in the Indian state of Kerala.

4) ACHIEVEMENTS AND WEAKNESSES OF PARTICIPATORY BUDGETS

47. You might be asking why are we talking about participatory planning instead of participatory budgeting.

48. We cannot ignore the contribution made by participatory budgeting, a process whereby people participate in the design and implementation of an annual investment plan, that is, in prioritizing where resources assigned to municipal public works and services should be invested. This process has been implemented in various regions across the world and has helped increase the level of people's participation in public policy making. It has also helped improve the performance of municipal governments and, above all, made municipal governance more transparent, while also benefiting the most disadvantaged sectors.[7]

49. Participatory budgeting can become an effective weapon in the fight against corruption and the diversion of funds. People not only prioritize certain public works and services but also organize themselves to follow up on their implementation and monitoring to make sure that allocated resources are used for the objective that had been decided on This also increases the chances that the works or services are carried out to the required standard of quality.

50. Participatory budgeting is also an ideal means for speeding up the administrative machinery, making it more efficient and decreasing bureaucracy given that so many eyes are monitoring the process and pressuring to make sure public works are completed on time.

51. When people see the efficiency and transparency with which resources that come from their taxes are used, they begin to feel more willing to comply with taxation regulations and are less prone to evade taxes. This tends to lead to an increase in municipal tax collection.

52. In times of economic crisis and budget cuts, when it is necessary to "tighten belts" because there are fewer resources than the year before, the method of participatory planning is particularly useful and revolutionary as it places in people's hands the decision as to what should be done with the scarce resources they have. There is a big difference between a people suffering cuts

---

7. In this regards see Marta Harnecker, Delegando poder en la gente: presupuesto participativo en Porto Alegre, Brasil (Habana: MEPLA, 1999).

when they are made from above and when the people themselves, via participatory planning, make these decisions.

53. However, this process also has its limitations.

54. On the one hand, given that the objective of participatory budgeting is to determine which public works or services should be prioritized given the resources available each year, the discussion carried out with participatory budgeting tends to focus solely on these issues rather than on longer term goals that can allow us to move towards the kind of society we want to build. The fact that participatory budgeting is restricted to the framework of an annual investment plan limits the scope and horizon of government actions.

55. On the other hand, in many cases, public works and services prioritized by the people during the participatory budgeting process do not fit within any plan, which can lead to chaotic development.

56. In contrast the participatory planning we advocate is not limited to discussing investment in public works and services that the population deems necessary. It goes further and proposes actions that affect society as a whole: the development of cooperative industries that offer employment to underemployed or marginalized sectors; finding sustainable solutions based on the natural and human resources available within the territory; the elimination of intermediaries in the distribution of food; mechanisms for the redistribution of natural resources, rents, etc. In sum, participatory planning should create the basis for a new, more just and humane society.

57. Thus, participatory planning is not in competition with participatory budgeting; rather, it seeks to go further. Ultimately, annual budgets should reflect yearly provisions within a longer-term plan so that investment plans included as part of these budgets represent the advances made in the implementation of the multi-annual investment plans.

5) Political importance of our proposal

58. According to the experiences we have studied, a mass decentralized participatory planning process can have a lot of positive political outcomes. Apart from those already noted above, when we speak about the positive aspects of participatory budgeting, we can add the following:

59. Although the process starts with a diagnosis of problems and deficiencies, **its aim is to orient people towards imagining the kind of community they would like to live in.** It helps stimulate them to think of initiatives that go beyond merely material things, such as the idea that emerged in Caracas when Aristóbulo Istúriz was mayor to get children to paint murals on street corners.

60. Participatory planning can help to transform the traditional logic of distribution of public resources that has always benefited those sectors with higher incomes, in order to now **favor greater social inclusion.** By promoting popular participation – especially among the most disadvantaged sectors - participatory planning becomes a powerful weapon for better redistributing public resources, thereby inverting priorities that previous governments had until now. Those that were previously humiliated and unprotected are now the most cared for.

61. Given that projected public works and services should emerge from a collective discussion based on national, regional and state or provincial development plans, and that projects are prioritized according to certain criteria, **investments are no longer carried out in an anarchic manner** or in line with the personal criteria of a particular mayor or governor.

62. Participatory planning is also an **instrument in the fight against clientelism and the exchange of favors.** As the community itself designs the project, the potential for cronyism is considerably diminished, as is the influence of administrative leaders, councilors or so-called

"managers."

63. **It strengthens the work of existing organized communities and promotes the organization of others.**

64. It can act as **an instrument with which to measure whether politicians and elected representatives are committed to participatory processes.** It reveals whether they are really willing to promote participation and allow people to exercise power.

65. **It is a school for popular education** and for promoting new values and new social relationships. As we said in the Preface to this book "those who participate learn to inquire about the causes of things, to respect the opinion of others, to understand that the problems they face are not exclusive to their street or neighborhood but are related to the global situation of the economy, the national social situation, and even the international situation. They learn that everyone's problems and every community's problems should be examined within the context of the reality of other people and other communities that perhaps face a much more difficult and urgent situation. Through this, new relations of solidarity and complementarity are created that place the emphasis on the collective rather than the individual."

66. Perhaps one of the most significant achievements of participatory planning is having been able to **motivate citizens' participation in the tasks of government, and to** facilitate their initiative and creativity. Citizens knowing about and deciding upon public issues in face-to-face meetings is one of the most concrete ways to create spaces for participation and strengthening grassroots organization.

67. Carried out properly, this process has nothing in common with the co-optation of popular organizations by the state or their dissolution into the state. On the contrary, through it other powers are created outside of the traditional institutions of the state, making it a highly revolutionary experience.

68. Lastly, as we said in the Preface, this form of planning is more than just the ideal instrument to achieve the full participation of citizens in the management of public matters. When people are involved in the process of planning, they no longer feel like beggars demanding solutions from the state. They feel themselves to be the builders of their own destiny.

69. In short, this process not only facilitates the creation of a plan, something that is tangible and visible for all to see, but **also helps transform the people who participate in it.** Those who involve themselves are transformed; they are no longer the same persons they were at the start of the process. They begin to not only worry about themselves, their self-interests; instead they think about their community, their territorial area, and finally, their municipality as a whole. They learn to express solidarity with those most in need.

CHAPTER II. VENEZUELA AND KERALA EXPERIENCES

70. Before going on to develop the theme of decentralized participatory planning (DPP), we would like to pause in order to briefly examine what most caught our attention about the experiences in Venezuela and Kerala.

1) THE ROLE OF ORGANIZED COMMUNITIES IN VENEZUELA

71. In Venezuela, after much debate and studying, it was agreed that the ideal unit for participation was the geographically based community.

a) What do we mean by community?

72. What do we mean by community? A community refers to a group of families that: live in a specific geographical space; know each other and can easily relate to each other; can meet without having to rely on transport; use the same public services and share similar economic, social and town planning concerns. We are therefore dealing with people who live in the same territory but do not necessarily share a common history, cultural traditions and political ideas. Within this geographical space we will find people with different beliefs and cultural traditions

73. The number of people that make up a community can vary a lot from one place to another. It is worth recalling that in Venezuela, after much debate and studying successful experiences in community organization (in particular, the Urban Land Committees, there are made up of 200 families organized to struggle for title deeds for the land they built their houses on, and Health Committees, that encompass 150 families with the aim of supporting local health clinics in heavily disadvantaged areas), it was decided that in densely populated urban areas, such as those with high-rise apartments and slums where tens of thousands of families live, the size of a community should range from 750 to 2000 people, while in remote rural areas, where communities form small villages, they could range from 100 to 250 people, and in indigenous communities, the size would be about 50 people.

74. These figures could be different for other countries depending on their reality. However, in no cases should we have communities in high-rise areas, slums or residential areas made up of 30,000 to 40,000 people.

75. Residents in these high rise areas or slums may share a common history and similar problems, but it is highly unlikely that they would all know each other and it would most likely be very hard to bring them all together for a meeting. Imagine how difficult it would be to organize a meeting of 2000 or more people. By proposing smaller spaces, we are hoping to create better conditions that can facilitate the active participation of residents in meetings dealing with community issues.

76. These smaller spaces are better suited to successfully dealing with problems such as rubbish collection, footpaths or footbridges, school absenteeism, at-risk pregnancies, crime or the lack of sporting, cultural or humanitarian initiatives, and involving residents in their resolution.

77. Now, each community is different from the next. In Venezuela there are some with an important tradition of organization and struggle, and that therefore contain various community organizations and activists. Others only have one or two organizations, and others perhaps have none.

78. The organizations we can find in a community in Venezuela include: urban land committees, social protection committees,[8] health committees and community health organizations, cultural groups, sports clubs, neighborhood associations, education missions, water roundtables, energy roundtables, Bolivarian circles, environmental groups, food committees, grandparents clubs, community housing groups, popular defense units, cooperatives, micro-enterprises, popular economy councils, and others.

---

8. Committees that attend to the most vulnerable sectors of society: the elderly and sick, people living in extreme poverty, etc.

79. In general, community organizations tends to work on their own, in many cases duplicating efforts and being less productive and effective than they would be if they were to work together in a coordinated manner.

b) Unified plan that brings together all community initiatives

80. President Chavez's idea was to create an organization that would bring together these diverse groupings into a single organization that could act as a community government. He called this organization the "communal council", although a more appropriate name would have been "community council" (See Annex V), leaving the name "communal council" for the next level of territorial organization: the commune[9].

81. And what is the best instrument for bringing together the different demands and organizational efforts of a community? Chavez had the brilliance to see that the best instrument for this was the creation of a single work plan dedicated to solving the community's most deeply felt problems. Bringing together all existing community initiatives into a single work plan saves effort and leads to much better results.

82. Chávez also said that the first task of the communal council should be to actively involve residents in the community in coming up with this plan.

83. However, the Venezuelan experience has also shown us that actively involving residents in the community **in coming up with a work plan should not be the first task of the communal council**; rather this should occur prior to the formation of the council, because it is precisely through this process that a community develops and is able to detect those people who are best suited to running this small community government that is closely tied to the people and is at their service.

84. In cases where conditions are not favorable for such participation, or where a community wants to promote participation but does not know how to, initiating a process of community planning can be a very useful instrument for enticing apathetic residents. Participatory planning is therefore not only valid for places where strong community dynamics already exist; it can be especially useful for creating such dynamics.

c) Promote community supervision

85. Another function of the communal council is to promote community supervision over all projects carried out in the community by state, community or private entities. It should also manage the resources granted to it or raised through its own initiative, via a community-based financial entity or its own system of accountability.

86. Each communal council should organize topic-oriented workshops for each of the most deeply felt needs of the community, for example: food, health, infrastructure, housing and habitat;

---

9. The most appropriate name would be "Community Council", while leaving the name "Communal Council" for the level of territorial organization immediately above it: the Commune. The Sub commission for Education of the Presidential National Popular Power Commission, at the time headed by Marta Harnecker, has published some useful material explaining what a Communal Council is, how it is formed and the task it should carry out. It was published as *Serie ABC Consejos Comunales*, Comisión Presidencial Nacional del Poder Popular, Caracas, 2006. It involved a series of 11 short pedagogical pamphlets. Appendix V outlines some of current thinking of how a Community Council should be organized.

education; sports and culture; communication, information and training (alternative media and others); security and defense (defense units).[10]

e) Ensuring an electoral result that reflects the will of the people

87. Once the number of workshops has been decided upon, residents should elect - in citizen assemblies - those neighbors they believe can best represent the community on the communal councils because of their leadership qualities, knowledge of the area, spirit of community work, willingness to work in a collective manner, honesty, and dynamism. Those elected are called spokespersons because they are the voice of the community. When residents lose confidence in them, they should be recalled, as they can no longer be said to be the voice of the community. Venezuelan activists refuse to use the term "representative" because of the negative connotations this term has acquired historically in the bourgeois representative system. Candidates for representative positions only talked to the community at election time, promising "all the gold in the world," but were never seen again once they were elected.

88. I think it is important to point out that in Venezuela, they discussed whether this community council should simply be the sum of the leaders of the different organizations that exist within a community or whether it was better to hold a citizen's assembly and let the assembly elect its spokespersons. The second option was agreed upon because reality dictated that the leaders of many of the existing community organizations had lost their legitimacy because they had lost their connection with the constituents that had elected them. Elections via assemblies allowed the local people to correct this situation. If the sectional leaders are carrying out their duties, then their names will undoubtedly be put forward in the assembly, and if they have popular support, they will be elected.

e) The Community Assembly: the maximum authority

89. While those citizens elected as members of the communal council come to form a kind of informal community leadership body, it is the residents of the area who, in assembly, get to exercise final decision-making power.

90. The citizens' assembly **is the highest decision-making body in the local community**. This is where sovereignty and the power of the people reside. Its decisions are binding on the communal council.

f) Giving priority to actions over words and speeches

91. Of course, it is very important to make sure voters elect candidates for the right reasons. The Venezuelan experience is very useful in this regard. It has shown us the importance of ensuring that the elections of spokespeople is properly organized and that people know who the candidates are not simply because of what they say but because what they have done. This is particularly the case for those people who don't have a prior history of activism and organizing in the community.

92. How can people best get to know their candidates?

---

10. The tasks of each working group should be undertaken in a collective manner by the different organisations that identify with a specific issue. For example, the group dedicated to social issues can involve the social welfare committee, the health committee, the food roundtable and other organisations within the community that support the struggle for healthcare and quality of life for all people, especially those living in extreme poverty.

93. The Venezuelan experience tell us, for example, that prior to electing members of the communal council, it has been very useful to **get candidates to collaborate in the carrying out of the demographic and socio-economic census**, as this involves them visiting families door-to-door. This manner of obtaining information not only provides an opportunity to collect data that is not useful found in institutional databases; it also puts candidates in direct contact with families in the community.

94. The Venezuelan experience, and other similar ones around the world, has demonstrated the usefulness of giving these people, together with those people from outside the community who want to help the community organize themselves, the task of **drafting a brief history of the community with the people**. [11] This is particularly helpful for ensuring that external collaborators do not steer activities in a certain direction without taking into prior consideration the reality they are working in.

95. Another activity that has proven itself to be very handy is organizing a **participatory diagnosis.** Such a diagnosis can help provide a better understand of the needs and most deeply felt desires of the people of a given community. This can also be a very good way for those with little background in organizing to get to better know the community they may become spokespeople for.

96. It is therefore not enough for candidates to simply give good speeches to get elected. It is important that they carry out small practical tasks in the community, such that residents can see for themselves their genuine vocation to serving the people. This is a manner of ensuring that candidates who are simply looking to use these posts as a springboard for a political career will get weeded out.

g) How to ensure a large and broad attendance

97. How can we make sure that the assemblies to elect the communal council involve the majority of residents, are genuinely representative of all the community and cannot be political manipulated?

98. The Venezuelan experience, along with some others, has shown that the way in which the assembly is convoked is very important. Often invitations are not extended to the more remote sectors of the community. On many occasions, it is mainly friends, acquaintances, those with similar politics who were invited, while others were left out. Furthermore, invitations tend to be general, with little effort made to go door-to-door. They are not linked to the concrete problems of a community, those that all or a majority of families face and are therefore easily recognizable.

99. Experience has shown us that the only way to guarantee attendance and avoid political manipulation is to make sure that people from all "spaces" in the community come along to the citizen's assemblies. No important decision should be made if one of these spaces is not represented in the assembly.

---

11. The documentary *Forging the future* shows how in a community experience in Pinar del Rio, Cuba, children were given the task of constructing this history by interviewing local residents that had the most knowledge about the community. Readers can view the material at: https://videosmeplaen.wordpress.com/participation-documentary/video-debate-cyclelearning-about-participation-without-an-instructor/ English subtitles.

100. What spaces are we referring to here? Every street, pathway, apartment block, building. In each of these there tend to live a small group of families who, due to living so closely together, share a deeper bond and relationship. We propose to refer to these small spaces as neighborhood areas.

101. As such, a community could be made up of various neighborhood areas. Each of these should elect someone that commits to turning up to these assemblies and speaking on behalf of the areas. Achieving this will undoubtedly involve an important amount of work across the whole community.

102. We can call these people **neighborhood delegates** to differentiate them from the spokespeople on the communal council's executive committee.

103. Having a delegate for each neighborhood area is very important for the functioning of the community assembly. His or her presence will ensure the election of **councils that are representative of all parts of the community and the variety of views that exist within it**.

104. To achieve this we propose that quorum not be determined by selecting an arbitrary percentage of the community in attendance. Quorum should take into consideration the presence of delegates from every corner of the community. Consequently, quorum for Citizen's Assemblies should require a minimum of one representative from at least 75% of families living in small communities, and at least one delegate from two-thirds of the neighborhood areas in large communities.

105. Achieving the presence of at least one person from each family living in the community would represent a complete success.

106. Moreover, the different experiences we have studied have taught us that it is very important to involve children, given they are generally more willing to collaborate in community tasks. They tend to not be weighed down by the apathy present among those older than them as a result of years of unfulfilled promises. They are also the social sector that, once they return home from school, tends to spend the most time out in the community. As such, we feel that it would be a good idea to set the minimum age for voting in citizen's assemblies at 12, rather than 16 or 18 as generally set out in existing voting laws.

107. One of the main problems this process of communitarian organization might face in places where it is carried out is that many people may fear that the government or political parties will manipulate the process, a fear often stoked up by interested factors. We have insisted on the need to avoid any political or other type of manipulation during the process of forming communal councils.

108. **This is not about creating communal councils that involve only supporters of the government.** All community institutions should be open to all citizens, no matter their political stripes. We can expect that many of those currently fooled by the media, seeing in practice the support they receive from higher levels of the government to resolve their community's problems will discover the reality of the revolutionary process through their struggle.

h) A team to help initiate the process

109. The Venezuelan process has also shown that popular protagonism cannot be decreed from above, but neither can it appear simply as a result of willing it from below. Nor does it emerge from one day to the next. It requires a process of learning that brings together the willingness to achieve popular protagonism through a conscious process to build it.

110. This process will occur more quickly if the people receive support from a group of

individuals, whether from the community or belonging to outside institutions that are trained in the area and have a broader perspective of the world.

111. These people could be members of a social, political or religious organization (we are thinking here of the grassroots Christian communities – *comunidades cristianas de base* – that played such an important role in Latin America) or a local government or institution willing to promote popular participation. However, regardless of their origin, their role should never be to substitute for the community. Instead they should facilitate the participation process, helping people discover their own potentialities. They should guide, point people in the right direction, save learning time by helping them avoid having to go through the process of trial and error, and learn together with the people by working with them.

i) Handing over financial resources to small projects

112. The participatory planning process[12] can take a while to be implemented at the municipal and territorial levels, particularly as time is needed to train the various participants and to create a database, both of which are essential for planning. This delay could lead to demoralization as people begin to think that the process will ultimately go nowhere, and that it represents just another broken promise. That is why we believe it is important to take on board Chavez's idea of handing over resources to communities so that they can carry out small projects. This should not be done in a populist manner in which funds are dispersed mainly to try to win political support for an upcoming election. Instead, communities should have to first organize themselves, come up with a community plan and, as part of this process, prioritize a project that could potentially be funded.

j) Small public works that had a big impact in Santa Tecla, San Salvador

113. A similar initiative, though this time at the municipal level, was implemented in the Salvadoran municipality of Santa Tecla[13]. While the participatory strategic municipal plan was being prepared, and faced with the need to provide concrete results, a decision was made to assign part of the funds designated to public works to projects the community was demanding (asphalt a street, fix up a school, provide adequate street lighting in a public square, etc.) These projects were referred to as "small projects with great impact" (POGI[14]). The idea emerged as a result of the need to demonstrate concrete results once the strategic plan had been developed and deal with the hundreds of demands emanating from residents.

114. Given that these small projects were of great interest to the population, and had been chosen by them, the community immediately began to identify with the larger project, involving itself in its execution and attempting to obtain resources over and above those it received from the mayor's office, whether by digging into its own funds or seeking international aid. We should recall that during their heroic revolutionary war, the Salvadoran people won the sympathy and support of an enormous number of NGOs, many of which continue to provide support today.

---

12. See Chapter V. Phases in the planning process.

13. For more information on the experience in this municipality, see the excellent book by Alberto Enríquez Villacorta & Marcos Rodríguez, *Santa Tecla. Gestión participativa y transformación del territorio*, Afán Centroamericana, San Salvador, 2009.

14. "Pequeñas Obras de Gran Impacto" pp.193-196.

115. This initiative helped break down the existing paternalistic culture. Its success lay in combining high levels of community participation with the decentralization of funds and their administration by organized residents. The municipal council at the time gave the community $1000, which they used to pay for inputs, contract labor and to administer the project overall. Once the project was completed, the community had to submit invoices and receipts to the major's office in order to be able to participate in future projects.

116. The implementation of the project involved a cycle that began with the organization of a project committee, elected in a neighborhood assembly, which was to come up with a design for the project. Then it would make a formal request for funds from the mayor's office, sign an agreement, get it approved and receive the funds. The next step was contracting the help required for carrying out the project, and then an evaluation of the project including its design and implementation.

117. While such a project was carried out, assemblies of neighbors were held to observe how the project was advancing and to continue raising funds. For its part, the mayor's office provided technical support via the heads of its territorial, infrastructure and citizen's participation departments. A regulation sets out the basic rules of the game for participants who are part of carrying out the project.

118. What is interesting is that there is no legal foundation for the decentralization of funds to citizens, yet this has not held back the government of Santa Tecla. Their argument has been that the municipal code does not contemplate this type of action, nor does it prohibit it. It is what we could call an "a-legal" initiative (neither legal nor illegal).

119. In Ecuador's case, in municipalities such as Pedro Carbo, in the Guayas region, communities in the rural parishes have received funds for small projects via the participatory budgetary process. In the case of Santa Ana parish, in the Cuenca Canton, the parish board, headed by Julio Álvarez (2009-2014), decided to hand over between $3000 and $7000 to each community that made up the parish for community projects that local residents deemed to be a priority.[15]

k) If there is a shortage of resources, hold a community project-ideas competition

120. It may turn out that so many communities express their desire to organize themselves in order to receive resources that the mayor's office will not have enough funds to cover them all. In this case, we propose organizing a competition in which the best project-ideas are granted the funds the mayor's office has available.

121. Some have pointed out that this manner of distributing resources to communities could lead to injustices as resources will tend to end up in the hands of better organized communities with greater capacity to come up with projects, and not those that most need them. Without denying that this could happen in the short term, in the medium and long term the possible negative effect of granting resources this way should be offset by the positive impetus that this will give to the unorganized communities to become organized. Those that are not organized will have an incentive to overcome their situation, with the aim of obtaining resources in order to deal with their most pressing needs. This will be reinforced if the organized communities that receive resources express their solidarity with those non-organized. As soon as a community expresses

---

15. Those communities that were located closer to the local rubbish dump were compensated by the fact they received more money.

their desire to organize themselves, they should receive external support to help them carry out their project (volunteers, activists, workshops, etc.).

2) THE EXPERIENCE OF DECENTRALIZED PARTICIPATORY PLANNING IN KERALA

a) Three levels of local rural self-government

122. In India, there exists legislation regarding participatory decentralized planning.[16]

123. Article 40 of the 1950 Constitution into practice establishes the need to organize "Grama Panchayats" (village or rural town governments) with as much power as is necessary to allow them to function as units of self-government. En 1992, amendments 73 and 74 were introduced into the Indian Constitution, giving the Panchayats constitutional status and laying the national basis for a process of decentralization. These amendments proposed the decentralization of administration via the creation of three levels of local rural self-government: the lowest level of self-government is the Grama Panchayats, that is, the village government, this is followed by the Block Panchayats, groups of villages organized into "blocks" or administrative units to carry out certain nationally funded development projects and lastly, the District Panchayats.

124. This legislation was strengthened due to the vision of certain political leaders such as the Prime Minister Rajiv Ratna Gandhi[17], who said that rather than using intellectuals that are not aware of the needs of the people to design development plans in capital cities and reducing citizens to mere beneficiaries of development, it was necessary to involve people in the process.[18]

125. However, this legislation has been applied in very few states. One of them is Kerala, one of India's most populous states. In Kerala, after much thought and research it was decided that the geographic and demographic unit for self-government most closely tied to the people in Kerala would be the rural village or town called "Grama", which is why the rural government is called Grama Panchayat (government of the town or village). Alongside the three levels of self-government in more rural zones, urban municipalities and municipal corporations exist in the big cities. Later on we will deal with how competencies, financial resources, equipment and personnel were transferred to these levels of self-governments.

b) Transfer of resources and competencies

126. In 1994, the government of Kerala passed the Panchayat Raj Act, thereby providing a solid legal basis for the system of local government and unifying the transference of institutions and personnel to local self-governments along the lines of the principle that everything that could be carried out at a lower level should be decentralized to that level, leaving for higher-up levels only those competencies that cannot be carried out at a lower level. This meant that the Grama Panchayats, the lowest level of self-government, had to assume many of the functions that were previously carried out at a higher level. This constituted an attempt to implement the concept of

---

16. Information taken from: Rosa Pinto Berbel y Tomás Rodríguez Villasante: *Kerala. La democracia en marcha. Los retos de la planificación participativa,* El Viejo Topo, España, 2011, pp.70-73.

17 Prime Minister between 1984-1989.

18 This information and what follows in the next few paragraphs have been taken from Rosa Pinto & Tomás Villasante, *Democracia participativa en Kerala*, 71-73.

subsidiarity that we briefly described in paragraph 40 and that is considered in greater detail below in paragraph 148.

127. In the Kerala experiment a third of all financial resources dedicated to development, as well as a large number of competencies, were transferred from that state level to the Grama Panchayats (governments in rural villages with an average of 25 thousand inhabitants), the lowest level governments.

128. A similar Kerala Municipalities Act was also passed in 1994 to cover the smaller cities.

129. This led to the emergence of two different administrative structures of local self-government: those in rural zones and those in urban areas. Currently, in the rural area there are 14 **District Panchayats** (the largest unit below the state level), 152 **Block Panchayats** (groups of Grama Panchayats set up by the central government for administration of centrally sponsored development programs) and 941 **Grama Panchayats** (rural villages) and in urban areas there are 87 **Municipalities** and 6 **Municipal Corporations**. Below is a diagram illustrating this situation.[19]

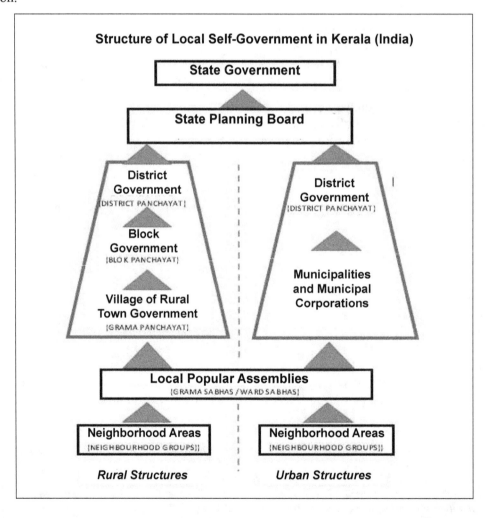

---

19. Richard Franke contribute to clarify some concepts. We have taken this diagram from Rosa Pinto and Tomás Villasante, Op.cit. p.110, and made some modifications to it.

130. In 1996 the Communist Party of India – Marxist (CPI-M) led a coalition of progressive forces that won a majority in the statewide assembly elections and that year launched the "People's Campaign" for decentralized planning. This campaign brought a fundamental change in the roles that the different levels of local and regional government would play from then on.

c) From the rural village to meetings in smaller areas: wards and neighborhood areas

131. The starting point for the People's Campaign was a full afternoon assembly of citizens charged with expressing the felt needs of their communities. During the entire afternoon, residents expressed their most deeply felt needs.

132. Once the lowest level of self-government had been decided upon, those responsible for the planning process in Kerala realized that convening an assembly of all residents in a densely-populated territory or town, implied having to hold assemblies of more than 1000 people, something that did not facilitate meaningful participation.

133. That is why they decided to hold popular assemblies (grama sabhas) not at the level of the village but instead at the lower level of the electoral wards they were divided into. Urban municipalities and municipal corporations (6 big cities in the state of Kerala in those years) also conducted assemblies in wards or electoral circumscriptions.

134. Meetings in the wards involved plenaries in which all those present and the smaller working groups dedicated to discussing different issues contributed, with the aim of ensuring the best possible level of participation. However, even these spaces turned out to be too large; accordingly in the third and fourth years of the campaign for some tasks they set up neighborhood areass (40-50 families) that began to carry out many of the functions of the grama sabha or ward assembly, such as discussing the local plan, revising the plan's implementation and selecting which people or entities should receive resources.[20]

135. Throughout the process it is made clear to people that they were making decisions about real investments in their communities and not just approving decisions already taken from above. [21][5]

---

20. "Many neighborhood groups (NHGs) became involved in settlement of family disputes, educational programs for children, health programs, cultural activities and rotating credit associations…. The representatives of NHGs often constitute a ward committee, which acts as an executive committee of the grama sabhas." T.M. Isaac & Richard Franke, Op.cit. p. 185. The issue of the neighborhood groups is more fully developed in M.P. Parameswaran, ***Democracy by the People, The Elusive Kerala Experience*** (India: Alternatives Asia, 2008), pp.121-144. It is impressive seeing just how many similarities exist between what Chavez proposed regarding the communal councils and the ideas of this Indian intellectual.

21[5]. See Richard Franke, Marta Harnecker, Andrés Sanz Mulas & Carmen Pineda Nebot, ***Estado Kerala, India, Una experiencia de planificación participativa descentralizada*** (Caracas: Centro Internacional Miranda, 2009) http://www.rebelion.org/docs/97086.pdf). Regarding this issue I would recommend reading T.M. Thomas Isaac & Richard W. Franke, ***Local Democracy and Development: The Kerala People's Campaign for Decentralized Planning*** (Lanham: Rowman & Littlefield, 2002) and Rosa Pinto & Tomás Villasante ***Democracia participativa en Kerala: Planificación descentralizada desde la base*** (Madrid, El Viejo Topo, 2011).

136. Subsequent stages of the campaign included additional assemblies, election of delegates to various specialized seminars, recruitment of volunteer technical staff from among retirees, prioritization of projects by the elected village or urban councils, and public monitoring and evaluation procedures.

137. Higher levels of administration were instructed in ways to fit local projects into regional plans and a massive education and experience sharing program was launched for activists at all levels. It was a very ambitious initiative that demanded the mobilization of the energies and resources of large sections of the society.

138. One of the strongest points of the PP process in Kerala was precisely the emphasis the organizers placed on training various participants: residents, technicians, representatives and volunteers. Different levels of training programs were created, each with its own respective manual, training camps, meetings and, later on, seminars where participants could exchange experiences.

139. There is a Kerala Institute of Local Administration (KILA) where, twice a year, elected representatives from different parts of the state come to participate in training sessions that last several days. One piece of information demonstrates the emphasis they have placed on training cadres: in just one year (2004-2005), 249 programs were run with 29,000 participants.

140. A lot of importance has also been placed on what they call "training trainers", that is, those people that go on to train residents in their own communities,[22] and training through practical experience. KILA also publishes a journal on local decentralized administration in English. It can be accessed at: http://kila.ac.in/node/61.

d) Decentralization of important financial resources to the lower levels

141. To inspire meaningful participation of ordinary people in these local assemblies, the State Planning Board decided to devolve 35 to 40% of development funds to the local levels to be allocated as they chose within certain broad limitations. This devolved fund was divided into two parts: 85% was for the local, block and district panchayats and 15% was for the urban areas, made up of smaller cities or municipalities and the 3 (currently 6) large cities called "municipal corporations" in the administrative English used in Kerala.

142. Of this sum of money, in the rural areas, the local village government[23][3] -- the Grama Panchayat (the lowest level of the decentralized structure) -- received around 70%; the following level, the Block Panchayat (rural municipality) 15%; and the District Panchayat, of which there are 14 within the state of Kerala, the remaining 15%[24]. As you can see, there was an evident

---

22 "In the first year of the campaign, 373 trainers at the state level taught 10,497 people at the district level, who in turn ran one-day workshops for more than 100,000 local community activists who became the backbone of the initial stage of the campaign. In 1998, 4,195 district educators received specialised training from 545 educators at the statewide level, and then ran workshops for 93,000 participants. In 1999-2000 there was more mass training, including a series of three-day workshops for women activists and elected representatives." (Richard W. Franke, Marta Harnecker et. al., *Estado Kerala, India: una experiencia de planificación participativa descentralizada* (Caracas: C.I.M., 2009).

23[3]. What we have referred to as the territorial area.

24. Rosa Pinto & Tomás Villasante, p.127.

decision on the part of the authorities to decentralize the bulk of the resources to the level of government closest to the people.

143. The urban area projects ran generally parallel to those of the rural panchayats -- including first starting at the ward level-(about 500 families). In the published literature on the People's Campaign, most of the detailed attention has been on the rural Grama Panchayats with less description of the urban planning process.[25]

144. Within the urban area allotment, 75% was weighted purely by population numbers, 5% by geographical area and 20% by an index of underdevelopment that included characteristics such as percent of former untouchable caste members, percent of houses without sanitary latrines and percent of houses without electricity. The emphasis was thus on delivering resources to bring up the quality of life of the most deprived groups.

e) Principles that govern the process

145. As part of the Kerala experiment, elected members of the statewide legislative assembly and the State Planning Board commissioned a study of the essential features and prerequisites of DPP. They engaged Dr. Satya Brata Sen, an academic who had played a role in a decentralization campaign in the Indian State of West Bengal earlier. Dr. Sen's Committee was officially called "The Committee on Decentralization of Powers."

148. This committee came up with the following essential components of a genuine process of Democratic Participatory Planning in its 1997 report to the elected state level Ministry:
• *Autonomy.* The different tiers of local government should be autonomous: functionally, financially and administratively.
• *Subsidiarity.* What can be done best at a particular level should be done at that level and not at higher levels. All that can be optimally done at the lowest level should be reserved to that level. (Note: we shall discuss subsidiarity in some detail later in this chapter). It is also referenced and described in part in Paragraphs 40 and 132.
• *Clarity of roles.* There should be conceptual and operational clarity regarding the role of each tier in the development process and a clear division of functions among the tiers.
• *Complementarity.* The functions of the different tiers should not overlap, but be complementary to each other.
• *Uniformity.* There should be uniformity of norms and criteria for the pattern of assistance or selection of beneficiaries for all the programs implemented in a local area irrespective of the sponsoring agency.
• *People's Participation.* Local self-government should facilitate the maximum direct participation of the people in development.
• *Accountability.* There should be continuous social auditing of the performance of the elected representatives.
• *Transparency.* People should have the right to information regarding every detail of the administration.

f) The contributions of the experiences of Kerala and Venezuela

147. The experience of Kerala is a valuable guide for understanding how decentralized structures for participatory planning function and the importance of the principle of subsidiarity for organizing the decentralization of functions and resources, along with the importance of making

---

25. Thomas Isaac and Franke, Op.cit. 2002, p. 91 y pp. 160-161.

special effort to raise awareness and train up the population to ensure full participation in the process. When carrying out this experience, it was shown that people's participation was greater in smaller spaces, the wards, and more so when dealing with small groups of neighbors, in what Venezuelans refer to as "neighborhood areas".

148. The participation of communities is the most specific contribution from the Venezuelan experience. This has enriched the process of participatory budgeting carried out in municipalities governed by Workers' Party mayors in Brazil and the experience of DPP in Kerala, India.

149. Venezuela's experience have demonstrated that the more positive impacts have come not from people participating in decisions over what public works projects should be carried out or what initiative should be included in the plans at higher levels but from people developing their own plan at the community level, those small territorial spaces of no more than 2000 inhabitants in urban areas and less in rural areas.

150. When such an organization does not exist in a municipality, the decentralized participatory planning process should act to stimulate its emergence and be a mechanism for promoting community organization. When people see that they can improve their living conditions, they feel more motivated to participate. We therefore need to identify these areas and create planning teams there.

151. Therefore, the ideal space for peoples' participation does not necessarily seem to be the ideal space for self-government, if we accept the classic definition of self-government as a "system of territorial units of administration that have autonomy to administer themselves."

152. Now then, to have this capacity to administered your self doesn't mean to ignore the necessary interrelation that should exist among the diverse government, and it is also necessary to clarify and we also need to clarify that not every form of self-government implies participation. There could be local governments that have administrative autonomy but are run undemocratically. When we use the term self-government, we are referring to people's self-government, that is, where the people govern themselves. In this sense, there is no self-government without full citizens participation, which means that we are talking about a process that can always be improved.

CHAPTER III. LEVELS OF PLANNING AND TYPE OF PLANS

1. TERRITORIAL DIVISIONS AND LEVELS OF PLANNING

1) TERRITORIAL DISTRIBUTION AND CORRESPONDING LEVELS OF GOVERNMENTS

153. After having studied Kerala's experience of decentralization and Venezuela's proposal for territorial decentralization, as well as examining other Latin American experiences with regard to the geographical distribution of their territories and their corresponding levels of governments, we have seen that experiences vary from one country to the next, and that the terminology used to denominate the different spaces and government levels varies widely, making it complicated to do any direct comparisons.

154. We can broadly distinguish the following territorial subdivisions and their respective government levels:

- **Nation**   national government (whether centralized or federated).

- **Regions** regional governments.

- **States, counties, departments**: states that are part of a federated state (Argentina, Brazil, Venezuela, Mexico...); **counties** within a central state (Ecuador, Chile...); **departments** that are in turn divided into counties (Bolivia). Each of these generally has a state or department government.

- **Districts or metropolitan areas.** Municipalities that cover a capital city within a state or a group of urban municipalities that cover a capital city.

- **Rural and urban municipalities or cantons.** Subdivisions of the previous level. In some countries they are known as communes.

- **Communes, parishes, villages or rural towns.** Subdivisions of municipalities. We have chosen to use the term "territorial areas" to denominate this territorial level. But here it is necessary to clarify that our concept embraces both rural and urban areas. Each of these should have a communal governments.

- **Communities, enclosures, small neighborhoods, sectors.** Subdivisions of communes. It is within these spaces that we propose to set up community councils (See Appendix V)

155. Each governmental level should come up with a Development Plan.

156. According to the experiences that we have studied, it seems that the best way to begin the process of decentralized participatory planning is to geographically subdivide the territory into spaces that are sufficiently small enough, in terms of size and number of inhabitants, to facilitate the process of popular protagonism as much as possible. Then should come, territorial units which can become self-government spaces; that is, spaces that can take on an important number of responsibilities that were previously carried out at higher levels and, at the same time, create conditions to generate sufficient revenue that can allow them to operate as autonomously as possible. Chavez's idea of the Venezuelan commune was that it would be the first level of self-government, the level of self-government that was closest to the people.

157. This autonomy will always be relative, since it will be necessary to work with the other levels of government.

158. For the purposes of this book, we will limit our discussion to the three levels of planning that are closest to the people:

(a) **Planning at the first level, the community** that, in geographical and demographic terms, is a relatively small territorial space (150 to 400 families in urban areas, more than 20 families in rural areas, and fewer in more remote areas) within which everyone knows each other and it is relatively easy to bring together the majority of residents to discuss the common problems. We have provided a general definition of a community in paragraph 72.

(b) **Planning at the second level, the territorial area:** a geographical space involving several communities that share common problems, aspirations and economic conditions; that use the same services; whose inhabitants are willing to work together on a common project developed in a participatory manner; and, most importantly, that is in the position to be relatively self-sustainable and self-governing.

c) **Planning at the third level, the municipality or canton:** a geographical space involving several territorial areas in the following step of the participatory planning process.

159. Unfortunately the term municipality does not mean the same thing in every country. In some countries it is used as a synonym for commune; in others, it is used to refer solely to urban

territories, as is the case in Kerala. In others, the term canton is used instead. Here we are using it to refer to both urban and rural territorial units.

160. It is possible that in small rural municipalities there will be no need for an intermediary territorial level, the territorial area, and that the municipality can be directly divided into communities. However, in large and medium-sized cities it is obvious that there will be a need to create assemblies at the levels intermediate level in order to ensure effective decentralization and participation.

161. It may be useful to consider a typology of municipalities, for example: rural, semi-urban, urban with low-density population, medium-sized urban, large cities. The forms of organization and the process of PP should be adapted to the conditions of each place.

162. From here on, we will limit ourselves to referring to what can be done, in a participatory manner, from the municipal level down through what we have called the territorial area to the community.

2. A PLAN FOR EACH LEVEL

163. The ideal situation would involve the central state deciding to decentralize an important part of the national resources designated for development, as has happened in Kerala, but there is no doubt that most countries are a long way from finding themselves in such a situation. [26] Nevertheless, we believe that this should not stop local authorities that want to kick-start DPP in their local area --namely municipal authorities -- from doing so by creating appropriate territorial subdivisions (territorial areas in our case).

164. This may require a process of struggle but such actions would facilitate training residents, through practical experience, to be able to become protagonists of the new society we want to build, one in which people's participation with a protagonist role is a central feature.

a) Development Plan

---

26. . In Venezuela, an ample legal basis for participatory planning exists in the Constitution and in a series of laws such as the Organic Law of Public and Popular Planning, the Organic Law of Popular Power, the Organic Law of the Federal Government Council and its regulation, the Organic Law of Local Public Planning Councils, the Organic Law of Communal Councils, the Organic Law of Communes, and the Organic Law of Municipal Public Power, among others. The situation is the same in Ecuador. There we have guidelines established in the Constitution, the National Plan for Good Living, the Organic Code of Territorial Zoning, Autonomies and Decentralization, the Organic Code of Planning and Public Financing and the Organic Law of Citizens' Participation. However, this is not the situation in the majority of countries, and even in those that have advanced a lot in this regard, it is possible that the issue of decentralization and other issues have not advanced far enough. That is why in many cases it will be necessary to move in advance of existing regulations, while ensuring we are not operating illegally. Ideally the municipalities that want to implement our proposal on participatory planning should be legally exempt by the central state from any blocking legislation so they will have full freedom to experiment with this new form of building a new society with the people.

165. The process of participatory planning at each level should be encapsulated in several documents: the (Multi-year) Development Plan, the Annual Investment Plan, and its corresponding Budget.

166. The Development Plan should have as its goal the full human development of residents, taking in consideration not only economic and social aspects but also spiritual. It should be a plan that dignifies those who live there and that promotes a harmonious and sustainable development.

167. This plan should be an instrument to guide for the actions that need to be undertaken in the municipality in order to achieve our desired goal, and should be revised and updated along the way. However in our model, this plan should not be drafted by municipal experts; instead it should be the result of the participation from all levels of the affected population who themselves should determine objectives, define priorities, select alternative proposals to achieve them and exercise social control over the plan's implementation and its possible revision.

168. And as the development of a territory is a long and complex process, it usually requires a time frame that is longer than a year. In many cases, it could take longer than a term in government. It is therefore useful to think of a plan that at least coincides with the length of term of government for the mayor and councilors, even if, there may be projects that need more than one or two terms in government to be completed.

b) Annual Investment Plans

169. As it generally takes several years to implement the Development Plan, it will be necessary to work out what actions and projects are to be carried out during each year and what resources will be needed to make this happen.

170. This means it will be necessary to come up every year with an Annual Investment Plan that takes into consideration the actions to be carried during that specific year and the resources needed.

171. It is obvious that there will be projects that require more than a year to complete. These projects should be spread out across the different annual plans.

172. This will be the case, for example, for those local governments that need to replace dozens of shacks with dignified homes. This requires large sums of state funds that the state generally grants on an annual basis to build a limited number of houses. As such, supposing that the Development Plan refers to building 40 new houses, and funds are only provided for 10 houses per year, the Annual Investment Plan should set a target of 10 houses.

173. The same can occur with large projects such as the construction of an aqueduct. This goal could perhaps take more than four years to complete and would span over two periods of government, with a new section being built each year. Sometimes the first year can be taken up solely by coming up with a technical plan for the project.

174. We have to take into consideration that, once the first Annual Investment Plan has begun to be implemented, future annual plans could modify the original the Development Plan based on the evolution of the plan itself or other changes in the situation (such as a rise or fall in the financial capacity of the local government. A Development should be a flexible tool.

c) Budget

175. Each Annual Investment Plan should be accompanied by an Annual Budget that contemplates all foreseeable income and expenditure for the relevant entity at any of the three levels we have used in our analysis (municipality, territorial area or community), including those outlined in the corresponding Annual Investment Plan. This budget should include income and

running costs (that correspond to maintaining services provided by the entity as well as general costs) and capital income and expenditure, which in the main part correspond to the projects in the Annual Investment Plan.

176. The complexity of a Budget will vary depending on the level of the entity. It is not the same to have to come up with a budget for a municipality, and in some cases a territorial area, that provides numerous services to a population, as it is to come up with a budget for a small community that possibly uses up all its funds financing its investment plan with small allocations made for general maintenance costs for the office space they operate out of (rent, electricity, heating) and work materials, among other.

d) Immediate Action Plan

177. Lastly, like we recommend to prioritize the projects that the community can solve with its own resources, with this type of projects a Plan of Immediate Action should be elaborated whose execution can begin as soon as possible without needing to wait for the completion of the process of coming up with the Community Development Plan. Moreover, we propose that within the Immediate Action Plan, we group together in the first phase all the simplest projects that don't require funding and that can be carried out even before the hole Immediate Action Plan is drafted and approved. Of course, the Community Assembly should first approve these projects.

3. NATIONAL PLANNING SYSTEM

178. When coming up with a Development Plan for each respective level, it is necessary to consider the development plans that higher levels have come up as well as feed off the plans of lower levels. In Venezuela's case, the Municipal Development Plan has to take into consideration the National Plan and the State Plan, as well as the Development Plans of the communities and communes. At the same time, the Municipal Development Plan should enrich the State Development Plan and the National Development Plan.

179. If, as we propose, we take as our starting point the plans developed by organized communities that is, the lowest and most participatory levels, and follow this up with plans developed in the territories in which the municipality is or will be sub-divided into, and so on, we can establish a National Planning System that will go "from the bottom up" and "from the top down," in a mutually complementary relationship, where the opinions of the people will have increasing weight to the extent that they are internalizing the concepts and practices of PP.

180. The idea is, therefore, that the municipal plan should be based on the territorial plans and these, in turn, should incorporate the proposals developed by the communities. The municipal plan should only add proposals that, because of their macro nature, are not included in the territorial plans.

181. Similarly, communities should plan and implement their own actions, taking as their starting point the resources they have available, both annually and for the longer term.

182. But, we reiterate, each level should not only discuss issues that correspond to it but should take into consideration the proposals made by other levels. More over, they should discuss and take a position regarding thematic priorities and large public works that the municipal council is proposing to carry out in the municipality. For example, a municipality leader might propose to build a hospital or university, or to create an overall plan for industrialization or agricultural and agro-industrial development to generate jobs and income for the population and produce as much as possible, on the basis of local capacities and potentialities. This is an example of how the municipality should propose public works that fall within its competencies, but these should be discussed and approved both at the territorial and the community level.

183. In sum, at each level, its participatory entities should work on the basis of the priorities formulated at lower levels to come up with and present projects that fall within the responsibilities of this level. These, however, should be discussed and voted on by the corresponding lower level. That is, people participate in the municipal planning process primarily via the assemblies in their respective territorial areas and communities.

184. It is important to note that throughout the first year of DPP at the municipal level, there will be elements of the municipal plan (territorial distribution, allocation of available resources, etc.) that will, by necessity, have to be worked out from above by the municipal council, even if they are later submitted to public debate. If significant opposition emerges to these proposals, the community and territorial assemblies will have to submit alternative proposals to the Municipal Planning Assembly.

CHAPTER IV. NECESSARY CONDITIONS FOR DECENTRALISED PARTICIPATORY PLANNING

185. The Venezuelan and Kerala experiences have led us to conclude that the following conditions must exist in order to ensure full peoples' participation in the planning process:

(1) Identification or creation of suitable planning units,
(2) Decentralization of competencies,
(3) Decentralization of material and human resources,
(4) Teams to help kick start the process,
(5) Explaining the process to the population and key actors involved in it,
(6) Training of participants,
(7) Prioritize according to capacities,
(8) Creation of a good database, and
(9) Information and transparency.

186. The existence of public policies like those in Kerala has been key to creating these conditions.

1) CREATION OF SUITABLE GEOGRAPHIC PLANNING UNITS

187. The first step that a municipal council must take if it wants to implement a process of participatory planning is to create suitable planning units within which this process can be carried out. In the next few paragraphs we discuss the problems inherited from past divisions of territories and administrative levels and areas.

188. This is one of the most serious problems that those in local government who advocate an increasingly participatory and protagonistic democracy face.

189. In many cases in Latin America, geographical and administrative subdivisions exist that date back to colonial times (such as parishes) that no longer correspond to any rational needs. There are numerous municipalities that have large populations, enormous *barrios* (neighborhoods), much bigger than many municipalities, side by side with extremely small municipalities. These distortions have negative repercussions on a just, equitable and efficient territorial distribution of resources and make it more difficult for the population to participate. That is why it is sometimes necessary to move towards a new political-administrative division of the national territory.

190. Small rural villages tend to be more suited to people's participation. Existing sub-divisions in densely populated urban municipalities often   need to be further sub-divided.

191. In many places, people have gone about establishing their own sub-divisions, using criteria such as demarcation of barrios, administrative zones and sub-zones, parishes, villages, electoral districts and other forms of municipal sub-division.

192. Each case needs to be analyzed on the basis of the experience and opinions of local residents. Some geographic and administrative spaces will need to be sub-divided while others will need to be merged.[27] There will also be cases where it will be necessary to go beyond borders that have been established as part of the political-administrative sub-division of the country. This is what occurred in the experience headed by mayor Julio Chavez in the municipality of Torres, in the state of Lara in Venezuela, where in 2007, new communal areas were created by merging communal councils from two adjacent parishes.[28] Some thing similar occurred in Libertador municipality, Carabobo, where Argenis Loreto, who was elected mayor in 2000, and his team worked on a subdivision of the municipality into what they denominated "social territories" that brought together various communities. In this case, some territories even extended into neighboring municipalities.[29]

193. Probably in the majority of municipalities in Latin America, the first step that a municipal government should take in initiating a process of PP is the establishment of territorial sub-divisions that facilitate the decentralization of resources and brings government closer to the people. This process of geographic demarcation will only be necessary at the start of the process of municipal PP. For the ensuing years, geographic sub-divisions will already exist, even if it might be useful to periodically revise them and work out some modifications based on experience.

194. If a national prevailing procedure about how to divide the territory does not exist, the ideal scenario would involve the municipal government developing a proposal for how to geographically divide up the municipality as a prior step to starting the actual planning process. This task should be carried out by the municipal government with the support of its technical experts, but should be ratified by the respective assemblies of the different levels of the process.

2) DECENTRALISING COMPETENCIES

195. In cases where national policies aimed towards transferring competencies from municipalities to geographic and administrative subdivisions (parishes, communes, rural villages, etc.) do not exist, another step that municipal governments should take, one that is more complex than the first one, is the decentralization of competencies to the territorial sub-divisions, applying the principle of subsidiarity, which we referred to above in paragraphs 40, 132 and 148.

196. This implies transferring to lower levels all the responsibilities they can take on their hands, while reserving the rest for higher-up levels. It is probably possible to transfer competencies in

---

27 Information taken from Rosa Pinto & Tomás Villasante, *Democracia participativa en Kerala*, 71-73.

28. See Marta Harnecker, *Transfiriendo poder a la gente. Municipio Torres, Estado Lara Venezuela,* (Caracas: Centro Internacional Miranda- Editorial Monte Ávila, 2008), paragraphs 165-166 & 199-212.

29. Marta Harnecker, *Gobiernos comunitarios, Municipio Libertador, Estado Carabobo, Venezuela*, Colección: Haciendo camino al andar, N°1, Monte Ávila, Venezuela, 2006, Capítulo II: Buscando el espacio adecuado, párrafos 18 al 37. Digital version available at: http://www.rebelion.org/docs/97077.pdf

resource management, tax collection, civil registry, administration of state companies, urban planning, surveillance and security, road asphalting, management of homes with elderly people and community soup kitchens, along with the general maintenance of infrastructure related to healthcare, education, culture and sports (See Appendix I: Diagram of the different levels of planning and their responsibilities).

197. This decentralization of responsibilities creates a framework for determining the type and amount of human and financial resources to transfer to each level of local government in accordance with the principle of subsidiarity that we introduced in paragraph 40.

198. A correct distribution of competencies among the different levels is a fundamental step towards avoiding the overlap of activities and many other problems such as lending excessive technical support to one level and not enough to another. Before transferring competencies, a study should be carried out, because it is only worth transferring competencies to a lower level if the conditions exist to successfully deal with them.

199. We have to be careful however to ensure that all transfers are well planned and agreed upon by the levels that these competencies will be transferred to. It is possible that territorial public entities might try to rid themselves of competencies that are problematic for them (for example, rubbish collection) and keep those they are most interested in.

200. It is not possible to set general criteria for decentralization of competencies as it depends on many factors. For example, while the centralized management of services such as sanitation and street cleaning might seem reasonable in a city due to economies of scale and the possibilities available for mechanization, it is obvious that in the case of a relatively isolated rural area with small communities, decentralized management would not only be possible but would in fact produce better results.

201. Another example is housing construction. It would seem that this should be a state or municipal responsibility, but in many cases it is more efficient to give communities the possibility of managing the construction of new houses that can replace existing substandard homes or improve them. Undoubtedly, they should receive technical support from the state or municipality, but they are the ones who know best their needs and priorities, and can contribute their voluntary labor. Moreover, there is much self-confidence to be gained when people solve problems for themselves.

202. Lastly, another example that can help clarify this issue is water management within a defined territory. This can vary depending on whether it is a rural or urban area. While small communities are best equipped to carry out this task and come to an agreement on how to distribute existing water supplies, in urban areas where piping systems exist to distribute water throughout the city, it may make no sense for one neighborhood to have control.

203. In any case, as we have already said, the essential principle that should be applied in decentralization is that everything that can be managed at a lower level should be managed at that level, and in order to make this possible the necessary resources and training in how best to manage those resources should be provided to the community.

3) DECENTRALIZING RESOURCES

204. The other fundamental premise of DPP is the decentralization of resources.

205. If resources are scarce and only a small portion is decentralized, then the territories and communities will lack the capacity to act.

206. Here we have to take into consideration material resources (financial, tools and equipment),

as well as human resources (staff). This is the only way to carry out an effective decentralization.

a) Financial resources

207. Where existing regulations did not foresee the possibility of decentralization, the municipal government could take initiatives in this direction.

208. In the Venezuelan municipality of Torres, the municipal government transferred the resources it had for public works to the 17 parishes so that they could carry out the projects they wanted to prioritize.[30] The fundamental criteria used to transfer monies were: size of territory (much of which was rural), number of inhabitants, population density and an index of inter-territorial compensation that Venezuela uses when providing funds to lessen inequalities between territories.[31]

209. In our opinion, we should follow the example of Torres when it comes to determining the amount of money to transfer to each territory. It is very important to use criteria that enable us to share available resources in the most equitable way; criteria that favor the poorest territories that have until now been the most neglected by the state. This way, we can slowly begin to reduce the socio-economic inequalities among territories (We outline our proposal for the kind of criteria and methodology to employ in Appendix III).

b) Equipment and personnel

210. In addition to transferring financial resources, it is also necessary to transfer personnel, that is, to relocate civil servants by taking them out of the central apparatus and deploying them in the community. There is also a need to provide offices and equipment.

211. The people required to form technical planning teams in each territory should be included among the personnel that should be transferred.

212. In Kerala, the lowest level of self-government, the Grama Panchayats, not only involves representatives -elected and recallable by the population – in governing roles, but also civil servants that previously operated in the central apparatus of the state and who today - thanks to the process of decentralization –carry out duties at the level of the village in areas such as health, education, sanitation, production, etc. Local governments also have buildings suited to fulfilling the functions of local self-government and the necessary logistics so that their personnel can work and attend to the population's needs.

213. In Venezuela, big strides have been made in terms of organization and popular participation, especially with the communal councils and communes (the lowest level of genuine self-government). To an extent, progress has been made in transferring funds. But there has been little advance made, except in a few cases,[32] in transferring competencies and human resources. The

---

30 Marta Harnecker *Transfiriendo poder a la gente.* Municipio Torres, paragraphs 105-128.

31 These are the same criteria that the nation uses for determining its budget, and that the Intergovernmental Fund for Decentralisation (FIDES) and the Law for Special Economic Allocations (LAEE) set out. They also put aside set amounts of funding for each parish, among them one that they called an emergency fund and another destined to science and technology and for the construction of schools.

32 For example, the municipality of Torres, in the state of Lara, Libertador in the state of Carabobo.

communes remain a long way away from counting upon the personnel and physical resources they require in order to function.[33]

4) TECHNICAL TEAMS TO PROMOTE THE DEVELOPMENT OF THE PROCESS

214. Decentralized participatory planning is not a process that can be generated spontaneously. Preparatory work is needed to create the conditions that can ensure the success of the process and, above all, raise awareness and mobilize the population so that from a passive population that demands public works and services it becomes an active population that takes into their own hands the resolution of many of their own problems.

215. As well as this preparatory work, we also have all the technical and material support work that is needed to take the planning process forward, and the monitoring and control of the process itself.

216. Political will alone is not enough to take the process forward or simply decentralizing human resources. As we will see when we look at the actors involved in the process, a municipality or other higher level entity that decides to carry out a process of participatory planning needs to create different teams at each level (municipality, territorial area and community) made up of volunteer technical experts and activists willing to take up these tasks.

217. These teams should work closely with the population, without substituting for them. Their support function is essential to creating confidence among residents involved in the process. They contribute experience and technical know-how, but above all provide the encouragement needed to help overcome any initial doubts and hesitations, which will naturally appear when embarking on any project for the first time.

5) RAISING AWARENESS AMONG THE POPULATION AND KEY PARTICIPANTS

218. Another fundamental condition for the success of the participatory planning process is ensuring that the population understands and agrees with the importance of their active and direct participation in planning to improving their lives both materially and spiritually, and that they adopt an attitude of greater commitment to the process. It is important to use a variety of ways to explain to the population why their active participation would be very beneficial for their family and their community.

219. To achieve this it is crucial to touch peoples' hearts. How do we do this given the current situation of generalized skepticism, where the dominant ideology leads people to believe in individual solutions, and where it appears as though there is no time to participate? We cannot go to the people and talk to them about a process they know nothing about and invite them to a meeting to "plan" in the abstract. We have to connect with them through their needs and most deeply felt desires, starting from the basis that every community, or sector within it, has its own characteristics and its own problems. A poor community could have problems with running water or electricity while a middle class community could have problems with crime and transit. As such, the desires of the residents in the first community are different to those of the second community. In the first, residents see obtaining access to water and electricity as the priority, while the problem of crime is not an issue. In the second, the fundamental desire is to see a police

---

33 It is worth pointing out that the Law of Transference of Competencies, Services and Other Attributions to Popular Power (November 2014) has still not been implemented.

post installed and patrols undertaken in the community. The way we invite people to participate will therefore be different depending on the place. In each case, we should hold a meeting to examine how the community could obtain its dreams. When people see the value of the meeting, because they can relate to the issues that will be covered, they will attend.

a) Awareness raising days

220. Awareness raising days should be held, involving talks, forums and assemblies, to inform residents of the process. It would be very useful to hold meetings for women, as they tend to be the best activists.

221. Advertisements and informational updates should be run in newspapers, on radio and television. Alternative media outlets could play an important role here. It may also be useful to distribute leaflets, hold expositions, convene meetings with parties and mass organizations at the local level, organize events at schools, stage cultural activities (concerts, street theatre). Announcements should be put up in places that residents frequent: shops, bakeries, pharmacies, schools, sports centers, cultural spaces, train stations and bus stops, etc.

b) Door-to-door visits

223. We need to make sure that invitations to attend the assemblies are widely delivered and that an effort is made to ensure that those present truly represent the interests of all residents. Door-to-door visits can be important for this, together with a small brochure that pedagogically explains the main issues and upcoming activities.

223. When residents of a community are not willing to open their doors, due to existing crime levels or opposition to door-to-door salespersons, it is important to look for other means to reach them and win their confidence. Only after this will it be possible to carry out door-to-door work. Sometimes organizing meetings where women are invited for a particular activity can be a good way to make initial contact.

224. We should not forget the importance of inviting and involving all political parties active in the community, so that community planning can be as integral and inclusive as possible.

c) Raising awareness among key participants

225. Together with raising awareness more generally, special emphasis should be placed on raising awareness among key participants in the process, that is, those people who will be in charge of certain tasks throughout the process.

226. They should understand and agree with the importance of citizens' participation for coming up with community plans, not only because this ensures that they reflect the most deeply felt aspirations of a community, but because it is through participation that people grow and develop.

227. Special care should be taken when transferring staff, especially from higher to lower planning units to ensure that it is not done in a mechanistic manner. Efforts need to be made to raise awareness among the public servants of the value of their new responsibilities for the development of their respective areas.

228. These participants should completely understand all the various steps involved in the planning process and their involvement in every activity.

229. It would be useful if the Team of Animators created a directory listing all those who make up the different social collectives that exist in the territory, the functionaries operating in all of the state entities at the various levels, and the institutions and people who may be able to lend their support to PP. Activist groups in the community should also do the same.

d) The Internet and its limitations

230. Although the Internet can be an important tool for convoking assemblies, we should never rely exclusively on this means. Often messages sent to groups or networks are not read precisely by those people that we are the most interested in inviting such as those who, because of their standout activism, tend to me bombarded with messages, or who because of their age or education level are not fully acquainted with the internet.

e) Meeting spaces

231. It is also important to choose a readily accessible meeting space to hold meetings that, where possible, is equidistant from the homes of all potential attendees.

232. The meeting space should accord with the plurality of views we want to be working with. It is not appropriate to; pick a particular religious hall knowing that there are people of different religions in the community; or the offices of a political party when people within the community are active in or support other parties; or a very luxurious place where people from a poorer background may feel out of place; or a place that is hard to access.

f) Meeting times

233. Furthermore, it is important to hold meetings and assemblies at an appropriate time. They should be held at a time that can facilitate maximum attendance. We should avoid work hours, those hours where women find it difficult to attend, or those that clash with television soap operas or sports telecasts that tend to be watched by many in the community.

6) TRAINING PARTICIPANTS

234. To ensure genuine participation in the planning process, it is not enough to simply have good attendance levels at the meetings. We need to be able to actively involve people in the process, thereby stimulating their interest at the same time as providing them with the basic theoretical and technical knowledge of planning that can allow them to participate effectively in the process.

235. It is not enough to simply transfer human resources and hope that citizens will participate to the maximum extent possible. It is also crucial to train technical personnel, elected representatives and the population itself, providing them with skills and experience that can help them to play meaningful roles in participatory planning.

236. We agree with Rafael Enciso, an economist who advised the Federal Council of the Venezuelan Government during 2013, who said that "transferring responsibilities without creating the minimum necessary capacities can mean that the medicine ends up being worse than the illness."

237. To achieve this we should organize training days for the technical experts, the members of the promotion team and the people who sign up to participate in the different working groups set up during the process.

238. The less technical courses can be open to the general public.

239. Training programs should be held at the different levels and, ideally, there should be manuals that summarize the principle ideas.

240. These courses should be given by people with academic training or with a large amount of practical experience. They can be recruited from outside the community: from universities or technical colleges, as well as state institutions and organizations of retired professional and technical experts.

241. These people should function as "trainers." In municipalities that are carrying out a process of participatory planning, the mayoral or district office should hold training days to train the trainers.

242. It is also useful to hold workshops to exchange experiences between communities or territorial areas that have initiated the process or between different neighborhood areas within the same community. It is also useful to analyze how the process is going with all the various participants with the aim of correcting in time any errors that may have been committed and detect weaknesses. This way, the people themselves become trainers, training other people in their community or territorial area.

243. Learning about other successful community experiences from other countries can also be very enriching.

244. An interesting pedagogical initiative could be to hold a series of video screenings in the neighborhood areas with documentaries made by the Centro de Investigaciones "Memoria Popular Latinoamericana" (MEPLA, "Popular Latin American Memory" Centre of Investigations). These documentaries present – in an attractive and pedagogical manner – various successful community experiences from different Latin American countries. Readers can find a concrete proposal for such a series online at http://videosmepla.wordpress.com/.[34]

245. These educational activities seek to break down the barrier between "those who know" (technical experts, public servants, politicians) and "those who don't know".

246. We should not forget however, that no training day could ever teach someone more than what they learn in practice by participating in the planning process.

247. Lastly, we want to point out that an important part of this training initiative should begin before the different participants assume their respective responsibilities.

7) PRIORITIZE ACCORDING ONE'S OWN RESOURCES

248. One of the most important factors for ensuring the success of any decentralized participatory planning process is making sure the participants understand that they should set goals that can be achieved within a short timeframe, using one's own resources and the active involvement of the largest number of people possible. They should not simply wait for the state or other entities – governmental or otherwise – to assign them funds to begin carrying out tasks. Even if external resources do not arrive, there are many initiatives that can be undertaken immediately.

249. But setting achievable goals implies a new way of diagnosing the situation; one that prioritizes those initiatives that can be implemented with the resources the community, territorial area or municipality has at hand.

250. If the diagnosis is not carried out with this criterion in mind, what tends to happen is that, rather than stimulating participation, people tend to remain passive, waiting for a higher body to resolve their problems, or they become disillusioned with the participatory process because the desired results are not obtained.

251. To give any diagnosis such a focus, the people should know what potentialities and opportunities exist in their surroundings, such as available volunteer labor, and the possibility of using scrap materials, fundraising, and organizing activities that can help raise money, etc. They

---

34. They are available with English subtitles.

should also investigate what opportunities a particular industry in the territory could provide in terms of helping them with their activities.

252. By letting our imaginations run free; we might find that we have at our hands an infinite number of resources that we previously had not seen.

253. Prioritizing aspirations that can be implemented with one's own resources means we can immediately begin executing priority public works, the results will be seen in the short term and, with that, the self-esteem of the people will rise, motivating them to participate with more enthusiasm in future tasks.

254. This prioritizing should not simply be the responsibility of the Planning Team or the Council; we should invite all neighbors to contribute to the diagnosis and provide ideas for solutions or possible alternatives.

255. This criterion is especially important at the community level. Ensuring that a community is capable of finding ways to self-finance all or part of its initial plan is a fundamental condition for the success of the process.

256. Moreover, the community dynamic that is awakened when people realize that problems can be resolved if everyone is willing to contribute their share tends to attract the attention of the state. Often, these communities are the first to benefit from state funds.

257. Readers can see for themselves what we are talking about in the aforementioned documentaries filmed by MEPLA.

258. Where the solution is too costly or complex and therefore out of the reach of the people, the communal, territorial or municipal council should present them as part of the participatory planning process to other government bodies.

5) GENERATING A USEFUL AND ACCURATE DATABASE

259. Another fundamental premise for DPP is the need to generate an accurate and up-to-date database in regards to the aspirations that the people have formulated.[35]

260. Some readers might be asking why are we restricting the database to a certain number of aspirations rather than talking about a database that covers all aspects of the community, territorial area or municipality.

261. Undoubtedly, the ideal situation would involve the most thorough database possible, but experience shows that often a lot of time is spent on building up a database, delaying the initiation of the planning process when, in fact, much of this data is not needed for coming up with the plan.

262. What sense does it make to investigate existing healthcare infrastructure, available healthcare workers, the most common diseases, how well pharmacies are functioning, the price of medicines, etc., if residents are happy with the healthcare they currently receive and are instead concerned with resolving aspirations to do with unemployment or school absenteeism, for example?

---

35. This important observation was made to us by Carlos García Pleyán.

263. Is it not more logical to focus our efforts on obtaining data that can allow us to more deeply analyze these issues, rather than dispersing our efforts trying to build a thorough database, which implies a lot of effort for little short term return?

264. Of course, a basic minimum of general data is required, but we recommend only delving deeper once the most significant aspirations of the population have been collected.

265. In the second volume looking at methodology, readers will find information on what to investigate and how to present the information when trying to compile a thorough database. But, we reiterate, this should not be our starting point or a prerequisite for beginning the planning process. We nevertheless think it handy to have data that can provide us with a more objective vision of our reality, while obtaining more data as needed in order to advance the community planning process.

266. Often, at the different levels of various state institutions or NGOs, we can find particular data, but nowhere is this data organized in a single place, much less at the community level. And this data usually does not tend to refer to social actors, something that for us, with our humanist and pro-participation focus, is central.

267. It can be handy to rely on a group of activists to compile this data.

268. This group of activists should seek the support of people who are knowledgeable in the areas they are investigating (school directors, family doctors, priests, local police officers). They should also visit the offices of local governments and other state entities to find more technical data, such as land use, types of soil, available infrastructure and any other information that could be relevant to studying a particular aspiration. This last activity could be transformed into a popular audit of how these public services handle statistical data.

269. It can also be useful to work with the community in coming up with a map that notes the boundaries of the territory, its roads, its educational institutions, health clinics, workplaces, shopping centers, churches, sports facilities, meeting and recreational spaces (library, cinemas, theatre, Infocenters), green spaces, tourist attractions, etc. This map should include basic demographic data.

270. We know that there are complicated methodologies for coming up with different types of maps. What we are suggesting is something much simpler, something without grand scientific pretenses but that is pedagogically useful, and especially useful for illiterate residents. Moreover, the map can help those who find it hard to deal with figures. Once clearly outlined on a map, a certain issue can become less abstract.

271. Children have a lot to contribute to this. They frequently detect things that adults do not notice. Schools in the community could include children's mapping into their curriculum. We should not forget that children are people with their own views and needs and that they have a right to be part of the process of shaping the reality they live in everyday and into the future.

9) INFORMATION AND TRANSPARENCY

272. Lastly, but not less important, a successful planning process requires that residents have the means to monitor its progress, ensuring transparency at all moments.

273. This means that all information relating to the process should be accessible to any interested citizen, during the development of plan as well as during its implementation. Debates in the different spaces should be public. Further below we will look at practical ways for achieving this.

CHAPTER V. PHASES IN THE PLANNING PROCESS

274. In any participatory planning process, it is possible to distinguish two different phases:
(a) Coming up with and developing the plan itself.
(b) Implementing the plan and monitoring to ensure it is properly carried out, and evaluation of their results.

1. DEVELOPING THE PLAN

275. Coming up with the plan is a complex process involving various steps
(see diagram page 47):

(1) Defining the desired changes
(2) Setting out priorities
(3) Exploring alternative courses of action for implementing the changes
(4) Coming up with projects
(5) Drafting the Development Plan, the Annual Investment Plan and the Budget, and at the community level the Immediate Action Plan.

STEPS IN THE PLANNING PROCESS

Defining the desired changes

Setting out priorities

Exploring alternative courses of action for implementing the changes

Coming up with projects

Drafting the Development Plan, the Annual Investment Plan and the Budget.

Implementing the plan

Monitoring to ensure it is properly carried out

Evaluation of results

276. Let us turn to look at what each of these steps entails.

FIRST STEP: DEFINING THE DESIRED CHANGES (ASPIRATIONS)

277. To transform our reality we need to know where we want to go; that is, we need to be clear on the characteristics of the kind of society we want to build. This entails being able to imagine the ideal reality we would like to live in.

278. We tend to analyze reality by simply focusing on problems. But when we do this we cut off the emergence of initiatives that only tend to come up when we begin to dream about the ideal community we would like to live in.

279. Imagine for example, a territorial area in which the walls of public buildings are covered in children's paintings done by the children themselves. Or a community that is poor but has a high level of solidarity, in which residents – despite not having access to public transport at night – feel safe because in cases of emergencies they can be sure they will be taken to hospital or a medical clinic because from within the community emerged an initiative in which people with cars take turns to make themselves available to support neighbors, thereby ensuring transport is always available in the community.[36]

280. We need to dream, but within certain limits because we have to start with who we are and the dreams we will build have to be compatible and in harmony with the characteristics of our reality.

281. The dreams of a rural municipality with a semi-arid climate cannot be the same as those of a municipality with an abundant water supply or a densely populated urban municipality.

282. In any case, we believe that there are certain aspects that should always be present in our considerations. We are thinking here of things such as culture, education, the economic situation, respect for the environment, sports, healthcare, infrastructure, the situation of groups that are marginalized or discriminated against, among others.

283. Furthermore, we need to think of how we would like to see our community, not only in physical terms but also in terms of the relationships among residents. Here we should keep in mind an aspect that we usually forget: the organizational one.

284. We need to find concrete ways to express our dreams in order to go beyond mere abstractions. These are what we call "aspirations".

285. For example, when dreaming of a safe, harmonious community, this can be expressed in aspirations such as: a community where we can feel safe walking down the road, where there are no break-ins or muggings, where the population is disarmed and drug addicts can be rehabilitated.

286. The final result of this step should be coming up with an initial list of aspirations (for more information on this step, see our forthcoming Second Volume on Methodology)

SECOND STEP: SETTING OUT PRIORITIES

287. After dreaming of the community, territory or municipality we want and having made these dreams more concrete by coming up with aspirations, we have to list them in order of priority at

---

36. See documentary Mi barrio echó a andar.

each level, as it is impossible to simultaneously implement all the aspirations, as we will never have all the necessary time or resources to achieve this.

288. One way of establishing priorities could be by voting: the aspirations that receive the most votes become the main priorities. But this method, while seemingly simple and democratic, can produce grave distortions because the hurried nature of the vote may not allow us to take into consideration all aspects of a particular problem, not to mention that it opens up the possibility of assembly votes being manipulated.

289. That is why we propose that during this step a detailed study of each aspiration be carried out and a points system be established in accordance with certain previously approved criteria, as a way of prioritizing aspirations in the most objective manner possible.

290. To do this we would have to analyze all the aspirations formulated in the previous step, pointing out the problems and potential threats that could impede them becoming reality, and the strengths and opportunities that could help us make them a reality. This information can help us to establish priorities.

291. To avoid doubling up on work, we propose that each level (community, territorial area, municipality) only study those aspirations that correspond to them.

a) Analyze each aspiration thoroughly

292. Before continuing, let's look at what we mean by some of the terms we have just used.

▪ What do we mean by community problems?

293. These are defined as those problems and issues that affect the normal and dignified functioning of daily life of residents in a determined locality: deficient basic services (electricity, water, sewers, drainage, asphalt); crime; unemployment; lack of recreational infrastructure (sports fields, cultural centers, parks, plazas); deficient social infrastructure (schools, medical clinics, childcare centers); lack of participation or community organization; social disintegration, loss or lack of identity, conflict-ridden or non-existent relations, among others.

▪ What do we mean by threats?

294. Threats refers to those elements whose presence or evolution, if not corrected, could impede the solution to, or aggravate, existing problems, or otherwise encourage new ones to appear. Threats can be internal to a community, territorial area or municipality (an increase in drug use among youth, a rise in the number of houses in a precarious state as a consequence of new residents moving in and building their own houses, etc.) or external (the construction of a highway that would divide the community in two, the expansion of large agro-industrial companies that threaten small local producers, etc.)

▪ What do we mean by strengths?

295. Strengths refers to the different resources present in a population such as: human talent (natural leaders, bricklayers, artisans, bakers, engineers, mechanics, teachers); willingness of residents to collaborate in community activities, prevailing sense of solidarity; worker collectives attempting to change the productive model; existing social organizations (urban land committees, health committees, social protection committees, cultural groups, sports clubs, religious groups, shopkeepers, volunteer groups); ethical values, history and positive traditions of solidarity and struggle; natural elements that favor certain economic activities (minerals, seas, lakes, rivers, beaches, fertile soil); existing infrastructure (schools, public buildings, factories, small productive units), among others.

- What do we mean by opportunities?

296. Opportunities refers to those outside elements the community can employ to their benefit: social programs carried out by the national government[37]; national, regional or municipal popular financial plans[38]; companies that are present in the territory or surrounding territories[39]; the existence of systems of non-mercantile exchange of products and services; positive relations with other entities that share the same vision, the presence of external forces working in the same direction (NGOs, women's movements, etc.); a favorable attitude in the media, among others.

- An example of how to analyze an aspiration

297. Lets look at how this is applied when analyzing one of the community aspirations mentioned above: the desire to be able to spend the night walking the streets without fear of being mugged.

298. One of the problems that exist in terms of this aspiration is that the streets in the community are poorly lit, which is why so many muggings occur. There exists the threat that violence may increase and armed youth gangs may begin to appear.

299. Among the strengths that exist that could help overcome this situation is the willingness of residents to involve themselves in volunteer street patrols.

300. Among the opportunities that exist is the fact that municipal authorities are concerned by the situation and willing to take measures to help overcome it. The necessary electricity grid also exists and the lampposts are in a good state, the only thing missing is lighting. Lastly, the state has offered to exchange scrap metal (of which there is an abundance in this community) for light bulbs.

b) Prioritizing aspirations

301. Once we have come up with a diagnosis of the existing situation in relation to each aspiration put forward, we need to establish a priority list to know where to start. This list should be developed using certain criteria that can enable us to give each aspiration a score.

302. The criteria we select should relate to the objectives we want to reach: in this case, as well as the criteria of urgency, the number of residents that will benefit, the cost of solving the problem, we would like to add, the extent to which it benefits the poorest sectors, women and youth, and how compatible it is with the protection of the environment.

303. As the possibility exists that using these criteria we could end up prioritizing aspirations that can only be resolved with external resources – something that, as we mentioned before, would lead to people remaining with their arms crossed waiting for others to solve their problems – we should add another criterion: capacity of the community, territorial area or municipality to make the aspiration a reality using their own resources.

304. But how can we make sure that we prioritize the aspirations that can be satisfied using one's own resources? By employing a method that will allow us to obtain the desired results.

305. The World Health Organization has a methodological proposal for obtaining these objectives. An adapted and simplified version of this method is outlined in Annex VI of this

---

37. In the case of Venezuela: Mercal, educational missions, army reservists, etc.

38. In the case of Venezuela: Fonendógeno, Peoples' Bank, Women's Bank, Fondemi, cooperative banks, regional credit funds.

39. And if these companies are managed by the community.

book. Readers can also see how it is applied in the documentary *Buscando el camino (método de trabajo comunitario),* which looks at what happened in the rural Cuban community of Guadalupe, in the province of Ciego de Ávila, when this method was applied[40].

306. The documentary shows how issues such as recreation, development of sports, and the fight against crime, among others, are successfully dealt with using the community's own resources.

307. As can be seen in the documentary, linking aspirations and problems to real possibilities of solving them was key to the development of this community. It made them feel strong and confident in themselves. When people could see that the problems impeding the materialization of their aspirations were being overcome, they felt they were capable of solving even bigger problems. They developed their capacities and more and more they became protagonists in the whole process. Unfortunately, this aspect is often not taken into consideration.

308. In sum, as we have said before and want to emphasize here, one of the most important factors in the success of a participatory planning process has been people understanding that, even if external resources do not arrive, there are many initiatives that can be taken up using the available resources and efforts.

309. This is not to say that we should set aside larger aspirations simply because they require external support to make them a reality. In some cases we should take these aspirations to entities that could assume the project themselves. In others, the community, territorial area or municipality could take on the project if they are able to obtain the necessary financing. In the latter case, such aspirations should be included in the corresponding development plan.

c) Defining sector-base priorities

310. This moment should also serve to help establish, if considered necessary, some flexible criteria in respect to the distribution of possible investment into sectors. These criteria will be denominated sector-base priorities.

311. We will call these criteria sector-based priorities. They could be very useful for avoiding a situation where some sector is left out when the plan is executed or where some problems are given exclusive priority to the detriment of others.

312. Although in some cases the municipality or higher up bodies may provide certain guidelines, the sector-based priorities should be discussed within the participatory planning process as a way of providing clear direction.

THIRD STEP: EXPLORE ALTERNATIVE COURSES OF ACTION FOR IMPLEMENTING THE CHANGES

313. After prioritizing the aspirations we should explore alternative courses of action for making a reality of those aspirations that we are in able to deal with directly, even if this might be via accessing additional funds.

314. When exploring alternative courses of action for satisfying a particular demand, we should take into consideration the previous analyses we have made regarding available human and

---

40. Link to the documentary: http://videosmepla.wordpress.com/documentales-de-participacion-popular/ciclo-video-debate/5-buscando-el-camino/ . The documentary is accompanied by a book by Marta Harnecker, *Buscando el camino (método de trabajo comunitario),* published in Cuba by MEPLA in 2000 and also available online: http://www.rebelion.org/docs/95168.pdf .

material resources, costs and impact of the proposal on the population, as well as what capacity exists to carry out the actions required to implement and maintain the project over time.

315. If when analyzing the aspirations we come across solutions that are beyond our capacities (for example, a community wanting to build a multi-function sports center) we should meticulously note these down in order to put them forward as demands before higher institutions without putting aside other solutions that can be implemented and that should be incorporated into the plan.

316. Each aspiration should be analyzed, reflecting firstly on what can be done in general terms to satisfy the aspiration and, secondly, how we should implement in practice these action proposals, pointing out the different activities we need to carry out and putting special effort to plan even the smallest details.

317. For example, in terms of our aspiration that youth get more involved in sports in order to avoid them falling into drug addiction, alcoholism or addiction to the internet as is so common among youth today, we could take many different initiatives or roads towards achieving this goal, such as: a) set up a group of sports promoters, b) fix up the sports field, c) set up a boys, girls and youth football teams in the community.

318. But, as we have previously said, it is not enough to come up with possible solutions; we need to think of what kinds of actions are required in order to, for example, set up these football teams. This would include motivating boys, girls and youth to sign up by visiting schools. And to make sure these visits are successful we need to avoid falling into improvisation and plan them with anticipation. We need to call the school director so that they can indicate the most appropriate time to visit and indicate whether it is better to meet with the youth in a large hall or visit each classroom individually.

319. Planning even the smallest details is important for ensuring our efforts are successful. Simon Bolivar use to say that battles are won or lost in the details.

320. In the second volume we will look at how to carry out this step.

FOURTH STEP: COMING UP WITH PROJECTS

321. After exploring the various alternative courses of action, we need to turn them into concrete projects, that is, outline them in a document that describes all the activities and tasks required to make the aspiration a reality. The activities need to be programmed and accompanied by the necessary technical information for their execution as well as their cost.

322. The number of projects will depend on how we group the alternatives that have emerged for making these aspirations a reality.

323. Depending on the type of proposal and its scale, we may find ourselves with both simple and more complex projects

324. It may be the case that the projects, particularly at the community level, are relatively easy and can be implemented by people in the community, for example painting a community school or fixing up a room so that children can paint there and watch kids television.

325. But communities and territorial areas, depending on the available human and material resources, and logically the municipality, can also take on more complex projects.

326. For example, in order to build social housing a technical project is needed. This generally requires the participation of architects, engineers and project managers to determine the technical characteristics of the project such as design plans, amount of cement needed, specific materials

required, etc. Even in these cases, ordinary people participating via the participatory spaces can improve the "technical" content of the project by offering solutions and alternatives for cheaper costs and making the project better suited to the real needs of the population.

FIFTH STEP: DRAFTING THE DEVELOPMENT PLAN, THE ANNUAL PLAN AND THE IMMEDIATE ACTION PLAN

327. After all the projects have been drawn up, we have to come up with a Development Plan. This should contain all the projects that can be carried out at each level with the resources available to them and also those projects that depend on additional funds that a state entity or NGO could provide directly. This document should point out the objective sought with each project, those responsible for it and the time needed to implement it. Moreover, so that we do not forget about our dreams, the plan should include in an annex those aspirations that at the community, territorial level or municipality cannot be made a reality because they are too complex and costly and therefore need to be presented to corresponding higher level institutions.

328. But as we will see in Volume II, a Development Plan is not simply a sum of projects. In the first place, it should be coherent with the sector-based priorities that have been established. It must also include other information that can allow us to quantify results in relations to the objectives being sought.

329. As we said in Chapter III, in some cases it can take many years to implement the Development Plan. Therefore, once it has been decided which projects will be carried out during each year of the plan, on the basis of the resources available for those years and the established sector-based priorities, an Annual Investment Plan should be drawn up as well as an Annual Budget that takes into consideration the income is available to finance expenditures such as recurring costs for that year and funds to be destined to the Annual Investment Plan.

330. The elaboration of the simplest budgets in the community projects will be relatively simple. More complex budgets will require a prior debate to determine how to distribute resources between running costs and investments and set priority areas for the former. We will define these criteria as "budgetary priorities."

331. Finally, as we said in in paragraph 177 of Chapter 3, an Immediate Action Plan needs to be developed so that the projects that the communities can carry out with their own resources can be initiated as soon as they are approved, without needing to wait for the process of coming up with a Community Development Plan to have finished.

2. IMPLEMENTION, MONITORING AND EVALUATION OF THE RESULTS

332. Given it would make little sense to come up with a plan that remained solely on paper, we believe that an integral part of the participatory planning process is its implementation and the processes to ensure it is correctly carried out.

1) IMPLEMENTATION AND MONITORING

333. The people should also monitor and control the implementation of more complex projects carried out by companies or specialized entities. To carry out these tasks, the people need to have the necessary instruments.

2) EVALUATION OF THEIR RESULTS

334. Once each project has been completed, it can be useful to carry out a brief balance sheet of the experience, pointing out achievements, difficulties and the way in which they were overcome. This can be very useful for future experiences.

335. A general balance sheet should also be drawn up of how the Annual Investment Plan was executed, analyzing its level of execution (if there are projects that were not carried out or suffered delays, the causes and any subsequent modifications to foreseeable income) and the results achieved in relation to the aspirations and whether they were satisfied.

336. This balance sheet should be drawn up prior to the conclusion of each Annual Investment Plan, as its findings could lead to rectifying the following Annual Plan which should be drawn up and approved prior to the previous one finishing so that its execution can begin immediately once the prior one has finished.

337. Similarly, shortly before the period has concluded for the (multi-year) Development Plan, a general balance sheet should be drawn up of its execution and the results achieved. This should be the starting point for coming up with the following Development Plan.

3) CONSOLIDATING OF WHAT HAS BEEN ACHIEVED

338. Given we are not simply dealing with building new public works, improving services or carrying out beautification initiatives, but also ensuring they are maintained over time, we think it is very important that once a project is completed (painting a school, building a kids park, etc.) a system is set up to ensure it is kept in a good state by, for example, setting up a neighbors' committee to look after it. Clemente Scotto, the former mayor of Caroní, Ciudad Guayana, Venezuela dubbed this action the "democratic consolidation of projects."

339. Lastly, we should not only monitor the progress of the public works being executed at each level and the services being provided; we should be attentive to the subjective situation of the people who live in the municipality, area or community.

340. We should monitor how relations between residents are evolving, how the different work committees and community organizations are working together, how the people view the actions of the government, where conflicts have arisen, etc.

341. It would be very useful to come up with tables and graphs with all this data to be able to visualize the overall situation at a particular moment in its development, see how the situation is evolving over time and be able to point out critical issues that have to be resolved.

PART II. INSTANCES AND ACTORS

CHAPTER VI. GENERAL CONSIDERATIONS

342. In order to put in practice a process of decentralized participatory planning (DPP) within a municipality (along the lines outlined in Part I of this book), a number of entities are required to take responsibility for the process at different levels. Also required is the participation of a series of actors. In this chapter, we will look at these organizational aspects of DPP and outline the various roles involved, starting with the municipal level.

343. Before doing so, we would like to highlight some aspects of how we believe the participatory planning system should function in general. It should combine direct democracy with delegated democracy, involving thematic forums as well as geographically based assemblies. At the same time, it should also involve a solid base of professional and technical volunteers and incorporate training workshops at all levels. Lastly, it should include entities for general coordination as well as entities at each level of the DPP process.

1) COMBINATION OF DIRECT DEMOCRACY AND DELEGATED DEMOCRACY

344. We said it should combine two forms of democracy: **direct democracy**, where everyone who attends an assembly discusses and debates what to do; and **delegated democracy**, where only representatives, delegates or spokespersons have the authority to make decisions. The first form of democracy occurs at the local community level; delegated or representative democracy occurs at the higher levels. We have preferred to use the term delegate and not representative democracy for the negative connotations attached to the latter term, which is generally associated with bourgeois representative democracy.

a) Direct democracy and its limits

345. Direct democracy is one form of democracy[41], without a doubt the richest form and the one which encourages the greatest possible protagonism. However, it has its limits. For everyone to be able to fully participate, the size of the group cannot be excessively large. It is difficult to

---

41. **Direct democracy** is a form of democracy in which power is exercised directly by the people in an assembly. ... Direct democracy differs from representative democracy, given that in the latter, power is exercised by a small group of representatives, generally elected by the people (Wikipedia). There are limited forms of direct democracy, such as popular initiatives, referendums (plebicites) and recall referendums. More recently, there has been talk of electronic direct democracy, involving the use of the internet and other technologies for electronic communication to consult and allow citizens to vote.

imagine direct democracy in a municipality with 200,000 people, and even less so direct democracy in large capital cities made up of millions of people.

346. We have to create a system that allows citizens to participate, not only in the small areas but also in all decision-making processes that affect their lives. This requires establishing some form of delegation of power from the local assemblies upwards to the higher-level deliberative bodies, but it must not reproduce the limits and deformities inherent in classic bourgeois representative politics.

347. Denying the possibility of delegation is to deny the possibility to decide on issues that transcend our local reality (community, workplace, classroom).

348. A correct critique of bourgeois representative democracy should not lead us to reject all types of representation. We criticize it not because it is representative, but because it is not sufficiently representative.

349. Representatives, delegates or spokespersons, are not given a blank check for a certain period of time like bourgeois representatives; rather they must be guided by the decisions and orientations of their constituents who evaluate their performance according to the tasks they have been assigned.

350. Here we have to clarify this is not the same as saying that their mandate is binding. They are not robots that receive messages and simply transmit them; they are responsible and creative people who, faced with the realities of other communities and territorial areas, must be able to modify the mandate they have received.

351. In the system we are proposing, two types of delegation exist: that referring to what we have called Planning Councils at the three different levels, and that referring to the respective Planning Assemblies. The reader will find a detailed explanation of both entities in Chapter VIII 2.

b) Delegated democracy assemblies and direct democracy assemblies

352. The DPP process we are proposing combines assemblies based on a system of delegation or delegated democracy, and assemblies in which citizens from a particular geographical area participate directly, that is, assemblies based on direct democracy. The system of delegated democracy assemblies applies to all higher levels. Direct democracy assemblies are held at the community level.

353. Not all attendees at the participatory planning assemblies in the municipal or territorial level have the right to speak and vote. Only those people who have been elected by their respective grassroots assembly have this right. Nevertheless, we recommend that in either case, the meetings should be open to the public with no restriction, so that any interested citizen can attend as an observer and monitor the process.

c) Delegation strengthens democracy

354. Some say that a DPP process carried out via representatives or delegates can lead to its bureaucratization and convert it into just another bourgeois representative process. According to these critics, what is required is a more democratic process based on assemblies and not a process based on a system of delegation or spokespersons. It is worth asking however: would an assembly of 200, 500 or 1000 people, in an urban territorial area that has more than 600,000 residents, be more democratic? Have these critics thought about who generally attends such assemblies? Is it not mainly those with vehicles, those who live close to public transport, those who can get there by foot, those who work for state institutions that free them up to be there? How many do not attend because they live far away or do not have access to transport, or because they have to work

in their corner shop to survive?

355. And in those large assemblies, who mainly talks and makes proposals? Is it not the same old leaders? Is it not those who are always trying to stand out? What about the opinions of the humble people who only feel comfortable expressing themselves in small groups and who are afraid to talk in large assemblies?

356. These are some of the considerations that have led us to propose a system of representation, delegation or spokespersons, that does not weaken but instead enhances the DPP process, because representatives come to meetings prepared and steeped in the problems and resources of their respective communities.

d) How to avoid a separation between the grassroots and their representatives

357. We understand the concern of those who warn that elected representatives can end up no longer being "the voice of their communities and territories" and instead start acting on their own volition, putting forward their own wish list. There is no better measure to avoid such deviations than to ensure that delegates have to report back to the community that elected them, thereby making the whole process as transparent as possible. Publishing the list of public works or services decided upon by the community in a public place and making the assembly of delegates open to everyone who wants to attend can do this. Where possible, it would be useful to publish this information on the Internet.

358. In some recent experiences with assemblies, such as those of Chilean students, the figure of "overseer", a kind of political commissar of the assembly, has been introduced to ensure that delegates comply with their mandate. The task of these "overseers" is to observe and ensure that elected leaders stick to what has been previously agreed upon.

359. Furthermore, it is important to take care with open assemblies because certain parties or economic groups (such as shopkeepers, transport drivers, etc.) may be able to pay others to attend in order to ensure one sector has a majority and can manipulate the decision-making process. Established interest groups tend to carry out planned actions to defend their interests. We should not be naïve to this reality.

360. Of course, it is also very important that voters correctly select whom they want to be their delegates. In this regards, the Venezuelan experience once again provides important insights. It has shown us the importance of ensuring that the process for electing spokespeople is prepared in a careful manner, where the people know who the candidates are, not only because of what they say but because of what they have done.

361. How can they get to know the candidates? The successful experiences of some Venezuelan communal councils has shown the usefulness of involving candidates, before elections occur, in the preparatory tasks for the process and in visiting families door-to-door. Through this process they are obliged to get in contact with each family in the community. It has also been useful for them to talk to local citizens in order to come up with a short history of the community. This has allowed them to better understand the reality of the community they want to serve.

362. Candidates will not be able to get elected simply on the basis of nice speeches because the community will have been able to see in practice how genuine their dedication to serving the people is. This approach can avoid the problem of electing people who are only interested in

positions as a launch pad for their own political careers.[42] Further on we will refer to who should be included in these assemblies at the different levels of the DPP process along with their respective tasks.

e) Citizens' participation in communities: a system of direct democracy

363. Participation in the DPP process should be open to all interested persons, regardless of political stripes, nationality, ethnic origin, sexual orientation and the like. They can and should attend and express their opinions and recommendations in grassroots assemblies in their community. As much as possible, they should actively participate in a variety of other ways: attending one of the working groups formed during the DPP process, following up on the implementation of public works projects, convening assemblies, etc.

364. At their grassroots assemblies, ordinary citizens should express their aspirations, collaborate in the creation of community databases, identification of problems, solutions, definition of priority issues, and recommendation of project ideas that can make their wishes for a better life become a reality. They should also participate in developing less complex projects, in the discussion and approval of their community's multi-year development plan, annual investment plan and its budget, and in the implementation, monitoring, and evaluation of the plan, as well as contributing their voluntary labor in the implementation of the various community projects.

365. As we have said, any citizen can attend the higher-level assemblies as an observer if he or she wishes.

366. As we noted, to ensure that a citizens' assembly is truly representative of the entire community, delegates (spokespersons) from all corners of the community should be present, even those who live farthest away.

2) PUBLIC FORUMS

a) Thematic forums

367. Until now, when we have talked about assemblies, we have been referring to those taking place at the geographical base of the DPP process. Often it is those individuals or groups that have the most needs that tend to feel more motivated to attend these geographic-based assemblies.

368. To enrich the DPP process with information and suggestions regarding the issues that most affect citizens, whether in general or in terms of a particular sector, we suggest that the municipal or territorial planning council organize public meetings for debating these issues. We have named these "thematic forums." They could also be held in a community to try and resolve a particularly complex situation that has arisen within it. Forums of this type tend to attract those who would not normally attend geographically based meetings: trade unionists, students, professionals and technicians, cultural and ecological movement activists, business owners, shopkeepers, farmers, etc.

369. For example, we know that in Venezuela, various areas in the Sierra de Falcón face a lack of water, and that a proposed aqueduct project has led to conflicts among people living in the area. This could therefore be an issue for a big forum to which interested residents and local, national, even international technicians and expert professionals could be invited. If we are dealing with communities in Latin America, international organizations such as the Caribbean Community

---

42. This is developed further in paragraphs 87 -88; 91-96.

(CARICOM), the SELA, the Bolivarian Alliance for the Peoples of Our Americas (ALBA), the Common Market of the South (MERCOSUR), and the Community of Latin American and Caribbean States (CELAC), could be strengthened if they were allowed to participate in these forums to provide support and facilitate the exchange of ideas.[43]

369. Sabemos, por ejemplo: que en Venezuela en varios territorios de la Sierra de Falcón hay gran escasez de agua y que existe un proyecto de acueducto sobre el cual hay posiciones encontradas. Este podría ser, entonces, el tema de un foro temático al que debería invitarse, además de a los habitantes interesados en este tema, a técnicos y profesionales expertos en la materia, tanto locales como de nivel nacional, y hasta de nivel internacional, si se considerara conveniente. Si se tratase de comunidades de América Latina: Caricom, SELA, Alba, Mercosur, Celac se verían reforzadas como entidades internacionales si se les diese la oportunidad de participar en estas funciones de apoyo e intercambio.

370. If a municipality has big health problems and other nearby communities put forward the need to improve healthcare, then a forum could be held to look at the issue from a holistic viewpoint. Health professionals and technicians should be invited to such a forum, along with delegates from health service providers and experts, so that they can contribute their ideas and suggestions.

371. We believe that in various Latin American countries, it would be worthwhile holding a national forum, or at least regional forums, on the issues of mining and natural resource management in territories where the indigenous people, the rural and African-American communities, have suffered the effects of this type of exploitation of their natural resources. The forums could provide a space for dialogue over the advantages and disadvantages of continuing with extractive activities and how conditions could be improved by changing the productive model.

372. There is also a need to think about a thematic forum that could particularly interest young people.

373. Although we propose that these forums not be decision-making forums, as is the case in Porto Alegre, we do think that their deliberations should nourish debates in the respective municipal or territorial participatory planning council. This would be of enormous benefit for the projects, proposals, reflections and suggestions that come out of these bodies. The forums should be held at the same time as the first level DPP assemblies are occurring in the organized community, the first level of the process, so that the results are available when the discussion to prepare the plan begins in the territorial area and the municipality[44].

374. Furthermore, they could play the role of a mass training school for councilors and everyone who wants to participate in the DPP process.

375. If forums are well planned and central authorities are invited, such forums could be ideal spaces for making authorities aware of local and regional issues, and increase their willingness to provide resources and institutional capacities for initiatives that can solve these problems.

b) Service forums

---

43. Based on feedback received from Ximena de la Barra on 28 July 2014.

44. In a forthcoming second book we will provide a methodology for these workshops.

376. An interesting idea that we have borrowed from the Porto Alegre experience is forums dedicated to discussing the situation of public services that are not meeting people's needs. The idea is to invite residents who want to participate as well as functionaries from the respective public service. In Porto Alegre this initiative was able to go some distance towards creating spaces for controlling the actions of the inherited bureaucratic apparatus. It also helped ensure that participatory budgeting assemblies did not become too focused on criticizing the bureaucracy, and instead concentrated on proposing solutions to existing problems.

3) TRAINING WORKSHOPS

377. It is important to plan for some training workshops for participants. These can be opportunities for sharing experiences in which participants teach other at various levels:
• At the technical level, to unify the vision and methodology employed by technical teams that will act as facilitators of the planning process at different levels (community, territorial area and municipality);
• For the Planning Councils, to provide territorial and municipal councilors with the necessary socio-political and technical knowledge they will need to fulfill their duties; and,
• For territorial delegates, to provide them with knowledge of basic planning and other concepts that will help them to understand DPP and act as promoters and evaluators of the process.

378. Workshops should start before these persons assume their respective tasks. They should be given precise information regarding the responsibilities for each level of the DPP process.

379. A degree program, masters or postgraduate course on territorial DPP could also be organized by one or more universities in the municipality. This would allow participants to receive academic credit for the training they receive in designing and implementing the municipal development plan. This could serve as an incentive for those who participate in such a complex process and is a credential they can incorporate into their work resume.

380. One of the main successes of the DPP experience in Kerala was the fact that they promoted mass training campaigns with the aim of breaking down barriers between those "who know" (technicians, functionaries, politicians) and those "who do not know."

CHAPTER VII. ENTITIES AT THE HIGHER LEVELS

1) A START UP TEAM

381. To develop the process of participatory planning the mayor should designate a small team of persons with technical knowledge of planning and with political qualities sufficient to organize the process initially, coordinating those meetings and actions that should be carried out at the municipal level to start it. Once the process has become institutionalized, this Star Up Team should no longer exist.

a) Legal framework

382. One of the tasks of the Start Up Team is to come up with a legal framework for the DPP process. This step could be bypassed if there already exists in this place a larger national plan. Then the plan itself will generate the necessary legal framework for responsibilities to be decentralized and resources transferred to the two lower levels: the territorial areas and the communities. When a national plan does not exist, the first step to be taken before embarking on

DPP should be to ensure that an appropriate legal framework exists, as occurred in the original municipal constituent process in Torres municipality, in the state of Lara, Venezuela. [45]

383. At its first meeting, this team should study in detail any potential existing legal obstacles to a genuine process of DPP and possible mechanisms for overcoming them in the municipality. Among these we cannot rule out the possibility of putting pressure on the national government and parliament in order to achieve this aim through the combined support of all institutions.

b) Identification of the geographical units where the process should be carried out

384. Another step that the Start-Up Team should immediately take is to summon a commission of experts to study the territorial classification that allows to create the geographical appropriate spaces so that the process of decentralized planning can be developed. Let us remember that it is about creating self-government spaces where many of the tasks that were exercised by the municipality until that moment can now be exercised in these territorial subdivisions.[46]

385. This means that the Team should carry out a preliminary subdivision of the municipality into territorial areas and communities, without concern for the fact that that Municipal Planning Assembly will be responsible for setting the final definitive boundaries.

c) Guidelines for the decentralization

386. This Team should also establish the guidelines of the program of decentralization to be developed by the Municipal Cabinet of Planning and Budget. It would thereby define the responsibilities and resources to transfer to the territorial areas and, in some cases, to the communities as well as the issues to keep in mind for the distribution of the resources among the territorial area and where appropriate, to the communities.

d) Formation of the municipal technical teams

387. Another task of this Team is to set up or ratify --in case they already exist--.the two technical teams that the process requires: a team specialized in planning and budget and another in tasks of promotion of the activities that should be done during the process to involve to the maximum of people in them. This last one will be called: Social Animators Team.

2) GOVERNMENTAL COORDINATION TEAM

388. An entity that serves to coordinate the work of the different participants within the process at a territorial level, avoiding any overlap of activities and functions, should also be created.

389. One of their tasks would be recruiting the technical cadres of the different institutions (ministries, specialized institutes, government agencies, etc.) to support the design and implementation of projects.

390. It is about assuring that the whole institutional machine starts to service the process of participatory planning, distributing relevant cadres among the different levels of decentralization and avoiding the duplication or conflict of responsibilities and functions.

391. The role of the Governmental Coordination Team is fundamental in the initial stages of DPP, when the biggest risk of lack of coordination exists. Nevertheless, it can also be important when, in the development of the process of planning, you proceed to design the projects and later

---

45. Marta Harnecker, *Transfiriendo poder a la gente...* Op. cit. Part I, Chapter II, paragraphs 23 to 77.
46. See paragraphs 131-132

on during the execution of these, to assure the coordinated participation of the different agencies and government services.

3) DISTINGUISHED ADVISORS COMMITTEE

392. We believe that the DPP process should be as non-partisan as possible. This requires that all citizens should be called upon to participate, contribute their ideas and collaborate in the variety of tasks involved in this process, irrespective of their political leanings.

393. In this regard, we believe the government of Kerala took an interesting initiative in 1996, when it launched the Campaign for Decentralized Participatory Planning across the entire state. To try to forestall any attempts by the opposition – which represented 40% of the state government – to boycott the campaign they decided to set up a High Level Guidance Council, and offered seats and roles on the council to opposition leaders. The council was comprised of 140 members of the Legislative Assembly, the 20 national parliamentarians that represented Kerala, high-ranking government officials, leaders of mass organizations, artists, writers, cultural leaders and former chief ministers.

394. We believe this initiative could be replicated at the municipal level in order to provide suggestions and to monitor the process as it unfolds. We will to refer to this entity as the Distinguished Advisors Committee.

4) TEAM OF VOLUNTEER PROFESSIONALS AND TECHNICIANS

395. Mass popular participation in the planning process naturally leads to the emergence of an endless number of projects that require technical skills. The ideal is that these skills will spread more broadly among the population. However, in the interim the support of an ever-increasing number of professionals and technicians will be required. Given that there are not enough professionals with the required educational levels working in state institutions to meet this challenge, it would be worthwhile calling upon the help of outside professionals and technicians who would be willing to volunteer support by providing communities with the knowledge required to develop projects and to ensure they are carried out correctly.

396. Agreements could be reached with universities, whereby students in appropriate disciplines could help with these tasks as part of their course work. Not only will this provide immediate support for the process but it will also educate the students themselves, developing them into the kind of experts the process needs.

397. A public invitation campaign could also be initiated to win over professionals and technicians who have time available to help out, especially those who are retired. As people today tend to retire while still being able to contribute to society, this could be an excellent avenue for them to continue being useful and maintaining their self-esteem.

398. An example of the potential for retiree contribution to decentralized participatory planning comes from Kerala State in India. In March of 1997, a few months into the "People's Plan Campaign" -- Kerala's version of DPP -- the State Planning Board that was managing the campaign ran into shortages of engineers and other specialists as the local bodies developed far more projects than the existing government bureaucracy could evaluate. The Planning Board placed the following ad in numerous publications across the state:

If you are a retired person, this may be the beginning of a new life. The State Planning Board invites you to give technical leadership to the local plans that people have prepared. We can join together to create a better tomorrow. At the same time you may be realizing a new meaning for your life after age 55. Send a brief letter and your résumé.

399. Within weeks, ten thousand retired experts had responded positively to the call.[47] These volunteers worked *ad honorem* for two or three days a week, although their food and transport costs were covered.

400. Thanks to the overwhelmingly positive response to the invitation, an unprecedented number of groups of technical volunteers were formed that, together with local civil servants, contributed to the campaign with a non-party orientation.

401. At the community level, they do not need to be professionals from an academic background. Often, the best people are those with a lot of practical experience and an interest in learning, as well as those with a special vocation for helping the community. Of course, they must have a professional attitude to their work, and at the same time be able to express themselves in a direct and simple manner, without using unnecessarily complicated language.

402. They simply need to be able to help with the overall process without necessarily being leaders capable of mobilizing the masses, as their role should be focused on helping to deepen debate, systematizing the information obtained and, above all, helping come up with, implementing and evaluating projects.

403. This technical support can be organized by formally establishing a technical team.

404. Some community leaders tend to overestimate the level of knowledge among the people and oppose the participation of people from outside of the community, particularly because of the arrogant and authoritarian attitudes of certain technical experts.

405. We value this knowledge and acknowledge that, on occasions, the knowledge and ideas of residents in a community has been more valuable than that of the technical experts, such as for example when studying waterways in the hillsides of Caracas.[48] But recognizing this should not imply dismissing the role of experts in the participatory planning process.

406. As evidence of our position, we believe it is important to remember what happened on the Venezuelan island of Margarita. A number of communities were demanding health clinics. A technical expert went to the island to investigate why this demand had become so widespread. Arriving in a helicopter, he saw the city and surrounding areas from above and realized that there were a lot of roofs made from asbestos, which, as is well known, can produce serious respiratory diseases.

407. The communities were suffering the consequences of this situation, which is why they were asking for health clinics. But when the technical experts explained to them the cause of their problems, they realized that to genuinely resolve the situation, the asbestos roofs had to be removed.

408. This exchange of knowledge led the people to understand that they needed to change the priorities they had established prior to receiving this information: rather that building medical clinics, the community chose to prioritize replacing the asbestos roofs with other materials.

409. This experience shows us the important contribution that technical expertise can make. In many cases, it can led to a qualitative leap forward in terms of understanding the reality around us

---

47. Thomas Isaac, T. M. and Richard W. Franke. 2002. *Local Democracy and Development: The Kerala People's Campaign for Decentralized Planning*. Lanham, MD: Rowman and Littlefield, p.106.

48. See the role of the technical water roundtables in Caracas in: Marta Harnecker, *Alcaldía de Caracas: Donde se juega la esperanza (*1995), paragraphs 254 to 269, in: http://www.rebelion.org/docs/95162.pdf y

and how best to move forward: rather than analyzing the effects, we begin to analyze the causes, and thanks to this can attack the problem at its roots, thereby avoiding the reproduction of its effects.

410. These volunteers should work with community activists, the technical teams of the mayor's office (or City Hall, "the District Headquarters" or other state institutions) to form, in the words of Tomás Villasante, **"a driving force of participation at all levels."**[49]

CHAPTER VIII. ENTITIES AND ACTORS AT THE LOCAL LEVEL

411. Having outlined these general elements, we will now turn to describing the entities and actors that participate in the DPP process at the three local levels: municipality, territorial area, and community.

412. We have grouped these entities into two main categories: technical support entities and entities based on citizens' participation (or participatory entities). The relations among these entities and levels are shown on Figure 1 below.

Figure 1: Entities at the local levels

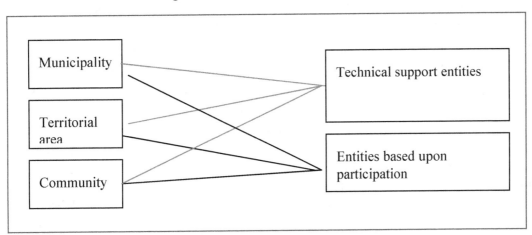

1. TECHNICAL SUPPORT INSTANCIAS AND PARTICIPANTS WITHIN THEM

413. Any DPP process that wants to put an emphasis on popular participation needs to be able to rely on people with technical preparation, organized into specialized groups, if it is to be successful.

414. Most of the technical personnel should come from the Mayor's Office. Nevertheless, given the enormous amount of advice required, it is vital to be able to rely on the participation of a

---

49. This concept is further developed in: Tomás Villasante, *Redes de vida desbordantes. Fundamento para el cambio de la vida cotidiana,* Cataratas, 2014, pp.186-193.

broad range of volunteers that can provide advice, particularly at the level closest to the popular base. The characteristics of these people and the entities they work in should be adapted to the requirements of the process at each level: municipal, territorial area, and community.

415. At the highest level, expert participation will be more necessary given the complexity of the challenges that need to be taken up. In the territorial area, expert participation will be greatly reduced, and even more so in the local community.

416. These experts will have to provide advice to the participatory planning councils at each level (municipality, territorial area, community) and at every step of the process of designing, implementing and monitoring their respective development plans.

417. Therefore, these technical personnel should fit the profile required to politically, theoretically and methodologically support the DPP process. Furthermore, they should assume responsibility for providing methodological orientations for events held as part of this process at all three levels.

418. It is advisable that the members of these teams are maintained in their positions during the whole process. Not being given continuity to their work can hinder the development of the process.

419. We need to distinguish between two different types of technical teams at the municipal and territorial level: the Planning and Budget Team and the Social Animators Team. At the municipal level, the first can be referred to as the Planning and Budget Cabinet. Moreover, there should be a team of coordinators at each level. At the municipal level we should add the Municipal Secretariats or D Secretariats or Departments (Finances, Education, Health, etc.).

420. At the community level, a Community Planning Team should assume the tasks of both teams, to both initiate the planning process in the community and ensure its proper development.

421. This Team should be a small group of people who, without seeking protagonism, are willing to dedicate time and effort to initializing and supporting community planning.

422. These people should have a lot of respect and authority among all sectors of the population and, above all, be convinced of the need to win people to the process. They should, as much as possible, have a basic grasp of the theory and practice of planning. They should be able to act on decisions, confront problems and find quick and creative solutions. And, of course, they should be willing to work in a dedicated manner as many tasks and responsibilities will rest on their shoulders.

423. This team can be set up by initiative of the community or by the community coordinator. The Mayor's office or another higher level authority should initiates the process and invites interested persons to participate and each community puts together a list of participants according to its experience and level of organization; some could have already begun a process of planning before the mayoral summons and might have appropriate committees already functioning.

424. But, in any case, the membership of this team should be ratified at the first DPP assembly. In fact, this first assembly could be a good opportunity not only to ratify but also to involve new people in the team in order to increase its diversity.

Chart 1: Technical support entites

MUNICIPALITY	TERRITORIAL AREA	COMMUNITY
Municipal Planning and Budget Cabinet	Territorial planning and budgetary team	Community Planning Team
Municipal team of animators	Territorial team of animators	
Territorial coordinators	Community coordinators	
Municipal government secretaries and heads of departments		

1).PLANNING AND BUDGETARY TEAMS

a) At municipal, territorial and community level

425. Before beginning the process planning as such In the previous phase, the municipal planning and budgetary team, in coordination with the mayor's office, should work to create the technical conditions required for kick-starting the DPP process in the municipality. Equally, the Territorial Planning and Budget Teams and the Community Planning Teams, once constituted, should prepare the conditions for the development of the process at their respective levels. And once the process is underway, they should guide and provide technical support during the different steps of the process. It would be useful to conform, within the Municipal Planning and Budgetary Cabinet, a team dedicated to providing informational and telecommunications support to the process.

b) Preparatory tasks of the Municipal Cabinet of Planning and Budget

426. The following are the preparatory tasks that should be assumed by this cabinet.

1. **To develop the general lines for the decentralization designed** by the Start Up Team. This may include:
(a) Sub-division of the municipality into territorial units.
Each territorial planning and budgetary team should also do the same in terms of sub-dividing their area into communities in any instances where such sub-divisions do not already exist
(b) Drawing up lists of responsibilities to transfer to territorial areas and communities.
(c) Logistical and human resources to transfer.
(d) Financial resources to decentralize, what proportion to assign to each territorial area and how much should remain in the hands of the municipal government.
(e) Approaches to distribute the financial resources among the territorial areas and in some cases directly to the communities

2. **To conform the technical work teams in the territorial level** (Planning and Budget Teams, Animators Teams) and Territorial Coordinators) that will give technical support to people's participation at the territorial level.

3. **To prepare the members of these teams** for carrying out their tasks and to organize a system of continuous formation training for the participants and the volunteers.
The best solution is the creation, of a permanent Commission on citizen education and participation.

4. **Prepare a timeline of activities**
 together with the municipal animators team. This timeline must specify which activities need to be carried out within each stage of the DPP process, including the preparatory stages, at both the territorial area and community level.

This is a very important step to ensure that the process is not slowed down at lower levels. It should indicate the activities to be carried out by the municipal participatory planning council, the entity entrusted with examining and approving, in the first instance, the development plan, the budget and the annual investment plan for the municipality, all of which must then be ratified and approved by the entities established by law. The timeline must be compatible with both the technical demands of the process and the deadlines set out by the laws corresponding to the DPP process.

The timeline should not only specify the activities that need to carried out; it should also indicate who is responsible for carrying them out, what material resources are needed, and an estimate of how long it will take to come up with the plan.[50]

The process of coming up with this timeline will help to organize and systematize the sequence of activities, guaranteeing that the activities of each team are coordinated, and that the necessary resources are available when they are needed.

5. To establish the budgetary forecasts, determining:
a) The revenues foreseen at municipal level including the box flow, keeping in mind that the revenues cannot be constant.
b) The expenses already committed for previous exercises (paying-off and interests of credits, rents, personnel, fixed expenses etc.) to determine the amount available.
c) Base for the formulation of the sectorial and budgetary priorities.

6. Draft a provisional set of guidelines for the municipal DPP
By guidelines we are referring to the set of internal norms that local entities have to abide by throughout the DPP process.
This regulation that incorporates the results of the previous tasks should be enriched and modified as the process moves forward, and should encompass the following issues:
a) Identification of entities and actors involved in the municipal DPP process.
b) Criteria for distributing resources.
c) Division of the municipality.
d) Methodology for establishing sector-based priorities
e) Municipal database.
f) Norms for electing and recalling delegates and their basic areas of responsibility.
g) Norms for electing and recalling councilors and their basic areas of responsibility.
h) Norms for discussion and debate.
i) Timeline of the municipal DPP process.
j) Methodology for designing and approving the development plan, the budget and the annual investment plan for the municipality.

7. Prepare the necessary prototypes
for the orderly development of the DPP process (forms and tables to fill out, model minutes of meetings, etc.). These support materials should be ready when setting up databases in each territorial area. This would ensure a uniform collection of information.

c) Preparatory tasks of the Planning and Territorial Budget Teams

427. Tasks of these teams:

(1) To study the program of decentralization elaborated by the Municipal Cabinet of Planning and Budget to see if it is necessary to take to the Territorial Assembly modification proposals.

(2) To propose the subdivision of the area into communities, in case this subdivision doesn't exist.

(3) To study the available resources in the territorial area for the realization of the territorial plan, the possible additional sources needed and a forecast of the available resources over the next few years.

(4) To designate the community coordinators for each area and those responsible for the corresponding Community Planning Team.

---

50. We have included material resources within the timeline because we have come across numerous experiences that have been stalled due to the wait for resources that never arrive.

(5) To draft their own timeline keeping in mind the community and municipal timeline.

(6) To establish the principles and mechanisms for the distribution of resources among the communities in case they have not been settled at the municipal level.

(7) To generate, consistent with the established practices at the municipal level, the principles and mechanisms for the determination of the sectorial and budgetary priorities at the territorial level.

(8) To develop in agreement with the established procedures at the municipal level, the procedures for the functioning of the Territorial Assembly and the Territorial Council.

d) Preparatory tasks of the Community Planning Teams

428. The tasks of these teams:

(1) To revise the proposed delimitation of the boundaries of the community to take to the community Assembly as a proposal for acceptance or modification.

(2) To study if it is convenient to subdivide the community in local areas and in affirmative case to carry out a subdivision proposal.

(3) To study the available resources in the community for the realization of the community plan, the possible additional sources of resources and a forecast of the available resources over the next few years.

(4) To establish their own work timeline keeping in mind the territorial and municipal chronogram.

(5) To document the internal norms at the community level that supplement the established process at the municipal and territorial levels.

(6) To make them aware the population and the main actors. of the DPP process that is starting up in their Communit

(7) To form the groups of activists.

(8) To gather information and come up with a basic database containing essential information about the community.

429. As it is logical, so much the formal appointment of the technical teams as the measures or the decentralization should have the formal, legal backing from higher levels of administration.

e) Tasks of the Planning and Budget Teams during the process

430. Once these steps have been taken, the municipal planning and budget cabinet, the Territorial Planning and Budget Team, and the Community Planning Team should undertake new tasks in support of the process at the municipal, territorial area and community levels.

431. The following table illustrates how the various technical tasks are distributed among the three levels of the DPP process. We begin our description of the technical issues at the higher levels where they are the most complex, pointing out which ones are also found at the lower levels. Then we present the issues around civic participation beginning at the lowest – or Community – level since the lower level plans create the basis on which the higher level plans should be developed.

432. Next the enumeration of these tasks: -- shown on Chart 2.

Chart 2: Planning and budgetary tasks during the process

MUNICIPALITY	TERRITORIAL ÁREA	COMMUNITY
Municipal planning and budget cabinet	**Territorial planning and budget team**	**Community Planning team**
1. Give workshops that provide basic knowledge on planning and public budgets to all participants.		
2. Give workshops on how to design development plans, budgets and annual investment plans to municipal and territorial councilors.		
3. Each year prepare the economic information required to initiate and manage the Municipal Development Plan, Budget and Annual Investment Plan of the municipality and for the evaluation of its execution.	3. Idem for the territorial level idem	3. Idem for the community
4. Create interdisciplinary and multi- functional teams (involving technicians from the respective departments of the municipal government and other state entities, experts volunteers, and people designated by communities) to help with the development of the more complex projects at all three levels of the process.	4. Support the design and implementation of projects within the territorial area.	4. Support the design and implementation of community projects.
5. Carry out a technical and financial evaluation of the more complex projects.	5. Idem at the level of the territorial area and for more complex projects that cannot be carried out solely at the community level.	5. Idem for simpler community projects.
6. Advise the Municipal Council regarding territorial area plans in order to avoid duplication or overlap, and propose alternatives where needed.	6. Idem for the Territorial Council in terms of revising community plans.	

7. To prepare the necessary documentation for the elaboration of the Development Plan, the Annual Investment Plan and the Municipal Budget, including: a) A Document summary on the characteristics of the municipality and the aspirations of their its inhabitants. b) A unique listing of municipal level projects to integrate into the overall Development Plan. c) A study of the available resources for the financing of the Development Plan and the foreseen calendar of revenues. d) A proposal for a yearly municipal budget in agreement with the budgetary approved priorities. e) Sectoral priorities to be considered in carrying out the Development Plan.	7. Idem for the territorial plans.	7. Idem for the community plans.
8. Provide the necessary technical adjustments to the Municipal Development Plan, the Budget and the Annual Investment Plan.	8. Idem for the territorial area.	8. Idem for the community
9. Provide technical support throughout each stage of the DPP process, in coordination with the team of animators.	9. Idem for the territorial area.	9. Idem for the community

2) TEAM OF ANIMATORS

a) In the three levels

433. As we said previously, a team of animators should be established side by side with the Planning and Budget Team at the municipality and territorial areas levels to promote participation and facilitate the logistics and organization of activities. At the community level, the Community Planning Team would carry out this function

434. Below (Chart 3 below), we outline the tasks this team should carry out to prepare for the DPP process as well as those it should carry out throughout the process.

Chart 3 Preparatory tasks of the teams of animators

MUNICIPALITY	TERRITORIAL AREA	COMMUNITY
Municipal Team of animators	Territorial Area Team of Animators	Community Team of animators
1. Provide copies of the provisional regulations on decentralized participatory municipal planning.	1. Distribute the regulations to members of the territorial council and assembly.	1. Make the regulations available to the community.
2. Make all the necessary preparations for the consciousness raising campaign among participants.	2. Carry out activities in the territory to help with the campaign.	2. Ídem in the community.
3. Set up and organize a body of volunteers.	3. Help with recruitment of volunteers.	3. Create activists groups
4. Create the municipal database with relevant information, including information obtained from appropriate state institutions as well as those passed on from the territorial level, with a special emphasis on the list of activists.	4. Idem for the territorial area which should be complement the information obtained from communities within the area.	4. Collect essential information.
5. Provide logistical and organizational support to establish the municipal council and assembly.	5. Idem in the territorial area	5. Idem in the community, with the support of the local activist group.

c) Rasks once the Planning Councils and Assemblies have been established

435. See Chart 4 below.

436. The Planning and Budget Team and the team of animators should coordinate with the technical teams that have been transferred from the municipality to the territorial areas, providing them with any logistical or technical support they might need. Efforts should be made to motivate the affected officials so that they willingly and enthusiastically accept the change in the physical location of their work.

Chart 4: Tasks once the planning councils and assemblies have been established

1. Maintain and expand the municipal databases	1. Idem for the territorial level	1. Idem for the community
2. Publish texts, statistical data and maps that are needed for training campaign participants.	2. Distribute this information in the territorial area.	2. Idem for the community
3. Coordinate and provide logistical support for the territorial social promotion teams.	3. Ídem for the Community Planning Teams in the communities.	
4. Carry out training programs at all three levels.	4. Ensure that designated people from the territorial area attend training relevant to their duties.	4. Idem for the community.
5. Take responsibility for convoking and publicizing events at the municipal level and assuring the logistics required for their smooth running.	5. Idem for the territorial area	5. Idem for the community.
6. Coordinate with and support the activities of the team of volunteers at the municipal level.	6. Idem for the territorial area	6. Idem for the community.
7. Select or come up with educational and training materials to use in workshops and other activities that form part of the DPP process.	7. Distribute the new material at the territorial level.	7. Provide the community with access to a library that houses these materials.
8. Organize workshops at the municipal level	8. Idem for the territorial area	8. Idem for the community
9. Organize assemblies at the municipal level.	9. Idem for the territorial area	9. Idem for the community
10. Organize thematic forums and forums on services at the municipal level.	10. Idem for the territorial area	10. Idem for the community
11. Select territorial coordinators from among the existing civil servants in the mayor's office or other state institutions.	11. Select community coordinators from among the existing civil servants in the territorial area.	

436. The Planning and Budget Team and the team of animators should coordinate with the technical teams that have been transferred from the municipality to the territorial areas, providing them with any logistical or technical support they might need. Efforts should be made to motivate the affected officials so that they willingly and enthusiastically accept the change in the physical location of their work.

3) TERRITORIAL AND COMMUNITY COORDINATORS

437. The process of participatory planning should have institutional personnel, assigned by each level of local government, that are dedicated to providing assistance to the territorial areas and communities. We will refer to them as territorial coordinators or community coordinators, depending on the level they have been assigned to.

438. Their task is to attend to particular requirements relating to the DPP process in the territorial area or community that have been assigned to them. They should act as liaisons between the municipalities and the respective territorial areas, and between the territorial area and the communities, regarding DPP.

439. They should work in tandem with the planning and budget team and the team of animators in their respective territorial areas and, when necessary, with the equivalent municipal teams. The community coordinators should coordinate with the Community Planning Team.

440. Given their roles, territorial coordinators should be persons who are well respected by all sectors. To avoid problems, the coordinators should not live in the geographic area they are assigned to coordinate. We recommend submitting their names for approval at the first citizens' assembly in the given geographical area. It would be detrimental to the process to impose a coordinator who is rejected by the community.

441. Their tasks at territorial and community level are shown on Chart 5.

Chart 5: Tasks of the coordinators

Territorial Coordina	Community Coordinator
1. Serve as a point of contact between municipal entities and the council and assembly in the territorial area they have been assigned to	1. Serve as a point of contact between territorial entities and the council and assembly in the community they have been assigned to
2. Mediate conflicts that might emerge between the municipality and the territorial area they have been assigned to	2. Idem between the territorial area and the community they have been assigned to.
3. Mediate conflicts that might emerge between communities within the territorial area.	3. Idem between different sectors within the community
4. Explain the draft regulations at the territorial area	4. Idem at the community
5. Provide the territorial área they are assigned to with general information they might require	5. Idem for the community
6. Help organize activities that should be held within the territorial area they have been assigned to.	6. Idem at the community level
7. Where no organized community exists, convene a citizens' assembly for the purpose of electing activists to help carry out the DPP process.	

4) MUNICIPAL LINE DEPARTMENTS OR SECRETARIATS AND OTHER STATE ENTITIES

443. Municipal line departments should collaborate by making available their socio-political and technical knowledge throughout the whole DPP process. There is no doubt that developing more complex projects requires the involvement of a group of professionals who have multi-disciplinary training and experience with community work. Technical expertise will be needed for structural calculations and technical specifications depending on the type of project, for example, building a bridge or wastewater system or asphalting a road. If human resources have not been redeployed from state institutions, ministries or other national entities, municipal departments should help facilitate access to technical personnel.

444. Municipal line departments should provide delegates with the technical information pertaining to their area of work, as well as information about any government proposals for structural works, projects and services in the area. They should also support the process of preparing projects in accordance with their responsibilities.

II. CITIZENS' PARTICIPATION ENTITIES

445. We propose establishing two citizen participation entities at all three levels of the DPP process: assemblies and councils.

(1) **Planning Assemblies**
   (a) Community Planning Assemblies with direct participation at the community level
   (b) Planning Assemblies with delegate participation at the municipal and territorial level.

(2) **Planning Councils**.

Figure 2: Citizen participation entities for DPP

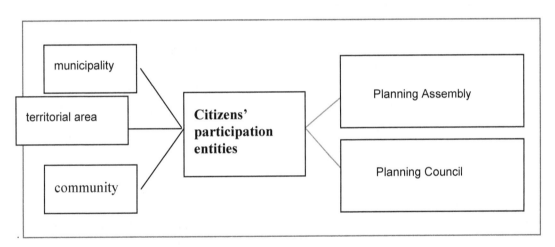

1) PLANNING ASSEMBLIES

a) Community Assemblies

446. **Community Assemblies** refers to meeting that are open to all members of a community, with no exclusions of any type, held in order to receive information, raise proposals or approve agreements on issues affecting the community. Among these issues are all those related to the community planning process, which require special sessions dedicated exclusively to these issues.

447. These assemblies have the last word in regards to important decisions adopted during the process. The other entities should implement the mandate given to them by these assemblies.

These assemblies should have a required quorum that is set out in the norms and regulations of the DPP process. We previously outlined our proposal in regards to a quorum that seeks to ensure all sectors or neighborhood areasof the community are represented.[51]

448. The assemblies should ratify or modify proposals coming to them from the Community Planning Team and, as we will see shortly, the Community Planning Council. A special quorum, clearly stipulated in the regulations, seems recommendable for the latter, to ensure that proposed modifications represent the sentiments of the whole community.

449. Later on we will point out the tasks that the Community Assembly should assume during the different phases of the process.

450. A good turnout at the first session of the assembly is very important for the subsequent development of the process. We should at all cost avoid beginning the process with a failure as this could demoralize people. Therefore, the convocation of the first assembly should occur once a sufficient number of people have said they are willing to attend.

451. If a quorum is not reached at this assembly, those present should analyze the reasons why people did not attend in order to rectify this for subsequent convocations.

452. Given that we want to ensure the participation of youth, women and ethnic groups that have traditionally been discriminated against, we should perhaps – as a step prior to the general assembly – hold preparatory meetings exclusively for each of these social groups or hold forums on issues that might be of particular interest to these groups. [52]

453. Let's look at how we envisage the content of the convocation for the first session of the Assembly. We want to spend some time on this, as numerous errors tend to be committed at this point in DPP.

454. Our proposal starts from the supposition that the community has never undertaken a participatory planning process. If it has, then undoubtedly the convocation will be different.

455. First, we recommend not using the term participatory planning when inviting people to the assembly. The reason is simply: these words mean little to the large majority of people. The best convocation is one that alludes to the immediate interests of the people.

456. Another important issue is determining the most appropriate day and time for the assembly. For example, in a rural community this could be after work on the farm ends for the day. In an urban community, where people do not usually get up as early, and particularly in those where the workday is divided into day and night shifts, it may be preferable to hold it later, perhaps at 8pm or on a weekend. Experience will allow us to determine the best time for each specific situation.

457. A convocation could go something like this:

We have a grave crime problem in the community. Come to a meeting this Sunday at 11am in the school hall so that between all of us we can come up with some solutions.

458. Or like this:

What changes would you like to see in your community so that your family and everyone in the community can live better? Come to a meeting this Sunday at 11am in the school hall where we will discuss this issue.

---

51. See paragraph 39.

52. See more in Thematic and service-focused forums, paragraphs 367 to 376.

459. The idea is that the activist group, entrusted with motivating people to attend the assembly by visiting them door-to-door, touch on the concrete problems facing families at a specific time in a particular community. In some cases it can be problems to do with crime, in others it could be a school that has collapsed or roads that are in a bad state, in another it could be the opening hours of particular services.

460. Without doubt, the best way to overcome the initial apathy is to offer some kind of material incentive. For example, if a municipality has decided to allocate resources via a contest for the best projects put forward in the community, the convocation could be the following:

> The local government has some resources set aside for public works in the community, but as the resources are limited, it has proposed a contest. The community that comes up with the best project will receive $60,000 to implement it. We want your opinion regarding what would be the best public works to carry out with these resources. Come along this Sunday at 11am to the school hall....

▪ *Meetings in neighborhood areas*

461. We have previously spoken (see paragraphs 100-105) about how small territorial areas, such as the neighborhood areas in Venezuela, are the best for facilitating participation.

462. We suggest holding meetings that are open to all residents to inform them of the process and facilitate the collection of aspirations of those living in the community. This can also stimulate social activism in support of the process, both for compiling the database and implementing some of the projects, as well as more generally for the process of monitoring and control of the plan.

463. Unlike the assemblies referred to above, the decisions taken at these meeting are not binding. That is why we refer to them as meetings and not assemblies.

464. The Community Planning Team should convene the first meetings. Community activists have the important role of promoting attendance at the meetings. During this phase, we should try to find those people in the community that could help activate others to participate.

465. Each neighborhood area should elect some people to take their proposals to the Community Assembly and the Planning Council. After being elected, they should be the ones responsible for convening the next meetings in the neighborhood area.

466. These neighborhood area delegates are very important for the smooth running of assemblies in larger communities. They can ensure that meetings are representative of all sections of the community and all ideologies and political positions that exist within it.

467. According to Argénis Loreto, the former mayor of the municipality of Libertador, in Carabobo, Venezuela, introducing the concept of delegate improves the quality of the community assembly. Referring to the experience in his municipality, he said: "Before, the citizens' assembly was an amorphous thing: sometimes you even had people from other communities participating. Now the makeup of the assembly is regulated in the municipal bylaws. They take into consideration the number of streets and the number of inhabitants per street. Each street should have at least one delegate and at most five. [...] To reach *quorum*, an assembly needs to, firstly, involve at least 50% plus 1 of the number of people that attended the first assembly and secondly, ensure every street is represented."[53]

468. We want to insist on the need to avoid all types of manipulation, political or otherwise. The participatory planning process should be open to all citizens, regardless of their political leanings.

---

53. Marta Harnecker, *Gobiernos comunitarios*... op. cit.

b) Planning Assemblies based on a system of delegation.

469. We call Planning Assemblies **with a delegation system** to the Assemblies that are carried out in municipality and territorial areas. Although anyone can attend, speaking and voting rights in these assemblies are limited to those who have been elected to represent their respective area (territorial areas at the level of the municipality; communities at the level of the territorial area,) and have responsibility for certain tasks in the participatory planning process.

470. All members of the Territorial Planning Councils within a municipality, in accordance with its subdivision into territorial areas, should be delegates to the Municipal Assembly. All members of the Community Planning Councils within a territorial area should be delegates to the Territorial Assemblies. To these councilors we have to add representation from each thematic forum and one from each forum focused on services.

471. They should actively and creatively participate in the DPP process, attending meetings and workshops in their territorial area, and commit themselves to working on relevant tasks during the process.

▪ *Tasks of the delegates*

472. The main tasks of the delegates are:

(1) Actively participate in the activities of the Participatory Assembly of which they are members, keeping themselves informed of the issues to be discussed and seeking out, if required, the necessary technical support.

(2) Take the demands and proposals from their respective geographic space to the assembly, provide information of the results of the assembly and report back on their actions to the Assembly of the geographical space they represent.

(3) Support the councilors in their respective geographic space to carry out all their tasks.

(4) Seek out technical support in order to be able to transform demands into viable projects.

(5) Monitor and manage the use of resources destined for priority projects and monitor the quality of project implementation.

(6) Attend meetings that help to: improve the diagnostic survey carried out in the relevant geographic area.

(7) Obtain a minimum level of training in planning and budgetary issues for exchanging personal experiences of carrying out their role among representatives from different territorial areas or communities; inform themselves on how the process is moving along, etc.

(8) In communities where delegates are elected on the basis of neighborhood areass, workplaces or places of study, such delegates should collect the demands from their respective grassroots meeting.

473. Some of the previously mentioned activities should also involve those who want to volunteer their available time to supporting the DPP process.

474. In sum, delegates have the key task of taking the concerns, wishes and opinions coming out of their grassroots assembly to the territorial assembly, and subsequently presenting the grassroots assembly with proposals that came out of the municipal or territorial level assemblies.

475. The delegates should be the main motivating agents of the DPP process at their particular institutional level.

c) Tasks

476. Tasks of the Planning Assemblies at all Levels:

(1) Learn about, discuss, and ratify the boundaries of the respective geographic sub-divisions (territorial areas, communities)

(2) Learn about, discuss, and ratify the procedures of the participatory planning process.

(3) Learn about, discuss, and ratify the criteria for assigning resources to various territorial áreas or communities.

(4) Learn about, discuss, and ratify the decentralization of responsibilities to territorial areas and communities.

(5) Learn about, discuss and ratify the rendition of bills about the economic situation at that level of decentralization has on the beginning of the process of implementation of the Plan of Development (multi-year) and the Annual Investment Plan.

(6) Learn about, discuss and approve the listing of aspirations from the relevant assemblies.

(7) Learn about, discuss, and ratify the list of prioritized aspirations for each level.

(8) Learn about, discuss and ratify the budget and sector-based priorities of the municipality and the corresponding territorial area.

(9) Learn about, discuss and ratify the major categoeris of expenses and the budget forcast.

(10) Learn about, discuss, and ratify the development plan, the budget, the annual investment plan (for all three levels) and any necessary modifications to these documents.

(11) Elect councilors to their respective planning councils and, in the case of the territorial and community assemblies, the two people to represent the assembly in the Council at the immediate higher level.

477. To reject the proposals that refer the points 1-4, 7, 8 and 10, it will be necessary to have a negative vote of the absolute majority of delegates (present or otherwise) of the assembly as long as two-thirds of the territorial areas are represented when the vote is taken at the level of the municipality, and two-thirds of communities when the vote is taken at the territorial area level. At the community level, the issue of a quorum has to be studied more closely as we are dealing with the participation of all citizens in the community. We suggest that one of the criteria to use is the one we previously mentioned: at least two-thirds of neighborhood area delegates of that community should be present.

d) Functioning

478. Although, as we shall see when we study the Councils, the job of planning should be carried out in relatively small collectives for reasons of efficiency, to ensure a democratic process we need to achieve transparency in planning. This is why it is fundamental that the corresponding assemblies ratify decisions regarding planning.

479. At the same time, given we cannot burden people with an infinite series of meetings. We should try to keep the number of assemblies to those that are strictly required to ensure that citizens are kept up-to-date and ratify what is being done. That is, assemblies should be limited to those moments where the most important debates need to be had and the most important decisions need to be made, having previously carried out the necessary work (providing support material, proposals, etc.) before each assembly in order to best maximize the use of time at these assemblies.

e) Sessions of the Assemblies

480. What moments are these?

▪ *Constituent session to begin the process*

481. We think that in the first year of the development of the participatory planning process, it is necessary to hold a session of the Assembly to formally initiate the process by approving the

procedures , the Timeline of Activities and the Methodology to be used (including the general criteria for distributing resources). And the corresponding Council or its Planning and Budget Team should inform the community about the resources with which it is endowed to move the Development Plan and the Annual Investment Plan forward . We will call this session a "constituent session."

482. It will not be necessary to repeat this session annually because the possible modifications to the procedures or the Methodology can be approved in any other ordinary assembly meeting.

483. Following this initial assembly, we think there are three moments in which a meeting of the assembly will be vital in the first and subsequent years:

▪ *First moment: to approve a unique listing of aspirations*

484. A first moment (first ordinary session), the assembly should collect the list of aspirations that will become the basis of the new Development Plan. In the other years, the assembly will simply ratify the aspirations previously approved and enact possible modifications and incorporate, where required, new aspirations that have emerged as the process has unfolded. Then they should ratify the budget and the sector-based priorities for the municipality and corresponding territorial area.

485. The Assembly must previously analyzed and studied the general economic situation in which the planning process will unfold once it has begun, including to learn about and approve the budget, the outstanding bills, the budget balance and the Annual Investment Plan of its geographical area including the global forecast of revenues and expenses for the following fiscal year.

486. Equally the Assembly should approve annually the implementation of the Development Plan and assess its results.

487. At the community level, this first session should elect the Community Participatory Planning Council and two councilors (one man, one woman) that will represent them in the Territorial Area Council. It should also ratify or modify the composition of the Community Planning Team. At the territorial level, in that session the assembly should elect two councilors (one man, one woman) to represent the area in the Municipal Participatory Planning Council.

▪ *Second moment: to approve the priorities*

488. A second moment so that the Assembly approves or modify the list of aspirations organized by priorities and the proposal of sector-based and budgetary priorities.

▪ *Third moment -- to approve the different plans*

489. A third moment comes when the Assembly votes to approve or modify the Development Plan, the Annual Investment Plan and the Budget for the following fiscal year.

490. To hold extraordinary sessions of the assemblies in the territorial areas may be necessary where the municipal or territorial council have observed duplication or overlap of projects or potential conflicts with other territorial areas or communities; likewise, if a municipal or territorial councilor, having seen the work being carried out by the council, believes it is necessary for the territorial or community assembly he or she represents to modify their priorities.

491. The process of participatory planning that we propose it is a linked process that goes from community to the municipal level, going through the territorial level. And it implies holding assemblies at the three levels. The order in which these assemblies should be held cannot be decided upon arbitrarily. For example, it seems obvious that in order to set up the Municipal

Assembly, the assemblies and councils of the territorial areas that make up the municipality need to already be set up; and to set them up, the communities will have had to have set up their respective assemblies and councils.

492. In a similar way, and as a general rule, it is useful for proposals and plans to emerge from the community assemblies, before taking them up to the territorial assemblies and finally approving them (if we are dealing with municipal issues) at the municipal assembly.

f) Invitees

493. As we indicated at the start of this chapter, it is important to ensure that assemblies are open to anyone who wants to attend. The assemblies should also invite prominent figures from their respective geographical area: school directors, doctors, notable sports figures, and religious leaders, among others.

494. At the municipal level, it would also be useful to invite a number of members of the municipal council (municipal legislative assembly) where it is responsible for approving the municipal development plan, its annual plan and budget, so that by the time it comes around to formally approving plans and municipal budgets, they have already participated first-hand in the debates that gave rise to the proposals they are voting on. We should invite not only the councilors that support the local government but also those from the opposition and independents. At the level of the territorial area, the local councilor that represents the area should be invited.

495. Of course, professionals and technicians who supported the process through their voluntary work should also be invited.

496. As in the case of the invitees to the Council, those invited to the assemblies should have the right to express their ideas at it, but voting should be restricted to the elected councilors mentioned above.

2) PLANNING COUNCIL

a) Guiding entity

497. The planning council comprised of councilors is the guiding body at each level of the DPP process.

498. The key function of the planning council is to draft proposals for the Multi-year Development Plan, the annual investment plan and its Budget at each level, and to guide them through preliminary approval. The corresponding planning assembly must give final approval.

499. To achieve this objective, the planning council must discuss and approve general guidelines for income and expenditure (budget outline) presented by the planning and budget team at each level. It is obligated to ensure that the aspirations of the people have been taken into consideration and transformed into specific public works and services.

b) Tasks of the Planning Council

500. To point out the tasks that the Planning Council should carry out at each level, we should bear in mind that before the DPP process officially starts, the municipal government, the municipal Start Up Team, and the Planning and Budget Cabinet have to come up with a variety of proposals that will help shape the process: the demarcation of territorial areas and communities; projections of annual and multi-year income and expenditure for the municipality and funds available for financing the municipal development plan; the decentralization of human, material and financial resources to territorial areas; criteria for distributing financial resources among the different territories; and provisional regulations that will guide the initial phase of the process.

501. These proposals are presented by the technical teams to their respective planning assemblies at all three levels of the process for them to study, analyze and debate. Final approval occurs at the first meeting of the municipal participatory planning assembly.

502. Below, we will look at the tasks of the planning councils, dividing them into two main groups: tasks that need to be carried out when the DPP process is initiated for the first time in a particular geographical space, whether that be at the municipal, territorial area or community level; and those that need to be carried out each year once the development plan has been established.

503. As higher levels need to feed off the discussions of those levels directly below, we will start by looking at the community level, then the territorial area, and finish with the municipality. When there are tasks that need to be carried out first by the community, then the territorial area and finally the municipality, we will use a stepladder format in the diagram to help visualize the process.

- *Tasks of the Planning Council the first year*

504. Let us see the tasks that the Planning Council should carry out during the first year when the process begins. These tasks are described in Chart 6 below:

Chart 6. Tasks for the planning council during the first year

COMMUNITY	TERRITORIAL AREA	MUNICIPALITY
Community planning council	Territorial planning council	Municipal planning council
1. Collate the conclusions from the community assembly that discussed proposals indicated in paragraph 500 and forward them to the corresponding Territorial Council.		
	1. To summarize and to consolidate the conclusions to those that their communities arrived regarding the proposals indicated in the paragraph 500 and to present them to the Territorial Assembly for their discussion and approval and to take them then to the Municipal Council.	

		1. To summarize and to consolidate the conclusions to those that the territorial areas arrived on the proposals of the paragraph 500 and to present them to the Municipal Assembly for their discussion and approval.
2. Develop procedures for the functioning of the community participatory planning council and for the functioning of the community planning assembly	2. Idem for the territorial participatory council and assembly	2. Idem for the municipal council and assembly
3. Revise and complete the database on the basis of the aspirations collected.	3. Idem for the territory	3. Idem for the municipality
4. a) Examine and compile the list of felt needs collected in the community assembly, determine which level they correspond to (community, territorial area, municipality) and prioritize each list. b) Present them to the Community Assembly for their approval. c) Elevate the listings of aspirations corresponding to the municipal and territorial level to the territorial corresponding Council. d) Invite those who are interested to set up working groups for the following step. .		
	4. Draw up a single list of felt needs that correspond to the territorial area level, and another one for the municipal level, in which the proposals coming out of the community assemblies are consolidated, added to and prioritized. b) Present these proposals for approval at the territorial assembly.	

		4. Draw up a single list of aspirations that correspond to the municipal level and establish priorities, taking into consideration the proposals coming out of the territorial assemblies. b) Present it to the Municipal Assembly for approval.
5. Concretize the aspirations of the community level in alternative courses of action. and to present them to the Territorial Council.	5. Idem for the territorial level and to present them to the Territorial Council.	5. Ídem for the municipal level..
	6. Study, with the help of the corresponding technical teams, the alternative courses of action . forwarded from the community level in order to detect any possible overlap or conflicts. Propose solutions and alternatives as necessary.	6. Idem for the project alternative courses of action forwarded from the territorial level.
7. Set up work teams with those interested in preparing projects that the community can carry out with their own resources. Hand over the more complex projects-ideas to the project elaboration team.	7..Set up work teams to prepare the territorial projects..	7. To determine in the more transparent possible form what state or private entity it will assume the realization of each project.
8. Negotiation about which projects should be incorporated into the community's annual investment plan.	8.Idem for the territorial level	8. Idem for the municipal level
9. Discuss and provisionally approve the development plan, the budget and annual investment plan, incorporating the projects that the community voted to include.	9. Idem for the proposed territorial development plan, budget and annual investment plan.	9. Idem for the proposed municipal development plan, budget and annual investment plan..
10. Present it to the Community Assembly.	10. Present it to the Territorial Assembly.	10. Present it to the Municipal Assembly.
11. Send the documents approved to the corresponding Territorial Council, after being ratified by the Community Assembly, and see what the inhabitants of the community can contribute in the execution of some projects.	11. Send the approved community and territorial documents to the municipal council.	11. Idem for municipal, , territoriales y comunitarios documents to the municipal, planning and budget cabinet, for the implementation of the development Plan, of annual investment plan and the Budget of the Municipality.
12. Prepare a timeline for the implementation of projects at the community level.	12. Idem at the territorial area level.	12. Idem at the municipal level.

13. Once the final versions of the development plan, the budget, and the annual investment plan have been written up by the Municipal Planning and Budget Team, all actors whether from institutional or citizens' participation entities should present these plans to the Municipal Legislative Assembly for its institutional approval.

- *Annual tasks*

505. Lets see now the annual tasks of the Planning Councils at the various levels (see Chart 7 below. page 92).

Chart 7 Annual tasks of the planning councils at the various levels

Community Planning Council	Territorial Planning Council	Municipal Planning Council
1. To revise – based on the experience of all previous years – the procedures for proposing, evaluating and approving projects and present the revised procedures to the local Community Planning Assembly.	1. Idem at territorial level and present the revised procedures to the Territorial Planning Assembly.	1. Idem at municipal level and present the revised procedures to the Municipal Planning Assembly.
2. To revise the preparation and implementation of the Budget and the Annual Investment Plan and present the appropriate revisions based on previous years experiences to the Community Planning Assembly.	2. Ídem for the territorial level	2. Ídem for the municipal level.
3. To carry out the steps 4 to 9 of the previous Chart III.6 on Tasks for the First Year of DPP to define the projects that will enter in the Budget and the Community Annual Investment Plan.	3. Idem for the Budget and the Territorial Annual Investment Plan-.	3. Idem for the Budget and the Municipal Annual Investment Plan.
4. To discuss and approve the proposals of the Budget and the Community Annual Investment Plan submitted by the Community Planning Team and, once constituted the Community Planning Council, by the Unit of Financial Management,[54] incorporating the projects.	4. Idem elaborated by the Technical Team of Planning and Territorial Budget	4. Idem elaborated by the Municipal Cabinet of Planning and Budget
5. To present the plan document to the Community Planning Assembly for their approval and to see what the inhabitants of the community can contribute in the execution of some projects.	5. Ídem for the Territorial Planning Assembly	5. Ídem the Municipal Planning Assembly.
6. To submit the proposal of Budget and Community Annual Investment Plan to the Community Planning Team and, once constituted the Community Council, to the Unit of Financial Management of the Community Council for their approval.	6.Ídem gpt the Territorial Budget and Annual Investment Plan to the Technical Budget and PlanningTeam.	6. Ídem for the Municipal Budget and Annual Investment Plan to the Planning and Budget Cabinet.
7. To draft a calendar for the implementation of the projects at the community level.	7. Ídem for the territorial level.	7. Ídem for the municipal level..
8. Once made, the final writing of the document is taken over by the Municipal Planning and Budget Cabinet, which then presents it to the Municipal Legislative Assembly for its approval		

54. See in Appendix V, paragraphs 58 and 59 on what it consists the Unit of Financial Management of the Community Council.

506. Another task the Municipal Planning Council could carry out is supporting the lobbying work of the Municipal Planning and Budget Cabinet and the mayor's office and municipal government in obtaining resources from national or provincial governments – that is, governmental units above that of the municipality – for projects that have been prioritized by the population at the lower levels, but that, due to their size, require a level of investment that cannot be covered by resources from the municipal government's coffers.

c) Councilors

507. "Planning **councilors**" refers to those people who sit on the planning councils.

508. The aim should be to elect people who are in the best position to carry out these tasks; those who are able to advocate and defend positions adopted by their respective planning assembly, while at the same time maintaining a holistic vision of the problems and potentialities of their respective DPP level.

509. Councilors should always seek consensus when selecting which projects to carry out. This consensus should be based on the priorities put forth by the communities and the territorial areas, and should fit within a comprehensive vision of the municipality and its territorial zoning plan, if one exists.

510. Below is a list of some of the characteristics they should share:

(1) Be among the most active in the community, demonstrate an interest in working for the community and always show concerne about what happens within it.

(2) Understand that it is not simply a struggle for the aspirations of their street, laneway, apartment block or school, but a struggle for the community's overall development, for this reason, is capable of changing his or her opinion and negotiating when presented with the full picture.

(3) Characterized by their ecumenical views and honesty.

(4) Well regarded in the community and respected by all.

(5) Have the necessary time and willingness to carry out tasks that are part of the process.

(6) Willing to receive the training required to carry out their tasks.

(7) Open to different ideas and seeking creative paths for carrying out the required tasks.

d) Election of councilors

511. This process will differ depending on whether we are dealing with the community level or with the two superior levels (territorial area and municipality).

512. **At the community level**, we propose that the Community Planning Team, which should have an overall vision of the community, be responsible for putting forward an initial list of potential members for the council made up of people who fit the aforementioned profile. However, anyone present in the assembly should be able to propose other names or themselves. The key point is to make sure that those who end up on the Community Planning Council are

committed to working together and sacrificing some of their time for the good of the community.

513. We suggest electing 25 to 35 people from the list to ensure that the council can function well. Of course, as with all our proposals, there should be a lot of flexibility on this depending on the characteristic of each community.

514. It is particularly important to try and achieve a real balance in terms of the participation of men and women, and in terms of other social groups (youth, elderly, ethnic groups, etc.). This should be defined in a very precise manner and not be left to chance.

515. We also believe these elections should be held after a period of time in which people have shown their interest and capacity to work for the community in a variety of meetings and tasks that have been organized prior to their election as councilors.

516. As well as these people we should add as observers two delegates from each neighborhood area (a man and a woman).

517. The elections should be done by secret ballot to avoid any issues or friction that could arise among people who have close personal relationships.

518. The Community Planning Council should be made up of the 25 (to 35) people who received the most votes and two delegates (a woman and a man) from each neighborhood area.

519. Working groups should be set up to facilitate the work of the council, and the candidates who were not elected should become part of these groups.

520. In terms of the communities, once they have been organized into Community Councils, these councils should take up the tasks assigned to the Planning Council, without the need for a specific election for this council.

521. If Community Councils do not exist, we suggest making use of the dynamic generated by the Participatory Planning Council to building them as a superior form of organization, so that they end up substituting for the Participatory Planning Community Council in carrying out its tasks (See Appendix V).

522. **For the territorial planning councils,** each community planning assembly should elect two councilors (one man and one woman) from the Community Planning Council to represent them on the territorial planning council.

523. If a thematic forum is held in the community, the forum should also send delegates.

524. Each planning council should propose candidates to be ratified or rejected at their respective assembly.

525. At the same time, **each Territorial Planning Assembly** should elect two people, a man and a woman, from among the members of the Territorial Council to become part of the Municipal Planning Council. If certain thematic forums have been held, a delegation from these should also be elected. The same should also occur for any forums that have occurred at the municipal level.

e) Councilors tasks

526. Along with the list above, councilors should carry out the following tasks:
(a) Attend regular meetings of the council and actively participate in the tasks decided upon there.
(b) Attend workshops to improve their knowledge (technical and otherwise) so as to be able to better fulfill their role.
(c) Seek necessary technical support.

f) Duration of terms

527. We suggest that the councilors' terms should last for the entirety of the multi-year municipal development plan. Their respective Planning Assembly should ratify their mandate on an annual basis. If any councilor loses the confidence of their voters, their mandate can be revoked at any time.

▪ *Creative mandate*

528. Even though they are members of their corresponding community or territorial council, territorial and municipal councilors should remain in permanent contact with their council of origin in order to collect and transmit information, while concentrating their efforts on the tasks of the higher up Council to which they have been elected (municipal or territorial).

529. Councilors should be able to defend at the higher level assemblies and councils the positions adopted in their respective grassroots assembly, while also being capable of listening to other councilors and modifying their initial position, if they become convinced otherwise on the basis of new arguments that have emerged through the debate. They are not robots that merely transmit the decisions of their communities.

530. A councilor may revise her/his community's decision on the priority of an issue as a result of discussions with other councilors that make them realize another community in the territorial area has a more urgent need: for example, the need to replace a pipe in order to re-establish the flow of drinking water could be viewed as more urgent than the wish of their community to paint the walls of their school.

531. If modification of priorities is proposed in any territorial planning council, councilors should be given time to return to their respective communities to convince their constituents of the new arguments that emerged in the council debates so that they may accept, on the basis of solidarity, the need to prioritize a public work in another community. Allowing people the opportunity to reconsider their decisions on the basis of new information provided by their councilors is important in terms of human development, one of the objectives of the participatory planning process.

532. If voters are not convinced, even after an educational effort has been made by the councilors – something we hope does not occur because we believe that people are capable of comprehending when provided with the arguments – and a large majority rejects modifying the priorities, the community councilors should resign since they have stopped being the voice of their community.

533. The municipal council should function in the same manner as described above when it comes to proposals from the territorial assemblies.

534. This process involves a constant stream of information from the bottom up and the top down, where the people carrying out their delegated tasks are in permanent contact with the grassroots, informing them of changes that are potentially being made to the original proposal, possible changes in priorities, public works proposed for different reasons, etc. Councilors should transmit upwards the reactions of the grassroots to the changes suggested by their delegate.

535. The councils do not operate in isolation when processing the plan or the budget outline; rather, they should periodically inform their assemblies of the advances made and the changes that have been introduced. When they present a plan or a budget to their respective assemblies for approval, they should convince the assembly with arguments, and if they are unable to do so, those assemblies should have the right to reject those proposals and suggest an alternative, as long as there is a sufficient quorum to do so. The procedures document should outline the norms for

electing and recalling councilors as well as their basic areas of responsibility.

536. The process described in the previous paragraphs may take time, but it is a price worth paying if we want to take seriously the idea of people's participation.

g) Permanent invitees to Councils

537. The following people should have a standing invitation to the Municipal Planning Council: the mayor and her/his executive secretary, two representatives from the planning and budget team and two representatives of the Animators Team.

538. At the territorial level, territorial coordinators should be invited, as well as two representatives of the Territorial Planning and Budget team, two representatives of the territorial team of animators and community coordinators.

539. At the community level, as well as the community coordinator and two representatives of the community planning team, it would be useful to include as observers those people who, because of their role in the community have a broader vision of it, for example, a school director, the local doctor, a priest, etc. That is, all those people who are active in or who exert influence in the community.

540. These people can only be observers; they can inform and give opinions, but they cannot play an active role in decision-making. Their presence is very useful because they can provide information and technical knowledge on certain issues.

h) Practical aspects of the functioning of the Councils

▪ Work hours and potential compensatory remuneration

541. An attempt should be made to elect people to the Council who have the greatest potential to carry out these tasks. They should also be able to find the time to attend meetings and workshops, and to support the various aspects of the participatory planning process.

542. The time councilors are required to dedicate to their DPP tasks should not interfere with their paid employment. Public and local holidays should be used to carry out activities that cannot be held during those times (tour of neighborhoods, workshops, etc.). If it becomes necessary to interrupt a councilor's paid workday, a compensatory payment could be arranged. The constituents should cover this payment, so that if they feel that said councilor is not complying with their mandate, they will be the most interested in replacing them. In any case, workers who are obliged to miss work should be legally protected in such situations from any potential employer punishment (such as dismissal or demotion).

▪ Organize by working groups

543. While making sure to not prejudice the fact that the agreements of the Council need to be discuss and approved in a plenary session in with which all members of the Council participate, we suggest organizing the Council into Working Groups by areas of interest, to achieve more efficient results. These groups should study and prioritize aspirations, come up with projects that correspond to their sector, and present them to the Council plenary for their evaluation in the corresponding assembly.

544. These groups should not only be made up of councilors. It could be very useful to involve other people with training or experience who are willing to volunteer their time to help out. It would also be very useful to count on the support of the people involved in the technical teams.

545. In setting up these working groups, we should seek to facilitate an internal dynamic of distributing resources on the basis of which groups have more participatory conditions.

Furthermore, in the municipal and territorial councils, if there is more than one councilor for the same organized community or territory, respectively, it is important that they work in different groups. It is also important to evenly distribute the professionals and technical experts among each group.

546. In sum, among the activities of a Council, we need to distinguish between the Plenary meetings in which all council members participate (these meetings will be simply referred to as "plenaries" from now on), Working Groups to work on different areas of interest and specialized thematic forums with the participation of other interested people. There are also, meetings with the corresponding Planning Assemblies to inform them of progress that has been made and debate results and the work of the specialists in the preparation of the most complex projects.

▪ *Human requirements*

547. To ensure we get the best out of the working meetings of the council, we should rely on a group of people to take responsibility for the following tasks:
(1) A general coordinator of the Council to give general presentations and decide on how to readjust work in progress according to the concrete dynamic of the process,
(2) A minute taker to take minutes of the meeting and record the time each activity takes,
(3) A logistics coordinator that can help facilitate the participation of people in the working sessions (organize chairs seats, paper, pens, etc.),
(4) A certain number of facilitators, which will depend on the number of working groups, and that are prepared prior to the meeting in terms of the issue and methodology,
(5) Moreover, we should have certain people who that have sufficient knowledge to take on the more technical aspects - depending on the level - of the design of the plan. They could belong to the planning and budget technical team or be professionals that are invited to participate, as we mentioned before.

▪*Material requirements*

548. There needs to be an adequate meeting room to hold open meetings, that can also be darkened to present videos and slides; and various small rooms for the working groups. At the municipal level, the rooms assigned by the Municipal Participatory Planning Council should also meet these characteristics. In the territories and communities, where normally there are no such rooms or spaces available, the best scenario would be to use a school or institution that has both large and small spaces.

▪ *Technical equipment*

549. As a minimum, all levels should have a computer, a video projector and a sound system.

550. But if a certain workshop or working group does not have these resources, they can use large sheets of paper to help facilitate debate and synthesize the work carried out.

▪ *Forms to collect information and the results of the debates*

551. The Municipal Planning and Budget Cabinet should, during the initial process, come up with forms or worksheets that simplify the collection of information and allow us to sum up the results of the debates (aspirations, priorities, etc.).

552. They should also prepare the necessary IT support to deal with this information, designing forms and worksheets. This facilitates the organization and utilization of the information.

553. Although the mayor's office should make an effort to provide communities and territories with technology the technological such as computers and their an Internet connection to allow access to distant information the treatment at distance of the information, in those cases where this is not possible, technical support at the territorial or municipal level should be made available to help them collate the data into the database.

▪h) Inspecting and diffusing available information

554. One of the first tasks for councilors should be to gain as full as possible a picture of the characteristics of their respective geographical space and its inhabitants, especially their main wants and needs, capacities and potentialities, as well as ideas coming from community activists.

555. That is why the mayor's office, in the initial phase, or the Municipal Participatory Planning Council later on in the process, should widely disseminate the results of its work in order to indicate the deficiencies and needs of the municipality and the territories, as well as the proposed allocation of resources, ensuring that all councils, whatever the level, have this information when they begin their work.

556. The councilors should be provided with complete details of the budget the council has inherited from the previous administration at the municipal, territorial and community levels including that of the previous years to show the expenditure patterns.

557. At the same time, organizers and activists should set up the means for complete citizen access to all documents and information including local materials and materials available on the Internet so that any citizen can access this information to assure complete transparency of the DPP process.

CHAPTER IX. OTHER ENTITIES

1). WORKING GROUPS AND WORKING TEAMS

558. Together with the entities we have already mentioned, DPP activists should set up working groups as needed to assist the assemblies and councils to carry out activities in support of the process, such as the listing of aspirations by thematic area, management of program implementation, exploration of alternative courses of action and evaluation of projects.

559. When the activities are relatively simple, these working groups can be quite homogeneous, but for more complex activities, the councilors and community supporters should encourage the participation of experts. These technical experts could come from other entities, from higher-level state agencies, and the expert volunteers.

560. We are talking here about genuine mixed working groups to facilitate an exchange of knowledge that can enrich the process: where popular knowledge that originates from practical experience is in dialogue with technical or professional know-how. The success of the DPP process depends on the collaborative effort of these diverse participants.

561. We are convinced that this can help us avoid populism and the manipulation of popular needs, as well as purely technocratic visions of reality.

562. In addition to the Working Groups, we suggest a separate name – Working Teams – for those groups that involve specialized technical assistants. Both Working Groups and Working Teams could be constituted by sectors and topic interests. The Working Teams of each sector, making use of the experience and potential specialized knowledge of its members, should study alternative courses of action that could help in realizing the goals appearing on the list of aspirations.

563. As an example, the following sectors could be set up: (1) Popular economy and endogenous development, (2) Education and sports, (3) Full social development (including health and the struggle against poverty and marginalization), (4) Housing and infrastructure, (5) Environment

(including rubbish collection and clean up), (6) Culture, (7) Security and civil protection.

564. We have said that this is just an example, because we should not create sectors if there is no reason for them to exist. If a community has no issues of crime and security, then it does not make sense to set up a group for that topic. The same could occur in a new community, with new building and recently inaugurated infrastructure. What sense does it make to create a group on Housing and Infrastructure there? Relying on the people to do the basic work of monitoring the progress of the situation should be enough to deal with any defects that could emerge.

2) GROUP OF COMMUNITY ACTIVISTS

565. Lastly, activists groups should be set up in the community to work closely with the community coordinator and the Community Planning Team. This can help contribute to the success of the process.

566. They should invite people to programmed activities and ensure consistent attendance from those who have committed themselves to participating in the Community Planning Council. This group is especially important when it comes to calling broad meetings of the entire community and working on the creation of a database once the aspirations have been collected.

567. The activist groups should:

- disseminate invitations for programmed activities and ensure a consistent turn-out from those who have committed themselves to participating in the participatory planning community council.
- collaborate in the creation of a community database.
- promote people's participation in the various work groups,
- promote voluntary labor to help with certain community projects

568. This is our proposal that, seeking to transform the current state of affairs, above all aspires to transform people in order to be able to build a more just an solidarian society. As we noted in the prologue, we hope that there will be local governments willing to put our proposal into practice so that on the basis of experience it can be enriched and corrected.

APPENDICES

569. In this diagram we can see how each level of the decentralization process has its own responsibilities and how a group of communities, in this case 6, make up a territorial area, and how 8 territorial areas make up a municipality. At the same time, each level has its own Participatory Planning Council.

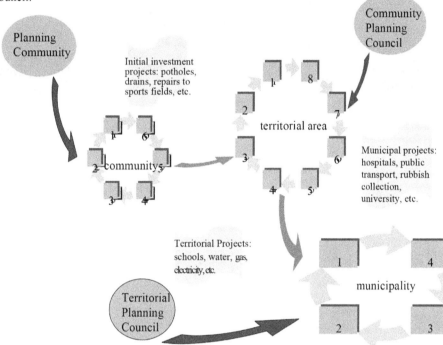

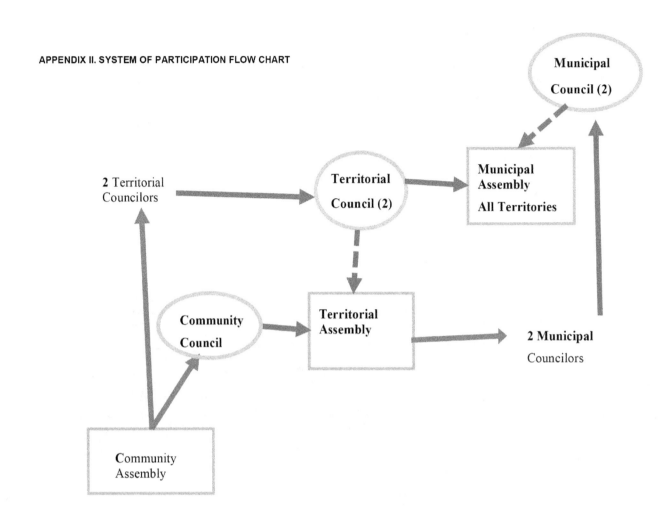

APPENDIX III. PROPOSAL FOR HOW TO DISTRIBUTE FINANCIAL RESOURCES TO TERRITORIES

570. In Chapter IV of this book, we said it was necessary to establish criteria that would favor the poorest and least attended to areas when redistributing resources to entities below the highest level. This would facilitate a gradual decrease in economic inequality among units at the same level. 55

571. Ideally, a national development plan would set out the amount of money to be transferred in accordance with these criteria.

572. Ideally, a national development plan would set out criteria for distributing resources among the different levels of decentralization according to predetermined general indices that favored those geographical area that are most disadvantaged.

573. However, we know that in many cases such a national plan will not exist, or that it may not deal with the issue of how to decentralize resources. A pilot project in participatory planning might be initiated within a particular geographic area (canton, municipality) well before any national plan is put in place.

574. In these cases, it will be up to that local government to set the criteria for decentralizing resources. The basic idea is that these criteria will favor the poorer territories as impartially as possible, avoiding clientalism and cronyism.

575. In this appendix, we will suggest some criteria to utilize and a methodology to employ in order to obtain these objectives.

576. This proposal should be presented to the Municipal Planning Assembly and discussed in the territorial areas and communities. If the proposal turns out to be widely rejected, then those citizens' assemblies that opposed it should come up with an alternate proposal to present to the Municipal Planning Council. The council should then discuss the issue again, and approve the new proposal if they agree with it.

a) Criteria by which to distribute resources to territorial areas

577. We believe at least two criteria should be taken into consideration: the level of deficiencies of certain services, and the size of the population of each territorial area.

578. The first thing we have to do to work out the level of access to services in a certain area is to draw up a table of deficiencies or needs that can allow us to see the approximate level of deficiencies each area or community faces.

579. The table should outline the overall situation regarding: a) roadway infrastructure (conditions and access ways), b) basic services (potable water, sewerage, street lighting, electricity in homes), c) healthcare, d) education, e) housing, and f) rates of unemployment and underemployment.

580. The socio-economic censuses carried out by organized communities in each territorial area can provide invaluable material for this table. In Volume II, where we refer to methodology, we broadly outline the data that should be collected for this census

---

55. See paragraphs 207 to 209.

581. We propose assigning points to each of the characteristics listed in Paragraph 7 above according to a pre-established scale in which more points are given to those areas that have the greatest deficiencies.

582. The territorial areas with the greatest level of deficiencies will therefore end up with more points and be given proportionally larger amounts when it comes to distributing funds.

583. It is possible that the characteristics of particular zones may mean we need to take additional criteria into consideration, for example: ethnography (greater or lesser presence of ethnic minorities), demography (level of dispersion of the population within a territorial area), and services already being provided by the private sector (shops, supermarkets, hairdressers, etc.). Nevertheless, given our more general focus here, we will only refer to the criteria previously mentioned.

1. ROADWAY INFRASTRUCTURE

1) ROADS

584. In terms of the conditions that roads are in, we should look at what percentages of roads are paved. If the territorial area has no paved roads, we should given them 5 points; if up to 25% are paved, 4 points; if it has more than 25% and less than 50%, 3 points; if it has more than 50% and less than 75%, 2 points; if it has more than 75% and less than 95%, 1 point; and if all roads are paved, 0 points.

2) ACCESS WAYS

585. In terms of access ways, we should look at whether areas confront a lack of road access ways. If this is the case they should get 5 points; if they have access ways that are unpaved and contain pot holes, 4 points; if they are unpaved but in good conditions, 3 points; if some ways are paved but with potholes, 2 points; if all ways are paved but with potholes, 1 point; and if they are in a perfect state, 0 points.

2. BASIC SERVICES

1) POTABLE WATER

586. In terms of potable water, we should look at the percentage of houses that have access to this service. If no houses in the area have access to potable water, we should give them 5 points; if less than 25% do, 4 points; if more than 25% and less than 50%, 3 points; if more tan 50% less than 75%, 2 points; if more than 75% have access, but there are still some without it, 1 point. If all the houses in the entire area have access to potable water, that unit should get 0 points.

2) SEWAGE DISPOSAL

587. We should look at the number of houses that have access to this service. If no houses in the territorial area have access to sewage disposal, we should give them 5 points; if less than 25% do, 4 points; more than 25% and less than 50%, 3 points; more than 50% and until 75%, 2 points; if more than 75% have access, but there are still some without it, 1 point; and if the entire territorial area has access to sewerage disposal, they should get 0 points.

2) STREET LIGHTING

588. We should give 5 points to those territorial areas that have no street lighting; 4 points if more than 75% don't have access; 3 points if between 75% and 50% of residents do not have access to street lighting; 2 points if less than 50% and more than 25% have no street lighting; 1 point if

25% or less of the population do not have access to street lighting; and logically, if the entire area has street lighting, they should get 0 points.

4) ELECTRICITY TO HOMES

589. We should look at how many have access to this service. If no houses have access to electricity, we should give them 5 points; if less than 25% do, 4 points; between 25% and 50%, 3 points; if between 50% and 75% have electricity, 2 points; if more than 75% have electricity, 1 point; and the area should get 0 points if all homes have electricity.

C) HEALTHCARE

590. We should work out what services exist in terms of providing medical attention in the area[56] as well as the number of ambulances available to transport patients. We should give 5 points to an area that has no access to medical attention and the number of ambulances available to transport patients; 4 points for those that contain some family medical centers, but not enough; 3 points if they have enough family medical centers; 2 points if they have enough family medical centers as well as access to a Comprehensive Diagnostic Centre (that houses a dentist, pathologist, etc.); 1 point if as well as what has been mentioned they have an ambulatory; 0 points for those that have a hospital, surgery theatre, an Integral Diagnostic Centre and sufficient family medical centers. We know that hospitals, surgeries and Integral Diagnostic Centers attend to all residents in a municipality, but it is nevertheless true that it is an advantage to the territorial area if they have these establishments located within their borders.

4) EDUCATION

591. We should determine whether there are enough places at all levels of the school system to cover the demand of the population in each area. If there are no schooling facilities, and students have to travel elsewhere to study, the area should get 5 points; if less than 25% of demand is covered, 4 points; between 25% and 50%, 3 points; more than 50% and less than 75%, 2 points; more than 75%, 1 point; and if the demand of the entire population is covered up until the end of high school, 0 points.

5) HOUSING

592. We should evaluate how many residents live in adequate housing. If none do so because they live in makeshift shacks, they should get 5 points; if more than 75% live in shacks or poor-quality housing, 4 points; if between 75% and 50% do not have adequate homes or live in cramped conditions, 3 points; if less than 50% and more than 25% live in poor conditions, 2 points; if less than 25% live in poor conditions, 1 point; and if everyone has an adequate home, 0 points.

6) LEVELS OF UNEMPLOYMENT AND UNDEREMPLOYMENT

593. Figuring out employment patterns requires evaluating the socio-economic difficulties facing residents within an area as a whole. Participatory planning is not simply about managing public investment in public works and services. It should also contemplate ways in which to promote and support the development of productive activities that help make territorial areas self-sustainable. That is why it is important to work out the level of marginalization and poverty in

---

56. Here we will use the names that these centers have in Venezuela.

each territorial area and locate where productive investment in things such as the creation of cooperatives is most needed.

594. We could use criteria such as the percentage of the active population that is out of work, employed in precarious work or the informal sector, or is underpaid.[57]

595. If more than half of the active population of an area find themselves in situations of unemployment or underemployment, they should be given 5 points, if less than 50% but more than 40% find themselves in this situation, 4 points; between 40% and 30%, 3 points; less than 30% and more than 20%, 2 points; between 10% and 20%, 1 point; and less than 10%, 0 points.

3. HIPOTHÉTICAL EXAMPLE

596. Once the criteria have been agreed upon, it will be necessary to work out the corresponding points tally for each area in order to establish a map of deficiencies. The databases generated in each geographical space will be very useful for this task.

597. To illustrate what our proposal might look like, let us take as a hypothetical example: a municipality that has 54,000 residents and has $100 million to distribute among five territorial areas. The first territorial area has 10,500 residents, the second has 12,000, the third has 9,500, the fourth has 10,000, and the fifth has 12,000. Evidently, there are two territorial areas with the same population (the second and fifth ones). However, as we shall see, the former has many more deficiencies than the latter. If we were to redistribute the overall resources according to population size, both would receive the same amount. However, if we want to favour the area with the most needs, we should use the tally and weighting system we have proposed above and which we describe in more detail just below for evaluating, in an objective manner, which territorial area has the most needs.

598. Below are the tables of deficiencies for the two areas with the same population size (12,000). Territorial area No. 2 has a number of important deficiencies in terms of access to potable water and sewage disposal, and an insufficient number of schools and medical centers, while Territorial area No. 5 only faces issues regarding road access ways.

---

57. Those that have or are seeking paid employment. We are not including here that part of the population that due to age or other reasons (looking after children, housework, etc.) are unemployed and not looking for work.

Table 1. Level of deficiencies in hypotheticalTerritorial Area N°2 with 12 000 residents

Level of Deficiency	100%	>75%	From 75% to 50%	From 50% To 25 %	< 25%	0%	Points
Potable water		4					4
Sewerage disposal		4					4
Street lighting					1		1
Education			3				3
Paved roads						0	0
Healthcare			3				3
Electricity in homes	5						5
Road access ways						0	0
Adequate houses			3				3
Unemployment		4					4
TOTAL							27

Table 2. Level of deficiencies in hypothetical Area No5 with 12 000 residents

Level of Deficiency	100%	>75%	From 75% to 50%	From 50% To 25 %	< 25%	0%	Points
Potable water						0	0
Sewage disposal					1		1
Street lighting						0	0
Education						0	0
Paved roads					1		1
Health Care					1		1
Electricity in homes					1		1
Road access ways				2			2
Adequate houses					1		1
Unemployment					1		1
TOTAL							8

598. If we carry out this same process for the other areas, we come up with the following table – Table 3 –area-wise disparities within the larger unit of which they are both a part, in which the number of total points is equivalent to the level of deficiencies in a territorial area.

Table 3. Level of territorial area disparities within the municipality we have choosen as an hypothetical example

	Territorial Area 1 Level of Deficiency	Territorial Area 2 Level of Deficiency	Territorial Area 3 Level of Deficiency	Territorial Area 4 Level of Deficiency	Territorial Area 5 Level of Deficiency
Potable water	0	4	2	5	0
Sewage disposal	1	4	2	3	1
Street lighting	0	1	1	2	0
Education	0	3	2	1	0
Paved roads	0	0	0	1	1
Health Care	1	3	4	4	1
Electricity in homes	1	5	2	3	1
Road access ways	1	0	1	1	2
Adequate houses	1	3	1	1	1
Unemployment	1	4	1	3	1
TOTAL	6	27	16	24	8

599. Once we also take into consideration the size of the population (a criterion to which we will shortly return), Table 4 (below) will not only allow us to see how we can best distribute resources among the different areas; it also offers us clues about the main problems facing the overall unit in which these five areas are sub-units. It is easy to see that there are certain deficiencies that more or less affect all territorial areas, such as a lack of medical centers, household access to electricity, sewage disposal and a lack of adequate housing. In other cases, problems are limited to certain areas (such is as access to potable water). There are also certain needs that only slightly affect, or do not affect areas in the larger unit, such as, in this case, road access.

600. This process can also allow us to appreciate range and pattern of disparities that exists within any unit made up of sub-units. In our example, two areas (those numbered 1 and 5) are clearly better off in comparison to the rest, an intermediary area (3), and two areas with severe deficiencies (2 and 4). As a result, the overall DPP unit contains severe internal disparities that need to be corrected.

601. Table 4 also allows us to compare and contrast the results with the priorities of the population of each area. That is, we can get a sense of how people subjectively view these deficiencies.

602. It is quite possible that when it comes time to discuss priorities, the population will adopt its own different priorities, despite the fact that these data have been widely distributed before the assemblies. Although we believe that the distribution of resources should be based on objective data, the selection of projects and the design of the plan and the budget must be based on the priorities established by the citizens themselves through the participatory planning process.

603. Once we have tallied the points and know the number of residents in each area, we propose using the following procedure to best achieve our aims.
Step one: multiply the existing population (column 2) of each territorial area by the points they obtained (see table column 4 in the following table).
Step two: add up all the numbers that we have come up with through this multiplication process which in this case gives us a total of 875,000 points (see Column 4).
Step three: divide the amount of resources announced at the beginning of the process as available ($100 million) by the total of points (857,000) this figure (which gives us a result approximating 114.29. This will be the point value (column 5).
Step four: multiple the point value 114.29 by the number of points each territorial area obtained when the population and points they received for the level of deficiencies were initially multiplied (see Column 4).

604. From column 6 on Table 4, we can see how by using this formula, Area No2, which has the same population as Area Nº5, but three times as many deficiencies, will receive about three times as many resources $37,028,571, while Area No. 5 only receives $10,971,429.

Table 4. Assigning resources per territorial area in a hypothetical example

Territorial área	Population	Points on Level of Deficiency	Total points (points X population)	Point value (total investment / total points)	Amount of resources assigned in $
1	10 500	6	63.000	114,29	7,200.000
2	12 000	27	32,4000	114,29	37,028.571
3	9 500	16	15.2000	114,29	17,371.429
4	10 000	24	24.0000	114,29	27,428.571
5	12 000	8	9.6000	114,29	10,971.429
TOTAL	54 000	81	87.5000	114,29	100,000.000

605. Independent of the aforementioned, a part of the resources transferred to the territories will have to be used to cover the costs of maintaining services that have been transferred over. This amount can be easily worked out by looking at how much it cost previously to run these services, for example, teachers' salaries if responsibility of the local primary school has been transferred. Another part of the resources handed over will have to cover running costs not committed with concrete services. Then, there will be those resources that are transferred for the purpose of investing in projects and worked out on the basis of the criteria indicated above. In order not to complicate the example, we have dealt with both criteria in their simplest version, knowing that both can be modified to take into account additional factors that we have not considered here.

606. In terms of deficiencies, we could say that since we are dealing with the distribution of resources to be managed by territorial areas that have assumed certain decentralized competencies, then these deficiencies should be ranked on the basis of those that can best be addressed at this level, due to the fact that they are issues that can resolve at this level. For example, if the electricity network has to be centralized in the hands of a municipal company, this deficiency should have its weight diminished in terms of being a criterion for assigning resources to local areas, as they will not have to assume the costs of improving the network. Alternatively, if responsibility over housing has been transferred to the territorial areas, its weighting as a deficiency should be increased, as the territorial areas will have to solve this problem.

607. On the other hand, we take into account population density; many deficiencies could be modified to take into account the degree of population dispersion. For example, dealing with a lack of road access for an area with a sparse population requires more resources than if the area's population is concentrated in a smaller area.

608. Whether to apply these modifications or not, will depend more or less on the level of territorial disparities within each municipality. For example, a municipality that contains both densely populated urban territorial areas and sparsely populated rural territorial areas should take into consideration the issue of population density, while a municipality that is entirely urban might view this issue as irrelevant.

APPENDIX IV. TIMETABLE

609. Throughout this text, we have referred to the need to come up with a timetable. Logically, the timetable will be very different if we are dealing with a planning process at the level of the whole municipality or one at the community level; and in both cases, if we are dealing with the planning process itself or the implementation of what has been planned, for example when we are planning the execution of a specific project.

610. What is important is that we remember that a timetable should incorporate all the steps that need to be taken, set out who is responsible for carrying them out and note the time it is expected to take. Moreover, when the timetable is for implementation, the required material and human resources to carry each step out should be included.

611. The reader should understand that what follows is just an example and not a rigid rule or model. The timetable each community comes up with should not be seen as a strict framework, but rather as a reference guide that can be adjusted when necessary in order to achieve the overall aims within a set timeframe. Each community should come up with their own timetable that is based on their own lived reality, which will be very different from one country to the next, and even within a country. A number of things need to be taken into consideration such as organizational traditions, the existing legal framework and local experiences. The most important thing is to ensure that all the necessary steps are included in the timetable and that the necessary time is set aside for each step. A timely delay should not be a drama if it is justified, but an accumulation of delays might be telling us that the timetable was wrong to start with or that something in the process is not functioning properly. We have to remember that the planning process is an interdependent process.

612. Let us first look at a generic timetable for the first year of the process that could be developed by the Municipal Planning and Budgetary Cabinet, surely the most complex one as it involves kicking off the process.

613. Over the following years, the time taken for each step will almost certainly be shorter because a general framework for the planning process will have been established, meaning it will only be necessary to introduce those modifications that experience has dictated are necessary. There will also already be a Multi-year Development Plan that will only need to be modified on the basis of how the implementation process is unfolding along with the appearance of any new aspirations.

614. The shortening of timeframes should allow for planning in the second year of the Development Plan to begin to being early on the basis of what has been implemented in the first year. This will allow for a first evaluation of both results and of the implementation of the Plan and Budget.

615. In the example below, the different steps of the planning process are set out. These steps are described in a more detailed and pedagogical manner in the second volume of this book.

616. Given that the start of the fiscal year differs from one country to the next, we have decided to not put dates on this timetable, and simply present a sequence of weeks.

TIMETABLE

Time sequence	Responsible entity	Actions
Week 1	Mayor's office	1. Designate Initiators Team (see paragraph 381). 2. Set up Governmental Coordination Team (see paragraphs 388-391). 3. Invite people to participate in a Distinguished Advisors Committee (see paragraphs 392-394).
Weeks 2 & 3	Initiators Team	1 Establish the basis of the process and program of decentralization (see paragraphs 382-387) 2. Enact legal framework (paragraphs 382 and 383) 3. Designate the geographical areas of the process (paragraphs 384 y 385) 4. Establish general guidelines for the decentralization of resources and responsibilities.(paragraph 386) 5 Set up the Municipal Planning and Budget Cabinet and the Municipal Social Animators Team. (paragraph 387)
Week 4	Municipal Council	Provide legal support for the decentralization program.
	Mayor's office	Formally assign people to the municipal technical support teams.

Time sequence	Responsible entity	Actions
Week 5	Municipal Planning and Budget Cabinet	1. Carry out preparatory tasks that will provide the technical and organizational bases of the participatory planning process, and come up wit a general framework for the participatory planning process (see paragraphs 426). 2. Set up technical working teams at the territorial level (Planning and Budget Teams and Social Animator Teams). 3. Designate Territorial Coordinators.
	Municipal Social Animators Team	Days of mass consciousness raising regarding participatory planning. Issue call for volunteer professionals and experts (see paragraph 395-410).
Week 6	Municipal Planning and Budget Cabinet	Continue developing the technical-organizational bases of the process initiated the week before.
	Municipal Social Animators Team	Continue campaign initiated the week before.
	Territorial Coordinators	• Visit their respective territorial areas. • Set up territorial technical teams.
Week 7	Municipal Planning and Budget Cabinet	Continue developing the technical-organizational bases of the process initiated two weeks prior and conclude this task by preparing the documentation that has been collected.
	Municipal Social Animators Team	1. Continue campaign initiated two weeks prior, now with the support of the Territorial Social Animators Teams. 2. Distribute documentation that has been drafted by the Cabinet among the territorial technical teams.
	Territorial Planning and Budget Team	1. Carry out preparatory tasks at the territorial level (paragraph 427). 2. Designate Community Coordinators.

Time sequence	Responsible entity	Actions
	Municipal Training Commission	Training days for the municipal and territorial technical teams on general planning issues: steps to follow and role of organized communities.
Week 8	Municipal Planning and Budget Cabinet	Based on the technical-organizational bases of the process, prepare a summary to be presented to the Mayor's office.
	Municipal Social Animators Team	Continue campaign initiated weeks prior, with the support of the Territorial Social Animators Teams.
	Territorial Planning and Budget Teams	Continue with preparatory tasks.
Week 9	Mayor	At a mass event, open to all those who are interested (and broadcast on TV) announce: 1. The start of the participatory planning process in the municipality, explaining the decentralizing process that is being undertaken and the role that organized communities will play in it. 2. Present the working teams. 3. Present the Distinguished Advisors Committee. 4. Present the Territorial and Community Coordinators.
Week 10	Municipal Planning and Budget Cabinet and Municipal Social Animators Team	For the next few weeks the technical entities at the municipal level will direct their activities towards supporting and backing the territorial and community technical entities in the task of initiating the participatory planning process, resolving doubts, contributing resources and, in general, collaborating with each other on their activities.

Time sequence	Responsible entity	Actions
	Municipal and Territorial Social Animators Teams	Organize issues-based or thematic forums at their respective levels. These will be held over the next six weeks.
	Community Coordinators	1. Visit corresponding community. 2. Set up Community Planning Teams.
Week 11	Community Planning Teams	1. Carry out tasks outlined in paragraph 428. 2 Set up a group of activists. 3 Workshop to train up activists (Intensive series of videos on experiences in other communities).[1][58]
	Municipal Training Commission	Intensive workshop on the first three steps for the Community Planning Teams.
Week 12	Community Planning Assemblies	**Constitutive Session:** 1. Approve or modify geographical delimitations. 2. Approve or modify the subdivision of the community into neighborhood areas. 3. Approve or modify the general framework of the participatory planning process. 4. Ratify or modify the membership of the Community Planning Team.
Week 13	Neighborhood meetings	**First round of neighborhood meetings** to make people aware that the process has started, collect aspirations and elect delegates to the Community Assembly. They are organized by the Community Coordinators and the Community Planning Teams
Week 14	Community Planning Teams	Review aspirations collected in the neighborhood areas and organize them by themes/issues.

_____

Time sequence	Responsible entity	Actions
	Community Coordinators	Begin the series of video-debates on successful community experiences in the neighborhood areas (1).
Week 15	Community Planning Assemblies	**First ordinary session**: 1.Report on work done in neighborhood areas. 2. Report on list of aspirations from each area and set up thematic groups to analyze them and, if necessary, add others. 3. Elect delegates to the Participatory Planning Council and two delegates to the Territorial Planning Council.
	Community Planning Councils	Carry out **First Step:** 1. Study the unified list of aspirations and come up with a definitive list. 2. Come up with forms to collect information for the community database.
	Neighborhood meetings	A second round of **Neighborhood Meetings** should be held to know the results of the first ordinary community assembly and plan out the work of going door-to-door to fill out the forms relating to the database. This should be organized by the community coordinator, together with the Community Planning Team and the neighborhood delegates.
	Community Coordinators	Continue with the series of video debates in the neighborhood areas (2).
Week 16	Territorial Planning Councils	1. Review decisions of the Community Assemblies regarding the general framework for the participatory planning process. 2. Prepare a Planning Assembly in their territorial area

6

Time sequence	Responsible entity	Actions
	Community Planning Team	With the support of the team of activist, it collect information for the database door-to-door in the neighborhood areas.
	Community Coordinators	Continue with the series of video debates in the neighborhood areas (3).
	Municipal Training Team	Training days for community councilors regarding socio-political and participatory planning concepts.
Week 17	Territorial Planning Assemblies	**Constitutive session**: 1. Study and approve or propose modifications to the general framework of participatory planning process. 2. Receive a report about the progress of the process at the community level. 3. Elect the two Municipal Councilors to represent the territorial area on the Municipal Planning Council.
	Community Planning Council	**Second step**: 1. Collate the information obtained in the neighborhood areas and organize the community database. 2. Continue with the diagnosis and prioritize territorial aspirations. 3. Prepare proposals for budgetary and sector-based priorities.
	Community Planning Teams	Come up with a list of prioritized aspirations and circulate this list among the members of the community.
	Community Coordinators	Continue with the series of video debates in the neighborhood areas (4).
Week 18	Municipal Planning Council	1. Study, and where necessary, propose modifications to the general framework of the participatory planning process

Time sequence	Responsible entity	Actions
		based on the decisions adopted in the Territorial Assemblies.
		2. Prepare Constitutive Session of the Municipal Planning Assembly.
	Municipal Social Animators Team	Carry out campaign to encourage attendance at the Constitutive Session of the Municipal Assembly.
	Community Planning Assemblies	**Second Ordinary Session** Approve or modify results from **Second step:** 1. List of the prioritized aspirations 2. Sector-based and budget priorities. 3. Incorporate volunteers into the Council Working Groups.
	Community Planning Councils	Present aspirations from the territorial and municipal level to the Territorial Planning Council.
	Community Coordinators	Continue with the series of video debates in the neighborhood areas (4).
	Municipal Traininjg Team	Intensive workshop for the Community Planning Teams on Steps IV to VI.
Week 19	Municipal Planning Assemblies	Constitutive Session: Approve or propose modifications to the general framework of the participatory planning process.
	Territorial Planning Council	Carry out **First Step:** 1. Travel around the territory covered by the area. 2. Come up with a single list of territorial aspirations.

Time sequence	Responsible entity	Actions
	Neighborhood meetings	Third round of neighborhood meetings: 1. Receive information regarding what was approved at the second meeting of the community assembly.. 2. Sign up those interested in participating in Community Planning Council's working groups, which are organized by the Community Coordinators, the Community Planning Team and the neighborhood delegates.
	Community Coordinators	Continue with the series of video debates in the neighborhood areas (6).
Week 20	Territorial Planning Assemblies	**First Ordinary Session:** 1. Study the economic situation in which the participatory planning process will unfold. 2. Approve and, where necessary, add aspirations to the list of aspirations from the territorial and municipal level.
	Community Council (Working Groups)	Carry out **Third Step:** Discuss alternative proposals.
	Community Planning Teams	Organize thematic community forums where it is deemed useful.
	Community Coordinators	Finish the series of video debates in the neighborhood areas (7).
	Municipal Training Commission	Training days for technical teams, councilors and volunteers regarding technical material related to the Budget and the Development Plan.
Week 21	Territorial Planning Councils	Initiate **Second Step.** • Continue diagnostic and prioritize territorial aspirations • Prepare proposals for sector-based and budgetary priorities.

Time sequence	Responsible entity	Actions
	Community Planning Councils (Working Groups)	Begin **Fourth Step**: come up with community projects.
	Community Planning Teams	Initiate tasks in preparation for **Fifth** Step.
Week 22	Territorial Social Animators Team	Disseminate results of Second Step and convene the second ordinary session of the Territorial Planning Assembly.
	Community Planning Councils (Working Groups)	Continue with **Fourth Step**. Finish coming up with more simple projects and continue working on more complex ones.
	Community Planning Teams	Continue preparatory task for **Fifth Step** and begin the first phase of the Immediate Action Plan with more simple projects that do not require financing or are linked to the completion of the project (1).
Week 23	Territorial Planning Assemblies	Second ordinary session: 1. Approve prioritization of aspirations. 2. Approve the proposal for sector-based and budgetary priorities.
	Territorial Planning Councils	Take municipal level aspirations to the Municipal Council.
	Territorial Planning Councils (Working Groups)	Carry out Third **Step**: Study alternative proposals for the aspirations in the prioritized list for the territorial level.
	Community Planning Councils (Working Groups)	Continue with **Fourth Step** (2) Complete simpler projects. Continue with more complex ones.

Time sequence	Responsible entity	Actions
	Community Planning Teams	Continue with tasks from previous week (2).
Week 24	Municipal Planning Council	Carry out **First step** : 1. Receive list of aspirations from the territorial areas. 2. Travel through the municipality. 3. Come up with a single list of municipal aspirations.
	Territorial Planning Team	Take alternative proposals that could affect other territories to the Municipal Planning Council.
	Territorial Planning Council (Working Groups)	Initiate Fourth Step: 1. Come up with projects for the territorial level. 2. Where necessary, come up with idea-projects, including conditions that need to be met by any bid for the tender.
	Community Planning Councils (Working Groups)	Continue with **Fourth Step** (3).
	Community Planning Teams	1. Continue with preparatory tasks for Fifth Step (3). 2. Prepare list of projects that can be included in the first phase of the Immediate Action Plan.
	Community Planning Councils	Approve proposed Immediate Action Plan.
Week 25	Municipal Planning Assembly	First Ordinary Session: • Study the economic situation within with the participatory planning process will unfold. • Approve or modify list of aspirations for the municipal level presented by the Municipal Planning Council. • Approve the basis on which sector-based and budgetary priorities will be determined.
	Territorial Planning Council (Working Group)	Continue with **Fourth Step** (2).

Time sequence	Responsible entity	Actions
	Territorial Planning Teams	Initiate preparatory tasks for **Fifth Step** (1).
	Community Planning Assemblies	Extraordinary Assembly to: 1. Approve first phase of the Immediate Action Plan. 2. Recruit support for carrying out projects and for ~~controlling~~ managing and monitoring their development. 3. Announce the start of its implementation.
	Community Planning Teams, coordinators and activists	Large community party to kick off the Immediate Action Plan.
	Neighborhood meetings	**Fourth Round of Neighborhood meetings** Receive information and seek volunteers for volunteer roles in the implementation of the projects in the Immediate Action Plan. They are organized by the Community Coordinator, the Community Planning Team and the neighborhood delegates.
Week 26	Municipal Planning Council	Carry out **Second Step:** 1. Continue with the diagnostic and come up with a prioritized list of public works to carry out at the municipal level. 2. Come up with proposals for budgetary priorities.
	Territorial Planning Council (Working Group)	Continue **Fourth Step** (3).
	Territorial Planning and Budget Teams	Continue the preparatory tasks for **Fifth Step** (2).
	Community Planning Councils (Working Groups)	**Finish Fourth Step** (4).

Time sequence	Responsible entity	Actions
	Community Planning Teams	1. Organize material and human resources required to carry out the projects in the Immediate Action Plan. 2. Finish preparatory tasks for Fifth Step.
	Community Volunteers	Carry out simplest projects and make sure this occurs properly.
Week 27	Municipal Planning Council	Carry out **Second Step:** 1. Continue with diagnosis and prioritize municipal aspirations. 2. Establish sector-based and budgetary priorities for the municipality.
	Territorial Planning Council (Working Groups)´	Continue with **Fourth Step** (4).
	Territorial Planning and Budget Teams	Continue the preparatory tasks for **Fifth Step** (3).
	Community Planning Councils	Carry out **Fifth Step.** Come up with a proposal for a Development Plan, Annual Investment Plan, Budget, and Immediate Action Plan.
Week 28	Municipal Council (Working Groups)	Finish **Second Step.**
	Municipal Planning and Budget Cabinet	Come up with a prioritized list of aspirations for the Municipal Planning Council.
	Municipal Social Animators Team	Widely disseminate the lists and carry out a campaign to promote the next Municipal Planning Assembly.

Time sequence	Responsible entity	Actions
	Territorial Planning Council (Working Group)	Continue with **Fourth Step** (5).
	Territorial Planning Teams	Continue with preparatory tasks for **Fourth Step** (4).
	Community Planning Councils	Finish **Fifth Step**: Come up with a Development Plan, Annual Investment Plan, Budget and Immediate Action Plan.
	Community Planning Teams	Draf final documents for the Development Plan, Annual Investment Plan, Budget and Immediate Action Plan.
	Community Volunteers	Begin to carry out simplest projects and make sure they are carried out properly.
Week 29	Municipal Planning Assembly´	**Second Ordinary Session**: 1. Approve the prioritized list of aspirations. 2. Approve the proposed sector-based and budgetary priorities.
	Territorial Planning Council (Working Group	Continue with **Fourth Step** (6).
	Territorial Planning and Budget Teams	Continue with preparatory tasks for **Fifth Step** (5).
	Community Planning Teams	Carry out campaign with the community to make available the proposed Development Plan, Annual Investment Plan, Budget and Immediate Action Plan.

Time sequence	Responsible entity	Actions
	Community Volunteers	From this week on, continue carrying out simplest projects and make sure they are carried out properly.
Week 30	Municipal Planning Council (Working Groups)	Carry out **Third StepI.** Analyze alternative proposals for prioritized aspirations at the municipal level.
	Territorial Planning Council	Approve the results of Fourth **Step.**
	Territorial Planning Teams	Prepare necessary support documentation to carry out **Fifth Step.**
	Community Planning Teams	Continue campaign with community to make available the proposed Development Plan, Annual Investment Plan, Budget and Immediate Action Plan
	Community Planning Councils	Prepare third ordinary session of the Community Planning Assembly.
Week 31	Municipal Planning Council (Working Groups)	Begin **Fourth Step** 1. Come up with idea-projects for the alternative proposals. 2. Prepare conditions to put the projects out for tender.
	Municipal Training Commission	Training days for technical teams, councilors and volunteers regarding technical material related to the Budget and Development Plan.
	Territorial Planning Council	Begin **Fifth Step** (1). Come up with a Development Plan, Annual Investment Plan and Budget.

Time sequence	Responsible entity	Actions
	Community Planning Assemblies	**Third Ordinary Session**: 1. Approve the Development Plan, Annual Investment Plan, Budget and Immediate Action Plan. 2. Receive information on progress regarding the execution of the first phase of the Immediate Action Plan. 3. Elect a Community Planning Council.
Week 32	Municipal Planning Council(Working Groups)	Continue with **Fourth Step** (2).
	Municipal Planning and Budget Cabinet	Begin preparatory tasks for **Fifth Step** (1).
	Territorial Planning Council	Continue with **Fifth Step** (2).
	Community Planning Teams.	Formalize the support documentation and present it to the corresponding Territorial Planning Council for it to integrated into the overall Municipal Development Plan.
	Community Planning Councils, Community Planning Teams, Community Activists.	Begin carrying out the second phase of the Immediate Action Plan.
Week 33	Municipal Planning Council (Working Groups)	Continue with **Fourth Step** (3).

Time sequence	Responsible entity	Actions
	Municipal Planning and Budget Cabinet	Continue with preparatory tasks for Fifth Step (2).
	Territorial Planning Council	Finish Fifth Step (2).
Week 34	Municipal Planning Council (Working Groups)	Continue with Fourth **Step** (4).
	Municipal Planning and Budget Cabinet	Continue with **preparatory tasks for Fifth Step** (3).
	Territorial Planning and Budget Teams	Begin drafting the necessary support documentation to finalize **Step V** and present for approval in the Territorial Planning Assemblies.
	Territorial Social Animator Teams	Begin mass campaign to disseminate the results of **Fifth Step** and convene Territorial Planning Assemblies.
Week 35	Municipal Planning Council (Working Groups)	Continue with **Fourth Step** (5).
	Municipal Planning and Budget Cabinet	Continue with preparatory tasks fo**r Fifth Step** (4).
	Territorial Planning and Budget Teams	Continue drafting the necessary support documentation to finalize **Fifth Step** and present for approval by the Assembly.

Time sequence	Responsible entity	Actions
	Territorial Social Animator Teams	Continue mass campaign to disseminate the results of Step V and convene Territorial Planning Assemblies.
Week 36	Municipal Planning Council (Working Groups)	Continue with **Fourth Step** (6).
	Municipal Planning and Budget Cabinet	Continue with preparatory tasks for **Fifth Step** (5).
	Territorial Planning Council	Prepare territorial assemblies.
	Territorial Planning Teams	Finish drafting the necessary support documentation to finalize Fifth Step and present for approval in the Territorial Planning Assembly.
	Territorial Social Animator Teams	Continue mass campaign to disseminate the results of Step V and convene Territorial Planning Assemblies.
Week 37	Municipal Planning Council (Working Groups)	Continue with **Fourth Step** (7).
	Municipal Planning and Budget Cabinet	Continue with preparatory tasks for **Fifth Step** (6).
	Territorial Planning Assemblies	**Third Ordinary Session:** Present and approve Development Plan, Annual Investment Plan and Annual Budget for the territorial area.

Time sequence	Responsible entity	Actions
Week 38	Municipal Planning Council (Working Groups)	Continue with **Fourth Step** (8).
	Municipal Planning and Budget Cabinet	Continue with preparatory tasks for **Fifth Step** (7).
	Territorial Planning and Budget Teams	Formalize the support documentation and present it to the Municipal Council for it to be integrated into the overall Municipal Development
Week 39	Municipal Planning Council	Approve results of **Fourth Step.**
	Municipal Planning and Budget Cabinet	Finish preparatory tasks for Fifth Step.
	Territorial Planning and Budget Teams	Formalize the support documentation to officially complete **Fifth Step**.
Week 40	Municipal Planning Council	Carry out **Fifth Step**(1): Come up with a Municipal Development Plan, Annual Investment Plan and Annual Budget.
	Territorial Planning Teams	Finish drafting support documentation for the Development Plan, Annual Investment Plan and Annual Budget and present them to the Municipal Planning and Budget Cabinet to be incorporated into the overall Municipal Development Plan.
Week 41	Municipal Planning Council	**Finish Step V** (2).

Time sequence	Responsible entity	Actions
Week 42	Municipal Planning and Budget Cabinet	Begin drafting the necessary support documentation to finalize **Fifth Step.**
	Municipal Social Animators Team	Initiate mass campaign to disseminate the results of Fifth **Step**.
Week 43	Municipal Planning and Budget Cabinet	Finish drafting the necessary support documentation to officially finalize **Step V**.
	Municipal Social Animators Team	Finish mass campaign to disseminate the results of **Fifth Step.**
Week 44	Municipal Planning Assembly	**Third Ordinary Session** Approve Development Plan, Annual Investment Plan and Annual Budget.
	Municipal Planning and Budget Cabinet	Consolidate all the documentation from the communities, territorial areas and the municipality in order to formalize the Development Plan, Annual Investment Plan and Budget for the municipality as a whole.
Week 45	Municipal Planning and Budget Cabinet	Continue consolidating all the documentation.
Week 46 and onwards	Municipal Legislative Council	Approve the Municipal Development Plan, the Annual Investment Plan and Annual Budget.

APPENDIX V.   CONSOLIDATING COMMUNITY ORGANIZATION

617. In Chapter 2 we said that coming up with a plan with the active participation of residents in the community should not be the first task of the Community Council; this should occur prior to its formation because it is precisely through this process that the community begins to develop and is able to detect the most committed people that are best suited to setting up this small community government that is tied to the people and at their service.

618. Now we will turn to the matter of how to consolidate a community's development that occurs through the planning process, converting it into an ongoing organization: the Community Council. This entity will be responsible for carrying out numerous tasks in the daily life of the community, most of which are broadly laid out in the plan.

1. COMMUNITY ORGANIZATIONS AND WORK AREAS

619. Below is our proposal for how to organize collective work in each community by creating structures that allow us to not only unite the efforts of community organizations that are already working on the same issue or theme but also those individuals that do not belong to an organization but due to their professional or personal inclination share the same interests. For example, when it comes to the issue of healthcare, this could include: a health committee made up of community activists, doctors and nurses from the community health clinic, those involved in a popular soup kitchen that attends to those in need, a grandparents club, etc. In terms of education, this could include: parents and guardian association, teachers, student organizations, the local Info Center, the school sports club, etc. In terms of housing, infrastructure and habitat: environmentalist groups, architects, a kids' patrol that educates people about recycling, etc.

1) THEMATIC AREAS AND WORKING GROUPS

620. We believe it is important to promote the creation of thematic areas in which work is done on a collective basis by the different organizations and people that identify with a particular issue.

621. We will use the name **working groups** to refer to these collectives, many of which would have participated in the process of coming up with the community plan.

622. Based on the work carried out by the Venezuelan educator Francisco Cañizales, we will delve into the seven possible thematic areas mentioned in Chapter IX[58]: Popular Economy and Endogenous Development; Housing, Infrastructure and Habitat; Education and Sports; Full Social Development; Culture; Communication, Information and Training; Security and Defense. Before doing so, we would like to clarify that we are not saying that every community council has to have thematic areas that cover all of these issues. There will be cases where it makes sense to group separate areas together; in other cases we may need to create new thematic areas.

a) Popular Economy and Endogenous Development

623. The area dealing with Popular Economy and Endogenous Development has as its objective the promotion of cooperatives and small family businesses, part of whose profits could go

---

58. Paragraph 552.

towards supporting some aspect of the community plan; generating jobs, diversifying production, guaranteeing food sovereignty; putting science and technology at the service of the people; recuperating popular technology and promoting endogenous development; and ensuring that the environment is looked after in the community. It should also maintain a permanent census of those who are unemployed, noting down their job qualifications and skills.

b) Education and Sports

624. The area of Education and Sports should guarantee that everyone in the community has access to a good education and monitor educational institutions in the community to ensure they are functioning well both academically and administratively.

625. At the same time, it should concern itself with making sure that no one abandons his or her studies, thereby halting any potential reversal in the process of inclusion. When a child or adolescent stops attending school, it should immediately find out why and take any necessary action to ensure he or she remains within the education system.

626. This is the best way to prevent crime. If every child and adolescent is permanently studying in school, the risk of their rights being violated or conflictive behavior emerging is reduced.

627. It should also design and carry out permanent training workshops for all members of the community on the issues of drug addiction, pregnancy, citizen's formation and everything to do with associative forms of production.

628. Special emphasize should be given to training in the area of recuperating historic and cultural values, both local and national.

629. It should seek to increase involvement in sports and recreation, making it accessible to everyone. In this sense, it should promote initiatives in integral recreation and popular tourism, as well as the creation of sports clubs and recreational groups. It is important to consciously work on this issue in order to ensure women are included, thereby overcoming the male-domination of sports.

c) Full Social Development

630. The areaih of Integral Social Development should focus on guaranteeing healthcare and quality of life for everyone, ensuring special attention for those living in extreme poverty (children, adolescents, women, the elderly, those with disabilities, the homeless), and organizing the local supply of food. This implies, among other things, maintaining a permanent community census that keeps track of which illnesses are most prevalent in the community, which families live in extreme poverty, violations of children's and adolescents' rights, mistreatment of women, the feminization of poverty, who the elderly, people with disabilities and homeless are, and the number of homes and where they are located.

631. All of this should be done with the aim of calculating the real scale of the "social debt" and coming up with projects to gradually pay it off.

d) Housing, Infrastructure and Habitat

632. The area of Housing, Infrastructure and Habitat should focus on guaranteeing appropriate housing and habitat, good infrastructure, optimum public services, adequate environmental conditions and a rational use of environmental resources in the local area. Furthermore, it should have full knowledge of the characteristics of the area in order to indicate the best locations for new buildings, those areas that are too risky to be built on and those that should be protected for diverse reasons.

e) Culture

633. This area should focus on ensuring full access to culture., This includes promoting activities in the community that help with the promotion of traditional festivals, artistic activities (music, dance, theatre, recitals, poetry, popular literature, puppetry, plastic arts), contemporary and traditional literature, artisanal arts, technical solutions that the people have come up with, traditional housing, culinary arts, traditional medicine, social and economic relations, culture of cooperative work, spirituality, popular religions, solidarian values and other.

634. It should promote the creation of an inventory of cultural patrimony and initiatives to collectively recover the community's history.

635. Another of its tasks should be training up community cultural activists.

f) Communication and Information

636. The area of Communication of Information should focus on promoting truthful and timely information via all possible forms of media (radio, audiovisual presentations, newspapers, photo exhibitions, Internet and others). This is a very important task given the direct repercussion it can have in terms of cultivating values, the defense of local, regional, national and continental identity, and contributing to the democratization of the media.

637. Various studies have shown that people tend to maintain themselves informed not just through the national or international media but also via the forms of media outlined in the previous paragraph.

638. It is increasingly common to hear talk of the idea that the democratization of information and communication should be tied to thinking of communities as producers and disseminators of content. Digital technology can be used for this purpose and at a very low cost.

g) Security and Defense

639. This area should focus on citizens' security, civil protection in the face of natural disasters, the organization of reservists, and the promotion of justice and peace via negotiation and dialogue, among other activities.

640. It should identify and attempt to contain risk factors in terms of neighborhood conflicts, crime, sale and consumption of drugs and gangs – which in a number of Latin American countries use guns to impose their rule in a community (like the "maras" in El Salvador[59] or the narcos in Mexico) – and work towards the prevention or minimization of damage from natural disasters (floods, landslides, earthquakes, etc.).

641. It could promote the creation of a peace and justice team in the community, a permanent security roundtable, a group dedicated to rescuing those in danger of falling into drug abuse or crime, a reservists unit, or a nocturnal community patrol to prevent burglaries, as occurs in a some rural areas in Latin America.

---

59 Criminal gangs tied to narcotrafficking, the sale of illegal guns, assassinations, etc. They emerged in the United States, but have extended their reach mainly to Central American countries such as Guatemala, El Salvador and Honduras. One of these characteristics is the different tattoos that cover the bodies and faces of their members depending on which gang they belong to.

642. It is important to ensure that as many people as possible take up different tasks and functions, so that a majority are playing a certain role in the community and feel that they are active protagonists. We need to promote and value the participation of everyone, avoiding situations where tasks are concentrated in one or a few people (many people doing fewer tasks, not fewer people doing many tasks.)

643. We have to make an effort to ensure that we take the natural attributes and qualities of each person into consideration when delegating tasks: the idea is that everyone does what they feel they are best equipped to do. There are those who can perfectly carry out a task when it comes to disseminating information but who are not capable of taking minutes during a meeting; there are those who have the qualities to promote cultural activities, others who can run training courses, and others that are good at numbers and accounting.

644. The first question we need to ask those who want to collaborate is: what do you like to do? It is important to make sure that everyone is happy doing what he or she is doing.

2. COMMUNITY COUNCIL

1. DEFINITION, FUNCTION, PRINCIPLES AND MEMBERS' PROFILE

a) What is a Community Council?

645. The Community Council is a space for the participation, unification and integration of the different community organizations, social groups and citizens that reside in the small territorial space we have defined as a community. It is a small government that puts into practice the decisions adopted by the community and where the organized people control and evaluate its actions.

646. It should also concern itself with involving all those willing to work for their community in community work, combatting all forms of discrimination. It should seek to win over natural leaders. It should look for ways to resolve conflicts that might exist within a community.

b) Who makes up the council?

647. We propose the Community Council be comprised of three bodies – the Executive, the Financial Management Unit and the Social Oversight Unit – as well as a support team, the Community Planning Team, created during the planning process.

648. The working groups covering different thematic areas (which we referred to in Chapter VII) should be tied to the council and be represented on its executive.

649. Depending on the characteristics of the community and the composition of the Community Council, it may be useful to create an Advisers Council made up of people who due to their capacity and vision could contribute a lot to the council's work but do not have enough time to take on the daily task of the council (school director, head doctor at the local clinic, etc).

650. The bodies of the Community Council should hold at least one coordination and progress meeting per month.

651. Participation in any of the council's bodies should be non-remunerated.

652. It is important that the council create a fund to help cover its functioning costs. The fund should be made up of contributions from the community or a percentage of the funds set aside for projects. The use of these funds should be based on collectively decided criteria. It is vital that the council account for all funds spent in a consistent and transparent manner.

c) Allow for flexibility when setting up the council

653. A word of warning: we should be very flexible when it comes to setting up Community Councils. We should always be looking to strengthen community organization. The organizational form we are proposing should never be allowed to act as a brake on the development of community-based initiatives.

654. We have to consider the reality that one community may be very different from another: for example, some are located in remote rural areas while others are located in densely-populated urban areas; Different areas will have residents with different political leanings or different levels of poverty; some contain a large number of natural leaders while others have a scarcity of leaders; some have a tradition of community organization and others lack this.

655. That is why we reiterated that one of the first things that a community that wants to organize itself has to do is work out what are the main problems its faces and what initiatives does it want to undertake to improve conditions in the community. Based on this it should create work committees to deal with these problems or initiatives. In an ideal situation, this would involve obtaining the commitment of leaders or distinguished individuals in the community for these tasks.

656. Based on all this, we can say that the structure and functions of the Community Council should be adapted to the reality of each community. If a law is created to regulate its functioning, it should only set out general guidelines and not go into excess detail.

657. For example, although we propose that all Community Councils should have a unit or entity dedicated to financial tasks, this does not need to be done in a uniform manner. Some communities already have their own financial entities: not-for-profit civil associations, agrarian banks, popular banks, etc. We should respect such forms of organization.

658. In the following model we offer a plan for how the council should be structured.

d). Its functions

659. The main functions of the Community Council should be:

(a) Bring together community organizations and promote the creation of new ones where necessary.

(b) Analyze what material and human resources exist in the community.
(c) Come up with community plans and oversee their execution.
(d) Organize residents to help out with resolving some of their problems.
(e) Represent the community in discussions with other communities and superior entities or spaces of participation.
(f) Promote social oversight in all activities carried out in the community, whether by the state, community or private entities (food, education, health, culture, sports, infrastructure, cooperatives, missions, and others).
(g) Administer the financial and non-financial resources of the community, regardless of whether they are a result of local initiatives or granted to it by other institutions.

Outline of the structure of a Community Council

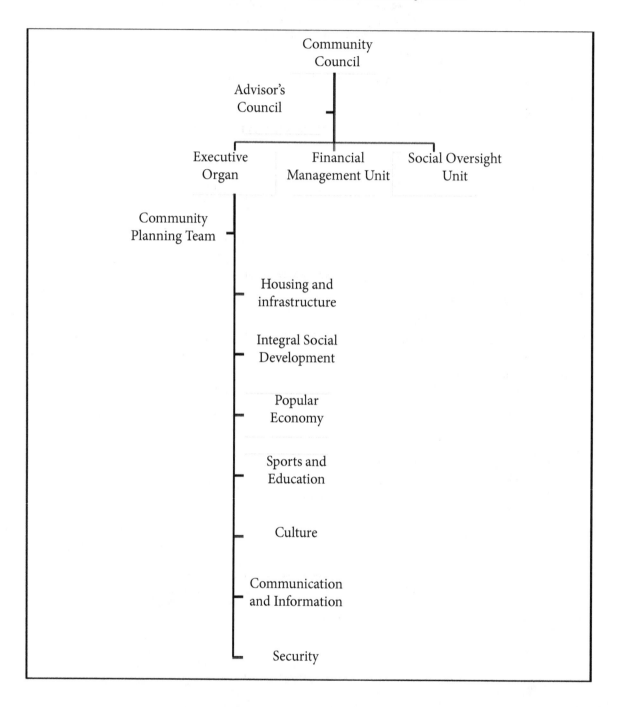

e) Principles that should guide its actions

660. A community councils' council's actions should be guided by the following principles:

(a) Team work: capacity to promote interaction between all members of a community.

(b) Responsibility: commitment to carrying out assigned activities.

(c) Co-responsibility: mutually agreed upon decisions and shared responsibility when working with a state institution.

(d) Transparency: maintain clear records: Present reports and balance sheets and correct and that are correct and up to date.

(e) Honesty: honorable conduct.

(f) Reportbacks: give regular presentations to citizen's assemblies regarding activities carried out and the use of resources.

(g) Equality without distinctions of race, creed, color, ethnicity, sex, age.

(h) Pluralism and respect for differences: give all residents an equal opportunity to participate, without discrimination of any kind (political, racial, religious, social).

(i) Solidarity: support and cooperate in the solution of personal or community problems.

f) Members' profile

661. These are some of the characteristics that candidates standing for the Community Council should have:

(a) Distinguished role in a diversity of activities having to do with community planning.

(b) A global vision of the community and specific knowledge of the area (school director, local doctor, priest, etc).

(c) Prestige and influence in the community.

(d) Willingness to work in a collective manner and without remuneration.

(e) Honorable.

(f) Dynamism.

3. STRUCTURE OF THE COUNCIL

662. Let's now describe in more detail each of the council's bodies.

1) EXECUTIVE

663. The Executive, as its name indicates, should execute the decisions of the Citizen's Assembly in relation to the functioning of the community council.

a) Functions

664. The Executive will have the following functions:

(a) Carry out decisions made in the Citizen's Assembly in which everyone participates and popular sovereignty is exercised.

(b) Work with the social organizations in the community, and promote the creation of new organizations where necessary, in defense of the collective interest and full development of the community.

(c) Coordinate everything that has to do with the functioning of the community council, the carrying out of its decisions and the communicating of these decisions to corresponding institutions.

(d) Be in charge of communications with other Community Councils as well as represent the community in other participatory spaces.

(e) Ratify or modify the Planning Team that will help with carrying out the community planning process. This team should be ratified by the Assembly, which has the right to veto candidates and propose others.

(f) Organize social volunteers for each of the work committees.

(g) Register the Community Council in accordance with the country's existing legislation (remember that in many cases, this Council must be legally registered in order to receive funds).

(h) Organize a system of community information.

(i) Coordinate community actions with those of decentralized state institutions.

(j) Request necessary support from the state.

(k) Coordinate citizen's pressure over the state when necessary.

b) Composition

665. The Executive could be made up of 29 members, of which the first 14 candidates could be proposed by the Working Groups (supposing that there are seven, one for each thematic area) to ensure coordination among them. Names for the other 15 spots could be put forward in the Citizen's Assembly. Gender equality should be ensured.

666. We want to point out that this is just a proposal: if a community has organized itself into fewer thematic areas, then the number of overall members will be less. In this situation, our idea is that the Assembly vote on the same number of candidates as those proposed by the thematic areas plus one more.

667. Once constituted, the Executive should select from its rank a person to fill the role of moderator, to preside over meetings and represent the Council when necessary. Furthermore, it should select one or two people to fill the role/s of secretary/ies.

c) Spokespeople and not representatives

668. The people who make up the Council should be referred to as spokespeople in order to point out the difference between our proposal and the bourgeois liberal democratic system, in which representatives tend to only reach out to people at election time, promise them the world and then, once elected, are never seen again.

669. We have taken the term spokesperson ("vocero") from the Venezuelan experience to refer to the members of the Executive as we believe they should be the voice of the community. That is also why they should be recalled if they are deemed to no longer reflect the thoughts or decisions of the community.

670. When we say the assembly should elect spokespeople according to work areas, we are thinking about the need to elect people who can best carry out tasks in these specific areas, tasks that go beyond the issues a particular organization may deal with.

671. For example, when electing a person to the community council to work on the issue of housing, we need to think of those people who have the knowledge and authority to coordinate a range of tasks and existing organizations in this area. It is quite likely that if the Housing Committee has already done a good job in this regard and maintains a level of prestige within the community, then the committee's spokesperson will be the best person to elect to the Community Council for the role of coordinating work in this area.

672. Furthermore, the community should have the power, if it so desires, to elect an expert in the area to this role if they have demonstrated themselves to be consistently active and willing to

collaborate, even if they do not belong to any of the already existing organizations in the community.

673. Similarly, if given a community's characteristics, there is a particular area of strategic importance (for example, Full Social Development due to the extreme poverty in the community), it is highly likely that the best community leaders will have dedicated themselves to this task. The same could occur in regards to Housing, Infrastructure and Habitat in a community that has mobilized itself to build its own houses. In these cases, we believe it is necessary to elect more than one spokesperson for the area, thereby providing those natural leaders in the community who are working in this particular are with an opportunity to be on the Council.

2) FINANCIAL MANAGEMENT UNIT

674. The Financial Management Unit is a specialized body of the Council, whose function it is to administer the financial and non-financial resources of the community. It should be comprised of three to five people.

675. The tasks of the Financial Management Unit are:

(a) Work out what material and human resources the community has available.

(b) Administer the financial and non-financial resources of the community, whether they be its own resources or those resources provided by external sources.

(c) Provide advice to the Executive and Community Planning Team during the process of coming up with community plans.

(d) Where necessary, act as a financing and credit institution for community plans.

(e) Manage the accounts of the Community Council.

3) SOCIAL OVERSIGHT UNIT

676. The Social Oversight Unit should control, monitor and supervise the use of resources that have been assigned, received or generated by the Community Council. It should be made up of three to five people from the community.

677. The Social Oversight Unit has the following functions:

(a) Monitor overall the administrative activities and ordinary functioning of the community council.

(b) Exercise control, monitoring and supervision over the execution of community plans.

(c) Prevent in time any irregularities or misuse of resources assigned to particular projects, services, programs and public works and suggest how to fix the problem.

(d) Carry out quality control over the construction of public works or provision of public services.

(e) Ensure diligence and honest conduct on the part of functionaries, public employees and social organizations.

4. ELECTION OF COUNCIL MEMBERS

678. Once the different thematic areas have been set up – many of which will have already been functioning as working groups during the participatory planning process – it is time to elect residents to the Community Council.

679. The election should occur via a secret ballot at a Citizen's Assembly. Voting for each of the three bodies will be different.

680. The spirit that should reign during these elections is that of integrating all the sensibilities in the community, rejecting exclusionary attitudes and avoiding a situation where any particular

orientation or tendency monopolizes positions on the Council. To ensure this, we need to come up with procedures that guarantee the presence of potential minorities and equal representation for women (open lists, voting for less candidates than positions available, etc.).

1) ELECTIONS FOR THE EXECUTIVE

681. As we previously said, the Council Executive might be made up of 29 members, 14 proposed by the Working Groups in each thematic area and 15 elected by the Citizens' Assembly.

682. In communities organized into neighborhood areas, two delegates from each of these areas should be incorporated into the executive as observers to facilitate coordination.

a) Who can be a spokesperson?

683. Anyone, irrespective of gender, involved with the community who is willing and motivated by the collective good, can be elected a spokesperson as long as:
(a) They have lived in the community for at least six months, except in those cases where a community has only recently been created or due to exceptional circumstances.
(b) Be over the age of 14.

b) Spokespeople proposed by Working Groups

684. To ensure that the Executive of the Community Council includes those who are most committed and with the most experience in community work, and it ensure that all areas are represented within it, thereby assuring coordination with the body, we have said that each Working Group should elect spokespeople to the Council.

685. In large communities, we suggest that each Working Group propose two spokespeople (a woman and a man). In small communities, where there may be fewer thematic areas, or in those where a particular thematic area tends to attract many natural leaders, we will need to work out the best way to do this.

686. Given that one of our objectives to create a team that is capable of working harmoniously within the community, it is important that residents feel comfortable with the team that makes up the Community Council. For this reason, we propose that if any candidate is rejected by at least 10% of voters, their candidature should be rejected.

687. If the assembly rejects a candidate, the affected working group should propose another name.

c) Spokespeople proposed directly in the Citizen's Assembly

688. The other 15 members will be elected by the assembly from among all candidates that have put their name forward before or during the Citizen's Assembly. To ensure gender parity, we suggest that the election be done via two separate lists according to gender, with the seven on each list that obtain the highest vote being declared elected. The 15th member should be the candidate with the highest vote between the two that came eighth in each list.

689. Being a member of a Working Group should not be an impediment to standing as a candidate for direct election. Rather, it should be seen as a positive quality that reflects the candidate's dedication to the community, as we shall see when we look at the profile of candidates.

2) ELECTION TO THE FINANCIAL MANAGEMENT UNIT

690. The election of the three to five members of the Financial Management Unit should be held during the same Assembly, once the Executive has been constituted and made a proposal regarding its composition.

691. They should be people who, as much as possible, are knowledgeable in economic affairs. If this is not possible, they should seek support from volunteers or institutions outside the community.

692. The Assembly should approve or reject some or all the candidates. If a candidate is rejected, the Community Council should propose new names.

3) ELECTION TO THE SOCIAL OVERSIGHT UNIT

693. The members of the Social Oversight Unit should be elected at the same Assembly where the Executive is elected, but in a separate election involving those candidates who unsuccessfully stood for the Executive.

694. To ensure the broadest possible representation, we suggest that each member of the Assembly only be able to vote for one candidate. The two male and female candidates with the most votes should be declared elected, with the fifth spot filled by whoever obtained more votes between the third-highest voted male and female candidate.

695. In line with the characteristics of its functions, we recommend lifting the age of eligibility to 18, and while financial training is not indispensable, it would be very useful if the members of this Unit were able to cope well with numbers, to make sure they are not put off or frightened when confronted with receipts, budgets and balance sheets. It is worth emphasizing that the most important characteristic for this responsibility is honesty and personal ethics.

5. CITIZEN'S ASSEMBLY: THE HIGHEST AUTHORITY

1) QUORUM4

696. Spokespeople should carry out decisions, but it is the residents in a community, through the Citizen's Assembly, who analyze, discuss, decide and elect.

697. Once again we insist that quorum for a Citizen's Assembly should not be determined by the percentage of the community that attends; rather, we need to ensure that all segments of the community are present.

698. As such, in small communities quorum should require the presence of at least one member of 75% of families in the community. In big communities, quorum should require the presence of at least two-thirds of the neighborhood areass.[60]

699. We also propose that the minimum voting age be 12.

700. The Citizen's Assembly is the ultimate authority in the community. Its decisions are binding on the Community Council. Sovereignty and peoples' power resides within the Assembly

2) FUNCTIONS OF THE CITIZEN'S ASSEMBLY

701. The functions of the Assembly are:

(a) Approve norms for coexistence in the community

(b) Approve statutes and constitutive acts of the Community Council.

(c) Approve the Community Development Plan, the Annual Plan and the Immediate Action Plan.

---

60. Regarding neighborhood areas see paragraphs 34 to 36.

(d) Adopt decisions that are central to the life of the community.

(e) Elect spokespeople to the Executive, the Social Oversight Unit and the Financial Management Unit.

(f) Recall spokespeople and other members of bodies of the community council.

(g) Define and approve mechanisms necessary for the functioning of the Community Council.

(h) Evaluate and approve the handling of financial matters.

702. Up to now we have outlined our ideas for how to organize the small community governments we have called Community Councils.

703. We are convinced that they are the fundamental pillars of any participatory and protagonistic democracy. Just as a house can easily crumble if it is not built on solid foundations, the same can occur with the new democracy we are trying to build. It will be sustainable to the extent that its base is strong, that is, if it is built upon good Community Councils as the smallest expressions of people's government.

VOLUME 2

Methodolgical Aspects

INTRODUCTION

1. This is the second volume of the book *Planning From Below*: *A Proposal for Decentralized Participatory Planning*. In the first book, and **especially** in the second part, we outlined the entities and participants involved in the three levels of planning – communities, territorial areas and municipality – along with their main tasks.

2. As we noted then, the main task of the entities at each of these three levels is to come up with a Multi-year Development Plan, a Budget, and an Annual Investment Plan for their respective geographical area, in accordance with the responsibilities and resources they have been designated. They should also monitor and control its progress.

3. We also noted the importance of allowing as much decentralization as possible, whereby anything that can be done at a lower level is carried out at that level. We also said that within this decentralization process, the territorial areas should be the level of government that is given the most weight.

4. Nevertheless, we believe that it would be useful for communities to have their own resources from the outset, so that their participation is not restricted to simply discussing aspirations for the territorial and municipal level; rather they should be able to propose, develop, and implement their own initiatives. This will help to raise the level of confidence they have in their own capacities and in the participatory process itself as a vehicle for providing quick solutions to some of their most immediate problems.

5. These resources could be obtained either through the decentralization process itself, with certain responsibilities and resources being assigned to communities; or through the provision of a small grant to carry out small-scale public works; or by assigning funds to specific projects selected via a tendering system (what we have referred to as small projects with a big impact in Part I, Chapter II of the first volume of this book)[1].

6. Utilizing the methodology we will outline below, we will suppose that in an ideal model responsibilities and resources have been decentralized to the territorial areas and that within the Territorial Annual Investment Plan, funds have been set aside for communities to carry out their own projects.

7. But the tasks of the communities and territorial areas cannot be limited to simply managing decentralized resources. To ensure citizens' participation throughout the whole process, we need to make sure that at each level, the entities do not limit themselves to simply outlining what they propose to do with their resources; rather they should present to higher levels those aspirations that due to their complexity or scale should be the responsibility of those levels or ones that are even higher.

8. In the opposite sense, it is obvious that at the territorial and municipal level, the corresponding entities will not be starting from scratch, as they should be taking into consideration the aspirations prioritized by the communities (in the case of the territorial areas) and the territorial areas (in the case of municipal entities), and integrating them into a single list of priorities out of which its projects will be selected.

9. Similarly, municipal and territorial budgets should take into consideration the priority areas set out by the territorial areas or communities, so that the budget outline reflects these priorities.

10. It is a back and forth process: we will regularly have to go back to a territorial area or community to explain why certain aspirations or priority areas have not been taken up, discuss

---

1. See paragraphs 113-119.

the reasons for this decision and look for a new consensus within the entity that first came up with them.

11. In Part II of Volume I, we outlined in detail the different tasks assigned to the different entities and participants in the participatory process. In this volume, we will explain in detail how the different participatory entities can carry out these tasks, both during the initial process and in successive years once the foundations of the decentralized participatory planning process have been established.

12. This is what we are referring to when we talk about the methodology of the process.

13. We are going to explain: how to create a database; how to formulate and prioritize aspirations and convert these into specific projects; how to come up with a Multi-year Development Plan and Annual Plans; and how to come up with budget priorities and integrate them into the overall budget outline. Lastly, we will look at how to implement, monitor and evaluate the progress of these plans.

14. We are conscious of the fact that a small community project, such as transforming an abandoned lot into a small plaza, will not be as technically difficult to come up with as a complex municipal project, like building a hospital. As we will explain in Chapter VI, the complexity of different projects may vary greatly, and undoubtedly more complex projects will require certain technical studies that we will not go into here. Our objective is to offer some general guidelines so that people without professional qualifications can come up with simpler projects, and identify the essential elements of more complex technical projects so that these projects are not distorted later on in such a way that they go against the initial objectives of the population.[2]

15. Similarly, we know that while a Community Budget or Development Plan is relatively simple to come up with and does not require special qualifications, at the municipal and perhaps even the territorial level, where a diversity of interrelated variables need to be taken into consideration when coming up with plans, we will require specialized technical expertise that the majority of the population does not have.[3]

16. This methodological book seeks to offer very simple and useful tools to those wanting to implement a process of participatory planning in their communities and territorial areas, so that they can successfully carry out the different steps involved in the process with as much participation as possible of the people who live in the geographical area. Without wanting to substitute for the necessary specialized knowledge that expert cadres responsible for promoting the process need to have, our objective at the municipal level is to identify the main aspects that neighbors should discuss and decide upon in the participatory process given the political consequences these issues have on the population.

---

2 See the concept "project-ideas" in Chapter VI.

3 Establishing the function of production or the interrelationship among variables demands a technical training in planning and econometrics. This training is essential for avoiding bottlenecks or distortions in the implementation of a Development Plan. For example, consider what would occur if a Plan proposed to promote agricultural production without taking into consideration existing deficiencies in transport networks and food storage.

CHAPTER I: DATABASE

17. We should never forget that to achieve the full participation of the people it is fundamental – as we said in Volume I – to touch the hearts of the people. We asked ourselves: how can this be achieved given the current situation where skepticism and the dominant ideology that reigns across the world leads people to think in terms of individual solutions and when it seems there is no time available to participate? We cannot reach the people by going and talking to them about a process they have never heard off. We cannot convene a meeting to "plan" in the abstract. We have to reach them via their most deeply felt needs and aspirations, taking as our starting point the fact that each community, or sector within it, has its own characteristics and its own problems. A poor community could face problems in terms of a lack of running water or access to electricity; a wealthier community could face problems relating to crime and transit. As such, the desires of the residents in the first community will differ from those of the second community. In the first, obtaining access to water and electricity are fundamental, while the problem of crime has been resolved. In the second, the fundamental desire is to obtain a police station and patrols. The way in which we will be able to reach people will therefore be different in each place. In each case, we should call a meeting to look at how the community can obtain want they want. When the people see that the meeting has a purpose, because they can relate to the issues that will be discussed, they will come.

18. We want to propose that data collection should start at the community level, and that the data obtained there should serve as inputs for the territorial area databases, which in turn will enrich the municipal database. Special attention should be placed on issues that generally tend to be forgotten, such as the environment and the situation of social groups that are often not taken into consideration: people with disabilities, older people, children and youth, people with a different sexual orientation, etc. It is also important to detect the key social leaders in each area to compile what we have called a Map of Activists.

19. It is important that the population participates in this process of data collection. This can be facilitated through the creation of groups of volunteers to help with collecting all the data that already exist in the offices of state institutions at the local level. This could serve as an interesting process of social auditing of the registries of these institutions. These groups of volunteers should also visit communities or territorial areas, together with a facilitator, with the idea of not only identifying problems, but also environmental characteristics and resources available in the area for solving problems. This would be very useful for identifying micro-ecozones.[4]

20. In Kerala, another interesting initiative was put into practice: group interviews with older residents to collect information on local history, with a focus on previous struggles to improve the lives of locals. A similar experience occurred in Cuba, where children did interviews in the community.

21. In the first phase, it will be enough to simply have essential data (demographical data covering age, gender, professions, etc.) that can be obtained from official censuses, while in the second phase will we need data that relates to the aspirations proposed. As we said in Volume I, we have to avoid spending too much time collecting more and more data, thereby delaying the

---

4. In Kerala they found that activists needed substantial amounts of training to correctly and usefully identify micro-ecozones.

start of the planning process when, in fact, much of this data will play no role in the development of the plan.

22. It is clear that we will not be able to carry out our work in the community if we do not have the minimum socio-economic data required. In this situation, we will have to focus our investigation on those issues that relate to the aspirations that have been formulated. It makes no sense to delve into the health situation of residents if no one has formulated an aspiration in this area because the people are happy with how things are at the moment. Each Planning and Budget Team should focus on questions relating to the areas that have been selected: for example, the aspiration to reduce unemployment could led us to delve into the issue of work, while the aspiration to resolve the housing problem could lead us to focus on this issue instead.

1) INFORMATION THAT COULD BE INCLUDED IN THE DATABASE

a) Cartographic data

23. We should request information from any state institution that has a map, plan, satellite photos or cadaster of the territorial area, or alternatively, create one, where possible, based on maps previously drawn up by the communities or territorial areas themselves. If none exist, then new ones will have to be drawn up.

24. For example, a map could be drawn up indicating soil fertility and potential uses (food production, construction, etc.), physical boundaries, existing limitations and zones that need protection (geological faults, mined land, wetlands, archaeological sites, eroded soils, flood plains), etc. The maps should also locate existing infrastructure such as main roadways, railway lines, aqueducts, power lines, sources and distribution networks for water and the disposal and treatment of sewage, etc.

25. This map could also indicate the problems and opportunities that have been detected during the data collection process. For example, it is important to know where those people with the most needs live, which neighborhoods have the greatest concentration of problems, which areas are privileged in terms of concentration of public services, green areas, etc. This information, together with that collected in the territorial areas, will enable us to produce maps detailing social disparities.

26. In Ecuador, a detailed guide exists to aid the technical work of the planners.[5] In terms of the site analysis, it talks about the "referential matrices" that have to be taken into consideration in the plans of each of the different territorial levels: province, canton[6], and parish.

b) Number and characteristics of residents

27. We need to know the number of people who live in the territorial area and, as much as possible, their characteristics: number of children, adolescents, adults, and older people; how many of them live in a state of abandonment or with a disability; number of unemployed people and general level of education; the average number of births per year; per capita income; ethnic origin; crime rates, drug addiction, and alcoholism; number of women with at-risk pregnancies; presence of sexually transmitted diseases; what illnesses are prevalent in the area and the main causes of death, among others.

c) Evolution of the population

28. It is also important to collate information on changes in the local population resulting from births and people moving away, and how these changes are affecting the characteristics of the population in the geographic area.

---

5. Guía de contenidos y procesos para la formulación de planes de desarrollo y ordenamiento territorial de provincias, cantones y parroquias: (Guide of contents and processes for the formulation of development plans and territorial classification of counties, cantons and parishes), Senplades, Quito, 2011.

6. In most countries these are generally referred to as municipalities.

d) Existing structures

29. We need to know the number of houses, schools, universities, health centers, workplaces, shops, shopping centers, sports fields, churches, and potential places to hold municipal meetings in the area, among others.

30. 14. We should not only collate quantitative data, but also note the conditions in which the buildings are in. We should, for example, consider if the buildings have deteriorated or have been maintained in a good state. We should also identify who looks after them and how they maintain the buildings.

e) Infrastructure

31. It is important to know what infrastructure exists and how well it covers the needs of the community, identifying the areas that are least covered by the existing infrastructure.

32. Here we are referring to electricity distribution, potable and household water services, rubbish collection and disposal, the state of roads (sealing of streets, maintenance of drains, lighting), public transport network, etc.

f) Economic activities and potentialities

33. We have to investigate what natural elements exist that could help with certain economic activities: mines, seas, lakes, rivers, beaches, fertile soil, proximity to rail lines, etc. Information regarding the various productive, commercial and financial activities carried out in the geographic area should also be collated, as well as information regarding whether they are run by the state or privately. We should know who owns what land, factory, business, and service. Moreover, it is important to know if any cooperatives, social property companies or other forms of productive associations exist as well as their quality level.

34. We have to work towards identifying the most important economic activities, as well as those that generate direct income and contribute to the daily maintenance of the population (small mechanic garages, clothing workshops, masonries, food halls, pubs, hairdressers, shops, restaurants, street vendors, tutors offering private lessons, taxis, etc.). We should also collate information on any bartering or non-monetary exchange systems that exist, and whether other economic activities and services could be carried out that could help the geographic area become more self-sufficient.

35. We should also see if any financial services exist (banks, credit groups, money lenders, etc.).

g) State of the environment

36. We should know of any environmental issues: contaminated waterways, productive activities that pollute the environment, logging, burning of rubbish in the streets, etc.

h) Forms of worker organization

37. It is important to investigate whether workers in the community are organized into trade unions or associations.

i) Social and human potential

38. We have to find out what the situation is in terms of the labor force (employed, unemployed, semi-employed) in the geographic area, breaking this down by gender, age, disability, nationality, and ethnicity. We also need to know what the situation is regarding labor rights.

39. We should know what human talent exists in the community: bricklayers, artisans, bakers, engineers, mechanics, teachers, sports players, artists, doctors, lawyers, farmers, among others, and how they are organized. We should also identify the natural leaders that exist in the geographic area. The success of participatory planning will depend a lot on them.

j) Socio-cultural traditions and activities

40. We should also find out the main cultural traditions of the locality and the socio-cultural activities that occur within it, such as traditional celebrations, events, competitions, tournaments, markets, etc.

41. In many cases it is easy to reach the people through such events.

42. In Cuba there was a very good initiative taken in a neighborhood that was generally regarded as a troubled area and that was able to turn its situation around thanks to the activities that families organized around a children's troupe[7].

k) Situation of women

43. As we are particularly interested in ending discrimination against women, we need to know their situation in detail (level of education, work situation, political participation, violence against women, etc.).

l) Situation of youth

44. In the same sense, we should know as much as possible about the situation of young people in the area, as they are another sector that we are particularly interested in motivating to participate.

m) Organized communities in each territorial area and their level of quality

45. It is also fundamental to have as much knowledge as possible regarding: how many organized communities exist in each territorial area; the quality of these organizations; if leaders are elected in a democratic manner; if they are able to mobilize an important sector of the population; if they meet frequently; if their meetings are creative and take autonomous decisions; if these communities have the capacity for self-management; if they have some financial entity to manage its resources; if they maintain some kind of social auditing; if they are open organizations or work behind closed doors; if they seek to broaden out their work or are happy to continue with what they are doing; if they are self-sustaining or rely on external economic support, etc. We also need to know those places where no community organizations exist but could be set up.

n) Existing sector-based organizations or interest groups

46. We need to know how many sector-based and interest groups exist. We should come up with a list of the social organizations that exist in the geographic area (cultural groups, sports groups, women's organizations, religious groups, student groups, environmental groups, farmers associations, fishers associations, shopkeepers associations, etc.) and their legal status. We should see if they are well known by the people in the area. It is also important to know their origins, history and purpose, and the quality of their organization: are their leaders democratically elected; are they able to mobilize important sectors of the population; do they meet regularly; are their meetings creative spaces and do they take autonomous decisions; are they able to carry out projects and are they currently undertaking a particular project; do their activists participate in some kind of systemic training; are they open organizations or do they operate behind closed doors; are they seeking to broaden out their activities or are they happy doing as they are; do they function in a completely independent manner or do they rely on external funding.

o) Problems that exist in the community

47. An analysis should be made of the issues that affect the normal and dignified everyday lives of residents in each geographic space, for example: lack of basic services (urban sanitation, electricity, water, sewers, asphalted roads), security problems, unemployment, lack of recreational infrastructure (sports fields, cultural centers, parks, plazas), lack of social infrastructure (schools, health clinics, childcare centers), etc. Special emphasis should be paid to

---

7. You can find books and videos on this situation online at http://videosmepla.wordpress.com/

issues such as contamination and other environmental problems, and the vulnerability of certain zones.

p) Problems that transcend the local community

48. We should not only detect the immediate problems of the geographic area. We should also detect those that transcend its boundaries such as, for example, issues with road access or transport services, which are problems that affect an entire municipality; or a faulty bridge that connects two communities.

q) External benefits that are received

49. There should be a register of all the social programs carried out in the community by the national government and national or international non-government organizations (NGOs). We also need to know how they are working.

r) Solidarity-based initiatives

50. We should also investigate what initiatives have been undertaken around social issues, for example: a club for the elderly, initiatives against drugs, renovating abandoned places for cultural activities and sports, among others. All of these initiatives are expressions of the spirit of solidarity among the residents in a given community and could be key to promoting the local development of the community in the future.

s) History

51. Generally no community starts from scratch. Therefore it is important to investigate if there were previous attempts to resolve, whether in a participatory manner or not, some of the community's problems. It is important to know how these initiatives were carried out, if errors were committed, what they did correctly and what was the final result.

52. It is also important to know if any initiatives are already underway to deal with specific problems and in what way they might affect the availability of resources to deal with the community's aspirations that had been detected during the process.

t) Legal framework

53. We should investigate what laws and regulations exist regarding the activities we want to carry out, for example: if there are regulations that protect the environment, or laws about carrying out public works that fall under the domain of the national or municipal government or the territorial area, and whether these need to be monitored to ensure they are adhered to.

2) CONSOLIDATION OF DATA INTO A SINGLE DOCUMENT

54. It is very important to have a single document that consolidates all the data obtained and helps to systematize the information in the most pedagogical manner possible, to facilitate its use in the following steps of the participatory planning process.

55. We suggest that when a summary exposition of the data collected by activists from the various organizations and those obtained by the residents themselves is presented, it should be combined with a PowerPoint presentation that contains photos or footage that provide images of the characteristics of the territory and its main problems.

56. In small communities, maps designed by the residents themselves could also be used.

57. It is important to correctly select the person or persons who will explain and outline the data. They must be able to do so in a pedagogical manner. They should avoid using very technical terminology. Everyone should be able to understand his or her presentation.

58. Collecting and synthesizing all the information in as pedagogical manner as possible will make it easier to use this information in the next steps of the participatory planning process and allow people to more clearly see their existing situation, the connection between different territorial issues, existing opportunities, and, based on this, determine priorities in an informed

manner. In particular, it can help facilitate the participation of children, youth and people with lower levels of education or capacity for abstract thinking.

59. It is often the case that the people presenting the data end up talking for too long, meaning that many of the participants become unnecessarily bored and the assembly loses its dynamism. That is why it is important to do some trial runs of the presentation before the assembly, to see if it is well prepared, sufficiently succinct and to time it to see how long it takes.

60. This data, organized into a single document, should provide an objective vision of the reality of each geographic space. It should provide us with a snapshot of the community.

61. An as we said in paragraph 21, forms should be designed in such a way as to collect the data that is of most interest, while making sure it can be easily filled out manually, thereby simplifying the collection process. We should aim to be as succinct as possible (See Appendix I).

62. If the technology exists, it is recommended that an easy-to-use and accessible electronic database be created. However, given the possibility that there will be communities where this is not possible, we are making available to the reader some model forms or sheets that can be filled out manually in Appendix I.

CHAPTER II.

DIRECT KNOWLEDGE OF THE LAY OF THE LAND

63. Along with the knowledge that can be obtained by coming up with the aforementioned database, it would be useful for community, territorial or municipal councilors to have more direct knowledge of what is happening in their respective area. Important information can be obtained by getting councilors to tour their geographic area, not only to see the situation with their own eyes, but also hear what those affected by the situation have to say.

64. In terms of communities, where we are speaking of relatively small spaces in which everyone knows each other, it may not be necessary to organize a formal tour of council members through the community. Nevertheless, if when studying the database certain doubts or contradictions emerge between what is reflected in the documents and the experience of certain members, it may be necessary to talk with those affected and, in some case, for an ad hoc group from the council to visit the specific area or areas to find out what the real situation is.

65. At the territorial and municipal level, without ignoring the contributions of council members and other people with direct experience (teachers, doctors, social workers, etc.), we think it would be very useful, even indispensible, that each council organize a tour of their territorial area or municipality to see what the situation is like.

66. To avoid a situation where the tour leaves participants with a distorted vision of the reality, council members should tour **the entirety** of the territorial area or municipality. If we are dealing with a large area, this tour should be done by bus or guided by a member of the Team of Animators[8] who can point out where the most significant issues that relate to the respective databases are.

67. After obtaining a general vision of the geographic area, the area should be divided up in neighborhood areas with interest working groups assigned to different areas.[9] Each group should

8. See more about the Team of Animators in paragraph 239-240.

9. The following paragraphs have been taken from a book we have been working on with Venezuelan economist Noel López since 2009 on municipal participatory planning.

be divided into sub-groups: one to play the role of "eyes" and the other the role of "ears". Those people who play the role of "eyes" should tour the area, visually detecting what the situation is like. Those people who play the role of "ears" should interview people, asking them to list the main problems that affect them and the solutions they have in mind.

68. Council members should not simply rely on their memory; they should note down the main things that people tell them in a notebook.

69. Moreover, the visit should not be done in a group as a whole but in an individual manner, or if necessary, in no more than groups of two. This will allow for more spontaneity in the interviews and, at the same time, allow more people to be interviewed.

70. To avoid doubling up, areas should be specifically designated to each member of each subgroup.

71. Unlike other tasks that will need to be carried out later on, in this case it would be useful for the technical experts to work on their own to then be able to compare the information they collect to that obtained by councilors.

72. It is important that this activity should be carried out while keeping in mind all aspects of the likely data needs of the local planning process, and not simply the issue that the group the council member belongs to is focused on when carrying out the tour.

73. Before visiting each area, the groups should have sufficient information to easily orientate themselves when studying the lay of the land: areas were people tend to congregate, sites of special interest, spaces where it is possible to find locals with a good knowledge of the area. At the same time, we do not think it is a good idea for councilors to tour those parts of the community or territorial area they have been elected to represent.

74. Although councilors tend to know the general problems in their territory or municipality, the tour can allow them to see situations that they may never have paid attention to before. Moreover, they will be obliged to compare their ideas with those of the people they speak to during the tour.

75. In this way, councilors can see for themselves the problems that most affect residents and those that most urgently require a solution. In many cases they may realize that the problems prioritized in some places are less urgent that others and, motivated by a spirit of inter-territorial solidarity, will feel the need to come out in favor of projects that were not originally theirs.

76. This same methodology can be applied to any *ad hoc* group where they have set up such groups in the community.

CHAPTER III.
FORMULATING THE DESIRED CHANGES AND TRANSFORMING THEM INTO A LIST OF ASPIRATIONS (FIRST STEP)

1. ASPIRATIONS AND MOTIVATING QUESTIONS

77. In Volume I, paragraphs 277-286, we referred to the need to try and imagine the kind of ideal scenario we would like to live in and not simply limit ourselves to pointing out problems. At the same time however, we said we needed to make sure we did not just come up with very abstract formulations; rather we needed to look for more concrete forms of expressing our desires or dreams. We referred to these as "aspirations".

78. We believe that, to stimulate the exchange of ideas, it would be worthwhile formulating questions that help neighbors identify what it is they want for their community.

79. Experience tells us that people tend to confuse aspirations with the ways in which to make them concrete. Therefore our questions should seek to avoid leading people towards imagining concrete solutions, as this should occur later on in the third step, which deals with exploring alternative ways to achieve the desired changes.

80. For example, imagine a community where a number of unemployed people live; one of the aspirations that will undoubtedly emerge is for all residents to have a dignified job. But rather than expressing this aspiration as a wish, solutions generally tend to be put forward, for example, create a cooperative to manufacture school uniforms as a way to create work.

81. To avoid these types of confusion, we recommend that facilitators come up with a few questions that can help generate discussion. We have to ask: how would you like or hope to see your community when it comes to the issue of employment?

82. In any case, if people continue to have difficulty talking about their aspirations and instead continue to only put forward solutions to their problems, we can help them identify their aspirations while noting the solutions they propose on a separate piece of paper, so that they do not feel as though their proposals are being rejected, while clarifying to the participants that we are noting them down so that they can be taken up again later on in the process.

83. Within these thematic areas we think it is important to motivate the participants to consider organizational aspects as a specific thematic area. Another aspect worth addressing is the issue of discrimination.

84. Appendix II will outline some examples of motivating questions for the different thematic areas.

2. METHODOLOGY IN THE COMMUNITIES (FIRST STEP)

85. Here we will distinguish between the first level of planning, the communities (and their respective neighborhood areas[10], where these exist), and the territorial areas and municipality. In our example we are going to suppose that neighborhood areas exist.

NEIGHBORHOOD AREAS

Activity 1. Collection of aspirations

86. Members of the Community Planning Team, who will be replaced by the Community Planning Council after the first year, should hold meetings in the neighborhood areas to explain the objective of the planning process, the different stages involved, the steps that need to be taken to come up with the plan and the way in which the work will be organized.

87. Next, they should explain in detail the first step. It is important to dream; therefore, it is worthwhile asking what kind of community we want to live in rather than taking the community's problems as our starting point.

88. We should then stimulate an exchange of ideas on this issue and orientate the discussion via motivating questions regarding different aspects of the community (see example further below) so that this vision begins to take the concrete form of specific aspirations. Peoples' opinions should be summarized and written down.

89. The list of aspirations that emerges from the neighborhood areas as a result of these activities should be handed over to the planning team. If a community is so small that it makes no sense to subdivide it into neighborhood areas, the list should emerge directly out of the Community Planning Assembly.

---

10. For more on the subject of neighborhood areas, see paragraphs 67 and 68.

Activity 2. Drafting a list of aspirations

90. The Community Planning Team should consolidate all the aspirations raised in the different neighborhood areas into a single list. An attempt should be made to merge those that represent essentially the same aspiration but are expressed in different ways.

91. Once this has been done, the aspirations should be organized thematically. Among the themes that tend to most frequently emerge are the following: Culture, Education, Economy, Environment, Sport and Recreation, Health, Infrastructure, Organization, and Human Relations.

92. Below are some examples of a unified list of community aspirations and of some thematically-organized aspiration lists.

Consolidated list of aspirations

A community where:

1. Healthy forms and spaces for recreation exist.

2. Traditional music from the zone can be enjoyed.

3. Artists that live in the community commit themselves to working with children on a diversity of initiatives.

4. Participation in sports is widespread.

5. You can go out at night without fear of being assaulted.

6. The streets and public spaces are well-lit.

7. Cleanliness reigns.

8. Sheltered bus stops exist.

9. Water is available on a daily level and in abundance.

10. Everyone has a job.

11. There are sufficient food supplies.

12. The various community organizations work in a unified manner.

13. Productive development respects the environment.

14. Everyone wants to participate

15. All types of discrimination are avoided.

16. Young people are working together in an organized manner.

List of organizational aspirations

A community where:

- The various community organizations work in a unified manner.

- Everyone wants to participate

- All types of discrimination are avoided.

- Young people are working together in an organized manner.

List of economic aspirations

A community where:

- There are sufficient food supplies.

- Productive development respects the environment.

- Everyone has a job

List of cultural aspirations

A community where:

- Healthy forms and spaces for recreation exist.

- Traditional music from the zone can be enjoyed.

- Artists that live in the community commit themselves to working with children on a diversity of initiatives.

COMMUNITY ASSEMBLY (WORKING GROUPS)

Activity 3. *Working groups look over the aspirations and add to list*

93. In the Community Planning Assembly, the Community Planning Team should set up working groups organized around the different thematic lists of aspirations. These working groups should see if all the aspirations are contained in these lists or if, for some reason, some have been left off.

94. Each working group should be given their respective lists (in hardcopy or electronic form).

95. To stimulate an exchange of ideas regarding other possible aspirations, we recommend using the motivating questions that we have included in Appendix II.

ASSEMBLY PLENARY

Activity 4. *The Assembly Plenary drafts up a new single list of aspirations*

96. After carrying out this activity with each working group, the Assembly discusses and approves or modifies the single list of aspirations and hands them over to the Community Planning Council so that they can begin the work of prioritizing the aspirations.

3. METHODOLOGY FOR COLLATING ASPIRATIONS IN TERRITORIAL AREAS AND THE MUNICIPALITY

97. Unlike in communities, this process requires prior work in territorial areas and the municipality. It requires collecting the dreams and formulated aspirations that communities have come up with and which fall under the responsibility of the higher levels of government.

98. In the following paragraphs we will describe the specific aspects of the process for territorial areas. When it comes to the municipality, the process is similar except for the fact that this level should focus on analyzing aspirations that have emerged from the territorial areas but fall within the responsibility of the municipality.

TERRITORIAL COUNCIL (PLENARY)

Activity 1. *Receiving aspirations that have emerged from the communities but whose realization is beyond their reach.*

99. The Territorial Planning Council should start by getting to know the aspirations that have emerged from the communities within its respective territorial area. These are aspirations that have already been prioritized by the communities, but which they recognize they do not have the capacity to realize by themselves with the resources they have and have therefore presented them to the territorial area or municipality.

100. The councilor that represents each community should bring the list of aspirations of his or her community. These lists should be pinned up in a visible place inside the meeting room.

101. All members of the Territorial Planning Council should closely read these lists and ask respective councilors for any explanations or extra information they feel is required.

102. The Territorial Planning Council, with the help of the Technical Planning and Budgetary Team, should make an effort to group together similar aspirations from the different communities, even if they have been formulated differently.

103. Once this has been done, they should organize themselves into thematic working groups.

Activity 2. *Tour through the territory*

104. With the aspirations presented by the communities at hand, a tour of the territory should be organized using the methodology outlined in Chapter II.

TECHNICAL PLANNING AND BUDGETARY TEAM

Activity 3. *Coming up with a thematic based list of aspirations*

105. The Technical Planning and Budget Team should draft a list that collates the aspirations that have come from the communities, along with new ones that might have emerged during the tour by the territorial councilors, to then group them by theme, noting which communities formulated them.

PLANNING COUNCIL: THEMATIC WORKING GROUPS

Activity 4. *Formulating desired changes for the territorial area and converting them into a list of aspirations.*

106. Starting with the list that corresponds to its area, each thematic working group should study, and if necessary reformulate, their respective aspirations. We suggest that the group should not limit itself to pointing out aspirations that resolve actual problems but should go further and make an effort to imagine the ideal scenario they would like to see when it comes to their thematic area.

PLANNING COUNCIL (PLENARY)

Activity 5. *Approving the proposed list of aspirations*

107. The Territorial Planning Council should look over the results of the different working groups and approve the proposed list of aspirations that have been grouped together by thematic area.

TERRITORIAL ASSEMBLY

Activity 6. *Approving the list of aspirations*

108. The Council should present the lists it has come up with to the Territorial Planning Assembly.

109. This Assembly should not be limited to simply taking note of the list of aspirations presented by the Council. Its members can propose new aspirations that have emerged as a result of the diagnosis of the situation previously carried out. If the Assembly approves some of these proposals, these aspirations should be added to the list with a reasoned justification as to why it was considered necessary to add them.

110. Out of the discussion should emerge a list of aspirations for the entire territorial area that, once approved by the Assembly, should be sent back to the Council so it can begin to work on prioritizing the aspirations.

111. 34. Below is a possible list of aspirations in the area of culture. As you will see, two aspirations are in bold. These aspiration were not in the initial lists presented by the organized communities, but rather came to light as a result of the deliberations of the working group for culture in the territorial area.

List of cultural aspirations

A territory in which:

• There is sufficient provision of secondary school level education.

- The possibility exists to access the internet for free in the territorial area.

• Cultural activities are not concentrated in the center of the territorial area.

• There are spaces that serve various communities in which cultural activities can access the most advanced technology

CHAPTER IV.
DEFINING PRIORITIES (SECOND STEP)

112. We said in the first part of this text that it is not possible to immediately satisfy all the collated aspirations due to resource issues such as time. Therefore we have to work out which ones should be given priority. To do this we have to analysis each one of the aspirations formulated in the previous step, note the problems and challenges that impede this aspiration from becoming reality, and the strengths and opportunities that could help us reach them. This information can help us determine priorities.

113. We proposed that the process of coming up with a list of aspirations should begin in the neighborhood areas and occur primarily in the Community Planning Assemblies, with the participation of anyone who wants to take part. To prioritize the aspirations, we propose something different: we believe this should happen within the Planning Councils.

114. We think that this debate requires a calm and profound study of each of the aspirations and should therefore be carried out in small groups in which all participants can fully express their opinions in order to be able to best reach consensus on the results.

115. These results should then be presented to the respective Planning Assembly for approval or modification.

116. Below, we will outline the activities corresponding to this step of the participatory planning process. Just as we did when formulating aspirations, we will distinguish between those activities that need to be carried out at the community level and those that should be carried out in the territorial areas and municipality.

1. METHODOLOGY FOR COMMUNITIES

Activity 1. (Plenary) Presentation of the single list of aspirations and explanation of the following steps in the process

117. The Planning Team should present the single wish list of aspirations, that by now has been cleaned up and organized, and explain the methodology that will be used in the next part of the process.

118. The team should propose the formation of working groups organized along the lines of the different themes that the aspirations have been placed under.

119. The team should explain that the existing situation regarding each aspiration will be looked at, taken into consideration the problems that might impede the realization of these aspirations, the challenges the community could face if the situation does not change, and the strengths and opportunities that could help make these aspirations a reality. The team should point out that this information will later help determine which aspirations should be prioritized. As such, it should be noted down in summary form on a large piece of paper or electronically so that it can later be presented in public.

Activity 2. (Working groups) Analyze the actual situation of the community in regards to each aspiration

120. The wish list of aspirations corresponding to each working group should be displayed alongside a clean sheet of paper where the results of the exchange of opinions can be written down (see below for example).

121. Given that other people (volunteer or publicly-employed experts) will be participating in these groups alongside councilors, norms should be established to ensure that priority is given to hearing councilors first and then the experts.

122. This is an activity in which the contribution of those with more technical knowledge can be very valuable. If, for example, participants end up focusing on the most apparent problems or challenges, the experts can broaden out these limited visions by using their knowledge and going to the heart of the matter.

123. Table 1 provides an example of how the worksheets could look like.

Table 1. Example of existing situation in a community in relation to each aspiration

List of aspirations	Current situation (problems, threats, strengths and opportunities)
Healthy recreation.	• There are no initiatives or spaces for recreation. • People are turning to alcohol. • Drug use is rising in neighboring communities and small-scale dealers are being to appear. • There is an open air cinema that could be converted into a space for recreation. • There are a number of people willing to volunteer to help in this area.
Cleanliness.	• Due to a lack of bins, rubbish is accumulating in unused lands. • Rats and diseases are beginning to appear in the community. • The people are very willing to collaborate in a volunteer cleaning up project. • The local rubbish tip could be transformed into a small plaza. • The mayor's office is willing to provide bins and organize rubbish collection in the community.
Listen to traditional music from the area.	• People mainly listen to foreign music. • There are groups who play traditional music.
Artists working with children.	• This aspiration does not have a specific problem as its starting point. • There are various artists who live in the community that are willing to collaborate. • Children have a lot of free time after school. • Schools have offered up their space.
Mass participation in sports.	• Lack of sports fields. • There is interest among young people to participate in sports. • There are people will to train them. • Parents are willing to collaborate. • There is an unused space that could be used for sports.
Possibility of going out at night without fear of being robbed.	• A lot of robberies occur. • Streets are not well lit. • Violence is on the rise in the municipality and armed gangs of youth have begun to appear. • Municipal authorities are concerned about this and are willing to adopt the necessary measures. • The poles and wires exist, what is missing are the light bulbs. • The state has offered to swap scrap metal for light bulbs. • There is a willingness among the community to carry out a program of volunteer neighborhood watch.
Others.	

Activity 3. (Plenary) Prioritization based on determined criteria

124. Once the existing situation in regards to each aspiration has been analyzed, we should being to establish priorities. To do this it is necessary to re-examine the single wish list of aspirations – which has now been enriched through the process of analysis mentioned above – and give each aspiration a score on the basis of criteria that has previously been agreed upon, by consensus, through a collective discussion.

125. The worksheet from the previous step should be displayed to help recall the various considerations made in the working groups. When scoring, it is worthwhile ensuring that the group that studied the aspiration speaks first, as they will have more arguments to help determine scores.

126. Afterwards, the Planning Team should explain the criteria that will be used to give out scores. These should been selected on the basis of the objectives we have set ourselves. In this case, for example, we want to: attend to the most urgent problems first; ensure that the measures adopted benefit the as many people as possible; ensure that the poorest, women and youth are given priority; not damage the environment; and, most importantly, ensure that the community can realize them using their own financial, material and human resources.

127. 16. We could add other objectives, such as: give priority to the elderly and people with disabilities, among others; alternatively, some objectives could be dropped. Nevertheless, certain criteria are essential such as attending to urgent needs, ensuring certain social sectors are given priority, issues of costs and the possibility of making the aspirations a reality on the basis of the community's own resources.

a) Criteria to use

128. Based on the above considerations, we suggest using the following criteria: 1) level of urgency; 2) number of people that will benefit; 3) level to which it benefits the poorest; 4) level to which it benefits women; 5) level to which it benefits young people; 6) respect for the environment; 7) cost; and 8) capacity of the community to realize the aspiration using its own resources.

129. To work out scores, a worksheet with 11 columns should be drawn up. The first column should outline the aspiration; the second should have a score based on level of urgency; the third, a score in terms of numbers of people that will benefit; the fourth, a score based on the impact on the environment; the fifth, a score based on how much it will benefit the poorest; the sixth, a score based on how much it will benefit women; the seventh, a score based on how much it will benefit young people; the eighth, a score based on cost; the ninth, the sum of all the previous scores; the tenth, a score based on the capacity of the community to realize the aspiration with the resources available to them; and the eleventh, a final score obtained by multiplying the numbers in column nine (total sum score) and ten (capacity of community). See below an example of a general list of aspirations with scores.

130. When establishing scores it is important to consider each individual aspiration on their own as well as how they relate to others, given that considering one aspiration without taking into account the others can lead to mistakes. For example, we might view a particular aspiration as urgent but when we compare it with other aspirations we might see that it is not as urgent as first thought. It would be worthwhile carrying out an initial evaluation and then going through each evaluation and revising our initial ones, as changes may occur on the basis of having considered all the aspirations as a whole.

b) Scores by criteria

131. Below we propose a scorecard for each criterion. The Plenary should approve or modify the proposal as they see fit.

132. The question that corresponds to this criterion is: can solving this problem wait or is the situation such that if it is not immediately resolved, it could lead to big problems for the community?

133. The parameters for establishing a score could be: A - very urgent (if not resolved immediately could lead to big problems for the community such as incurable illnesses or deaths); B - urgent (should be resolved in the short term, otherwise it could have negative effects on peoples' lives); C - can wait a bit (if not dealt with could produce negative effects but will not integrally affect the lives of people); D - not urgent (if not dealt with may produce discontent but will not lead to big problems); and E - it is a good project but if not realized will not negatively affect anyone. We propose giving four (4) points for A, three (3) points for B, two (2) points for C, one (1) point for D and zero (0) points for E.

Criterion	Parameters	Score
Level of urgency How urgency is a solution to the problem needed?	A – Very urgent	4
	B – Urgent	3
	C – Can wait a bit	2
	D – Not urgent	1
	E – No deadline	0

■ *Number of people that will benefit*

134. To work out a score we should ask: will realizing this aspiration benefit the entire community, more than two-thirds of the community, more than a third of the community, less than a third of the community or only those who proposed it? The parameters for establishing a score could be: A – everyone; B – more than two-thirds; C – more than a third; D – a third or less; and E – only those who proposed it. The following scores could be given: four (4) points for A, three (3) points for B, two (2) points for C, one (1) point for D and zero (0) points for E.

Criterion	Parameters	Score
Number of people that will benefit What is the percentage of the community that will benefit?	The whole community	4
	More than two-thirds	3
	More than a third	2
	A third or less	1
	Only those who proposed it	0

■ *Level of respect for the environment*

135. To work out a score we should ask: will realizing this aspiration benefit the environment or will it produce some kind of negative impact, and if so, how much of an impact will it have?

136. The parameters for establishing a score could be: A – benefits the environment; B – no damage; C – has a negative but controllable impact; D – has a big negative impact, but its benefits outweigh its negative impacts; and E – has a big negative impact, causing large-scale and irreparable damage. The following scores could be given: four (4) points for A, three (3) points for B, two (2) points for C, one (1) point for D and zero (0) points for E, because we

cannot give any points to a project that will have such negative consequences for the environment and, as such, for the future of the community itself.

Criterion	Parameters	Scores
Level of respect for the environment How will realizing the aspiration affect the environment?	A – Benefits the environment	4
	B – No damage	3
	C – Some damage, but certain measure can be taken to limit them	2
	D – Damages outweighed by other benefits	1
	E – Enormous damage	0

• *Level of benefit to the poorest sectors*

137. To work out a score we should ask: will this have a particularly large impact on the situation of the poorest? Will it improve their situation and therefore reduce existing social inequality?

138. The parameters for establishing a score could be: A – it is specifically directed at improving the situation of the poorest; B – it will indirectly affect the situation of the poorest in a favorable manner; and C – it will have no particular impact on the situation of the poorest.

139. The following scores could be given: four (4) points for A, two (2) points for B, and zero (0) points.

Criterion	Parameters	Score
Level to which it will benefit the poorest Will it have any particular effect on the situation of the poorest?	A – It is specifically directed at improving the situation of the poorest	4
	B – It will indirect affect the situation of the poorest in a favorable manner	2
	C – It will have no particular impact on the situation of the poorest	0

140. In this way, an attempt is made to favor those aspirations whose realization will improve the situation of those social sectors that until now have been ignored and therefore have the greatest amounts of needs. This should be the central objective of all governments seeking to move towards a post-capitalist society. This same model can be applied as a way of implementing positive discrimination in terms of gender, age, race, culture, disability, etc.

• *Level to which it will benefit women*

141. To work out a score we should ask: Will realizing this aspiration particularly and directly benefit, indirectly benefit or have no effect on women?

142. The parameters to work out a score could be: A – particularly and directly affects women; B – indirectly benefits women; and C – has no specific effect. The following scores could be given: two (2) points for A, one (1) for B and zero (0) points for C.

143. As you can see, we have suggested a higher score when referring to impacts on the poorest than for women. This is because we believe that the first priority we must have is to move in the direction of a society based on a more just redistribution of wealth, which, it should be said, will benefit an important number of women as the poorest women are generally doubly exploited: at work and at home.

Criterion	Parameters	Score
Women Do women directly or indirectly benefit?	A – Directly and particularly benefits women B – Indirectly benefits women C – Has no specific benefit	2 1 0

▪ *Level to which it benefits young people*

144. To work out a score we should ask: Will realizing this aspiration particularly and directly benefit, indirectly benefit or have no specific benefit for young people?

145. The parameters for establishing a score could be: A – particularly and directly affects young people; B – indirectly benefits young people; and C – has no specific effect. The following scores could be given: two (2) points for A, one (1) for B and zero (0) points for C.

Criterion	Parameters	Score
Youth Do youth directly or indirectly benefit from this?	A – Directly and particularly benefits young people B – Indirectly benefits young people C – Has no specific benefit	2 1 0

▪ *Cost*

146. This criterion presupposes a very general appreciation of how much it will cost to realize each aspiration. It is possible that during discussion different solutions may be proposed; if so, it would recommendable to consider the cost of the cheapest option, that is, the solution the community is in a better position to carry out.

147. In estimating the cost it is also important to consider ongoing running costs. That is, when calculating the cost, we need to consider two different aspects: on the one hand, how much it will cost to realize the aspiration and, on the other, how much it will cost to maintain.

148. This is an important consideration because a recurring problem with many community projects is that once realized, they are often abandoned to their own destiny, with no regards given to whether they need to be maintained to avoid rapid deterioration, and ultimately leaving the community in the same situation it was before. Furthermore, sometimes we design projects thinking only about the physical aspect without considering the personnel required to make it function (for example, building a school, without thinking about teachers and support staff).

Therefore, we should not forget this second aspect when giving a score to a project on this criterion.

149. We should ask: how expensive will the cheapest solution be and how much will it cost to maintain and ensure its continued functioning?

150. The parameters for establishing a score could be: A – no cost; B – very cheap; C – some cost, but the community can cover it; D – expensive and therefore requires some level of external funding; and E – very expensive, therefore requiring large amounts of external financing. The following scores could be given: four (4) points for A, three (3) points for B, two (2) points for C, one (1) point for D and zero (0) points for E

151. Why do we propose giving a higher score to those that are cheapest? Because we want to prioritize those aspirations that are easiest to realize.

Criterion	Parameters	Score
Cost How expensive will the cheapest solution be and how much will it cost to maintain and ensure it continued functioning?	A – No cost	4
	B – Very cheap	3
	C – Community can cover cost	2
		1
	D – Expensive	0
	E – Very expensive	

• *Capacity of the community to realize aspiration with own resources*

152. To give a score we should ask: what is the capacity of the community to realize and maintain the aspiration?

153. The parameters for establishing a score could be: A – complete capacity; B – a lot of capacity; C – little capacity and requiring additional external resources; D – no capacity.

154. The following scores could be given: three (3) points for A, two (2) points for B, one (1) point for C and zero (0) points for D.

Criterion	Parameters	Score
Capacity of community to realize aspiration How capable is the community of realizing and maintaining the aspiration?	A - Full capacity	3
	B - A large capacity	2
	C - Little capacity	1
	D – No capacity	0

• *A formula to achieve our objective*

155. We have given a zero (0) score to those aspirations that cannot be resolved with the community's own resources.

156. Why? In order to be able to use a mathematical formula that will allow us to exclude these aspirations from our priority list.

157. This is how it works. To establish whether to move ahead with realizing a certain aspiration, use a formula that adds up all the scores from the aforementioned criteria (urgency; number of people that benefit; level to which the poorest, women and youth benefit; respect for the environment; and cost) and multiple this figure by the score it received for the last criteria (community's capacity).

158. This last part (multiplying by 0) is key to determining whether to move ahead or not. If the community has no capacity to realize the aspiration because it requires a large amount of resources, it will be discarded even if it obtained a high score for all other criteria, because this is all annulled when multiplied by zero, the score it received for the last criterion.

159. This is because any number multiplied by zero will give zero as its result.

160. This formula is much easier that it first appears and is ideal for prioritizing, in the most objective manner possible, the problems a community can resolve.

c) Applying the criteria to an example

161. Let's take an example of a potential aspiration a community might share: daily access to abundant water in a community where no water infrastructure currently exists.

162. Given that finding a solution to this problem is urgent, as various outbreaks of illnesses have occurred, one leading to the death of a child, it is given a score of 4 in terms of the criterion of urgency.

163. Given everyone will benefit from the realization of this aspiration, it is given a score of 4 in terms of the criterion of number of people that will benefit.

164. Given clean water is fundamental for looking after the environment, it is given a score of 4 for this criterion.

165. Although it benefits everyone in general, this would indirectly have a more positive effect on the situation of the poorest, given this sector has the least possibilities of finding alternative sources of water; therefore it is given 2 points in terms of this criterion.

166. Given women indirectly benefit as they are the ones who most use water, it is given a score of 1 in terms of this criterion.

167. Given young people will benefit as much as the rest of the population, it is given a score of 0 on this point.

168. Given that solving this problem is expensive - it requires installing a water distribution system for the entire community as many households have until now relied on individual wells that are drying up - even if maintaining it is not, it is given a score of 1 in terms of this criterion.

169. But given that the community has neither the resources nor technical and legal capacity to build this system, it is given a score of 0 in terms of the criterion referring to community's capacity to realize aspiration. Therefore, if we add all the scores, with the exception of the last one ($4 + 4 + 4 + 2 + 1 + 2 + 1$), we get 18. However, if we multiply 18 by 0, the score for the last criterion, we get zero ($18 \times 0 = 0$).

170. Those aspirations that receive a final score of 0 are automatically eliminated from the list of prioritized aspirations in the Community Development Plan, as the community cannot resolve these with the resources it has at hand.

171. Nevertheless, we should point out that when we say they "are automatically eliminated from the list of prioritized aspirations in the Community Development Plan" we are not saying that the people have to give up on the idea of realizing this aspiration, just that they will not be among the projects the community includes in its plan. Later on we will see that these aspirations can be realized by other entities.

172. Let's look at a completely different example: the aspiration of having access to a diversity of activities and spaces for healthy recreation.

173. Given its realization is not as urgent as other problems in the community, such as the previous example we looked at, it is given a score of 2 in terms of this criterion.

174. Given that realizing this aspiration would particularly benefit youth and children, but also the family as a whole as parents will feel it less likely that their children may turn to drugs or crime, it is given a score of 4 in terms of the criterion referring to number of people who will benefit.

175. Given the project does not damage the environment, it is given a score of 3 for this criterion.

176. Given it indirectly favors the poorest, who are the ones with the least access to other forms of recreation, it is given a score of 2.

177. Given it indirectly benefits a large number of women who are constantly concerned about how their children are spending their free time, it is given a score of 2 for this criterion.

178. Given it directly benefits young people, it is given a score of 2 according to this criterion.

179. Given it is possible to make use of the physical and human resources the community has available, making this issue cheap to resolve, it is given a score of 3.

180. And lastly, as it is completely feasible to resolve this issue and the community is willing to provide the resources required, it is given a score of 3, the maximum score for the last criterion.

181. If we add all the scores with the exception of the last one $(2 + 4 + 3 + 2 + 1 + 2 + 3)$, we get 17; and if we multiply this by 3, we 51 $(17 \times 3 = 51)$.

182. Let's look at one last example: aspiring to have a clean community by resolving the issue of rubbish collection. This is an aspiration that is seen as important by many because due to the rubbish on the streets, rats have started to emerge from the rubbish tip that has formed on an unused lot. This is generating illnesses that are affecting the health of the poorest, who tend to live near the rubbish tip, but at the same time it affects everyone who passes through the area and has led to the community being seen in a very negative light. Only a small group of families are not suffering the consequences of this problem.

183. Given the problem needs to be urgently solved as it is contributing to a worsening of the situation caused by the lack of potable water, it is given a score of 4 in terms of the criterion referring to urgency.

184. Given it will benefit the majority of the population, with the possible exception of the more wealthy who have their own rubbish bins, it is given a score of 3 for this criterion.

185. Given it will benefit the environment, it is given a score of 4 for this criterion.

186. Given it will indirectly benefit the poorest, it is given a score of 2 for this criterion.

187. Given women will not benefit in a particularly different manner from the rest of the community, it is given a score of 0 for this criterion.

188. Given this is not something that particularly affects young people, it is given a score of 0 for this criterion.

189. Given it is estimated that solving this problem will cost less than solving the water issue (it only requires providing bins and organizing collection because a new fleet of rubbish trucks are already available), it is given a score of 2 for this criterion.

190. And given that neighbors in the community are willing to volunteer with the support of the rest of the community, to clean the rubbish tip and transform it into a small plaza for the benefit

of all, as well as maintain it, it is given a score of 2 in terms of the criterion referring to resources available in the community.

191. If we add all the scores with the exception of the last (4 + 3 + 4 + 2 + 0 + 0 + 2), we get 15; and if we multiply this by 2 (15 x 2), we get 30.

192. We have looked at three aspirations:
  Access to daily and abundant water   0 points
  Activities and spaces for healthy recreation   51 points
  Clean community   30 points

193. The aspiration that received the highest score was recreation, following by clean community, while the issue of water was eliminated.

194. All the aspirations should be analyzed in this manner. Those that receive a higher score according to this formula are the ones the community should attend to first. Those aspirations that cannot be immediately resolved are automatically eliminated from this prioritization process, as their final score is zero, but they should be incorporated later on into other lists, as we will see further below.

195. Below, Table 2 provides an example in which we have only selected a few aspirations from the 14 we outlined above.

Table 2. Generating a list of aspirations with scores

	Urgency	Population	Impact on nature	Impact on poverty	Impact on women	Impact on youth	Cost	TOTAL SCORE	Capacity to resolve	FINAL SCORE
Safe neighborhood	3	3	2	2	1	1	1	13	3	39
Abundant water	4	4	4	2	1	0	1	16	0	0
Healthy recreation	2	4	3	2	1	2	3	17	3	51
Clean	4	3	4	2	0	0	2	15	2	30
Well lit	3	3	2	0	1	0	2	11	1	11
Free of unemployment	2	3	2	4	1	1	4	17	0	0
Respect for environment	1	4	4	0	0	0	2	11	3	33
Artists working with children	1	3	2	0	1	2	4	13	3	39

196. 83. It is very likely that when formulating aspirations, some will emerge that are clearly out of the capacity of the community to resolve themselves; that is, they are territorial area or municipal level aspirations. These aspirations should be included in a list that the Council should work on in a similar fashion to that outlined above applying the same criteria to establish a list of priorities.

197. 84. Why do we think this should occur? Because even though we know that when these aspirations reach the final criterion (capacity to resolve) they will receive a zero score, it is important that when higher up levels establish their order of priority of these aspirations, they can take into consideration the priority that communities have given to each aspiration.

198. 85. It is important that when the Council is applying the different criteria, it should have in mind the impact of the various aspirations on the community itself. That is, to determine the urgency or impact on the population requires having to look at this in the context of the existing situation of the community.

199. 86. In this way we will come up with a prioritized list of aspirations that are deemed to fall within the responsibilities of higher up entities (See Table 3).

Table 3. List of aspirations that are the responsibility of higher up levels

Aspiration	Urgency	Population	Impact on nature	Impact on poverty	Impact on women	Impact on youth	Cost	TOTAL SCORE
Carry out a sustainable endogenous development	2	4	3	2	0	0	0	11
Ensure productive development respects the environment	3	4	4	0	0	0	0	11
Efficient transport service	3	3	2	2	0	1	0	11
Access to hospital attention	4	4	3	2	1	0	0	14
Guarantee emergency medical service to the whole population	4	4	4	2	0	0	0	14
Better land distribution	3	2	4	4	1	1	0	15
Access to a sufficient offer of secondary school education	3	2	3	2	0	2	0	12

Aspiration	Urgency	Population	Impact on nature	Impact on poverty	Impact on women	Impact on youth	Cost	TOTAL SCORE
Access to a sufficient offer of professional training and university education	2	4	4	2	0	2	0	11

PLANNING TEAM

Activity 4. Draft a prioritized list of aspirations.

200. After the Planning Council as a whole has determined the score corresponding to each aspiration in accordance with the established criteria, the Planning Team should draft up three lists of aspirations on large paper.

201. **he first** should be a list of those aspirations that received a final score higher than zero, ordered in terms of highest to lowest score. The aspirations in this wish list are the ones to be analyzed, exploring various alternative solutions and any projects related to them. These projects will become part of the Community Plan and will initially be ordered according to the score obtained by the aspiration it will help realize.

202. **A second list** should include all those aspirations from the first list that the community can resolve with its own resources; that is, all those that were given a score of 3 in terms of this criterion. They should be given special consideration, as the projects that help realize these aspirations will become part of the Immediate Action Plan.

203. And **a third list** should be drawn up with those aspirations that were eliminated due to the fact they obtained a final score of zero, and fall within the responsibilities of higher levels of government. They should be ordered according to the total score they received for all criteria without taking into consideration the score obtained for the last criterion (community capacity to resolve), which in the case of these aspirations was zero. This list should be given to the corresponding Territorial Council as community demands.

204. These three lists should be revised and approved by the plenary of the Community Planning Council.

205. Let us look at some examples of the three different lists in Tables 4, 5 and 6.

Table 4. List 1: Aspiration to be included within the Community Development Plan

Aspiration	Urgency	Population	Impact on nature	Impact on poverty	Impact on women	Impact on youth	Cost	TOTAL SCORE	Capacity to resolve	FINAL SCORE
Healthy recreation	2	4	3	3	2	1	2	17	3	51
Artists working with children	1	3	2	4	0	1	2	13	3	39
Safe neighborhood	3	3	2	1	2	1	1	13	3	39
Respect for the environment	1	4	4	2	0	0	0	11	3	33
Clean	4	3	4	2	0	0	2	15	2	30
Well lit	3	3	2	0	1	0	2	11	1	11

Table 5. List 2: Aspirations included in the Immediate Action Plan

Aspiration	Urgency	Population	Impact on nature	Impact on poverty	Impact on women	Impact on youth	Cost	TOTAL SCORE	Capacity to resolve	FINAL SCORE
Healthy recreation	2	4	3	3	2	1	2	17	3	51
Artists working with children	1	3	2	4	0	1	2	13	3	39
Safe neighborhood	3	3	2	1	2	1	1	13	3	39
Respect for the environment	1	4	4	2	0	0	0	11	3	33

Table 6. List 3: Community demands to higher up corresponding institutions

Aspiration	Urgency	Population	Impact on nature	Impact on poverty	Impact on women	Impact on youth	Cost	
Abundant water	4	4	4	2	1	0	2	17
Free of unemployment	2	3	2	4	1	1	4	17
Better land distribution	3	2	4	4	1	1	0	15
Access to hospital attention	4	4	3	2	1	0	0	14
Guarantee emergency medical service to the whole population	4	4	4	2	0	0	0	14
Access to a sufficient offer of secondary school education	3	2	3	2	0	2	0	12
Carry out a sustainable endogenous development	2	4	3	2	0	0	0	11
Ensure productive development respects the environment	3	4	4	0	0	0	0	11
Efficient transport service	3	3	2	2	0	1	0	11
Access to a sufficient offer of professional training and university education	2	4	4	2	0	2	0	11

COMMUNITY PLANNING ASSEMBLY

Activity 5. *Explaining to the community the process followed, its results and future steps*

206. Once the three lists of aspirations have been drawn up, an Assembly with the whole community should be held where a pedagogical explanation of the process followed is given along with the final results.

207. The Assembly should ratify the results, requesting clarifications where required, and if necessary opening up a debate. To avoid discussion becoming too dispersed, we recommend it be centered on the criteria adopted and its application, and not on the final scores, which are simply the result of applying the criteria.

208. Once clarifications have been made, or debate finishes if this occurs, the Assembly can approve the Council proposal or suggest amendments. In the case of the latter, we recommend applying a special quorum to ensure that any amendments suggested represent the sentiment of the whole community.

209. Afterwards, it should be explained that the next step will be to set up thematic working groups to look at the actions that will need to be taken to implement the aspirations the community can carry out with its own resources, and those aspirations that will be presented to higher levels. Those present should be encouraged to join the working groups that will study the various possible actions that could be taken to realize these aspirations.

210. In regards to the aspirations included in List 3 that the community does not have the capacity to resolve, they should be collected together with the scores they achieved in forms that have been prepared by the Municipal Planning and Budgetary Cabinet to be presented to the corresponding Territorial Council.

2. METHODOLOGY FOR TERRITORIAL AREAS AND MUNICIPALITY

211. It is up to the Territorial Planning Council to establish priorities for the aspirations that correspond to the demands made by the communities within its territorial area, as well as those that the Territorial Assembly has voted to include.

212. In the same way, it is up to the Municipal Planning Council to establish priorities for aspirations at the municipal level that have been received from the territorial areas, along with those that the Municipal Assembly has voted to include.

213. In this section, we will describe the methodology corresponding to a Territorial Planning Council, which can also be applied to the Municipal Planning Council, with the different that in the latter case, aspirations would come from the territorial areas.

TERRITORIAL COUNCIL (WORKING GROUPS)

Activity 1. Study aspirations.

214. Once the Territorial Assembly has approved the lists of aspirations by thematic area, the Territorial Planning Council should set up thematic working groups to study the aspirations that fall within their corresponding area, in a similar way to what we outlined when we spoke about communities (study problems, threats, strengths and opportunities).

TERRITORIAL PLANNING COUNCIL (PLENARY)

Activity 2. Prioritizing aspirations.

215.. These aspirations should now be evaluated. For this, the Territorial Planning Council should used the same methodology that we outlined when talking about communities; that is, applying the same criteria and points score, but this time with reference to the territorial area. This should provide us with a table very similar to the list of aspirations from the previous section.

216. However, we should add an addition criterion that takes into consideration the score that the Community Planning Assemblies gave these territorial-level aspirations.

217. To establish this new criterion, we could combine two elements: the number of communities that have proposed a particular territorial level aspiration and the scores it received.

218. In this case, the score for this criterion could be calculated using the following double-entry table.

219. On the one hand, we should look at the number of communities that raised this aspiration:
* 2/3 or more communities in the territorial area;
* More than 1/3 but less than 2/3 of communities;
* 1/3 or less communities.

220. On the other hand, we should look at the average score each aspiration got (excluding the criteria of cost and capacity to carry out aspiration), remembering that the maximum score is 20 points:
* 15 points or more
* Between 10 and 14 points
* Less than 10 points.

221. Table 7 can allow us to come up with a score based on this combination of elements.

Table 7. Evaluation of the demands expressed by communities

		Number of communities that have raised the same aspiration		
		More than 2/3 of communities	Between 1/3 and 2/3 of communities	Less than 1/3 of communities
Average score	15 points or more	5	4	3
	Between 10 and 14 points	2	3	2
	Less than 10 points	3	2	1

222. Let us look at how this can be done:

223. In the Community Planning Council, we will need a large sheet of paper that we can put up on the wall where we can collect the data from the community and its aspirations.

224. Let us suppose that there are seven communities in the territorial area. We would write the territorial level aspirations presented by the communities and the score each one of them obtained.

225. In one column we put the total sum of points obtained and in the last column the quotient of this sum divided by the number of communities that include the aspiration in its list (for example, if six communities raised the first aspiration, we divide by six; if five communities raised the second, we divide by five, and so on).

Table 8. Score by community for cultural aspiration

Aspiration	A	B	C	D	E	F	G	Total	quotient
There is sufficient provision of secondary school level education.	16	12	0	16	16	18	12	90	15.00
The possibility exists to access the internet for free.	17	0	14	0	11	11	13	66	13.20
Interested young people have the opportunity to study theater and music.	0	14	0	12	13	0	14	53	13.25

226. Using this table, we would have a situation in which the first aspiration has been raised by

six communities, which is more than two-thirds of communities in the territorial area, and has an average score of 15, meaning it gets a score of 5 for this criterion.

227. The second aspiration was raised by five communities, which is also more than two-thirds of communities in the area, but its average score is 13.2, which is less than 15, which means it gets a score of 4 on our table.

228. Finally, the third aspiration was only raised by 4 of the 7 communities (less than two-thirds) and its average score was 13.25, meaning it gets a score of 3 on our table.

229. Given this, the list of territorial level cultural aspirations would look like this:

Table 8. Prioritized list of territorial level cultural aspirations

Aspiration	Urgency	Population	Impact on nature	Impact on poverty	Impact on women	Impact on youth	Community Demand	Cost	TOTAL SCORE	Capacity to resolve	Total
There is sufficient provision secondary school level education.	2	4	4	2	1	2	5	1	21	0	0
The possibility exists to access the internet for free in the territorial area.	1	2	2	0	1	2	4	1	13	2	26
Interested young people have the opportunity to study theater and music.	1	3	3	2	1	2	3	2	17	3	51
Cultural activities are not concentrated in the center of the territorial area.	0	3	3	2	1	1	0	3	14	0	0

230. The aspiration added by the Territorial Planning Council would get zero points for the criterion "Community demand", given that none of them mentioned it. Nevertheless, in the Territorial Planning Assembly that is held to approve the priorities, delegates from the different communities can incorporate aspirations as their own, as long as the delegates from the community have voted in favor of it with a qualified quorum.

231. In this case, the points an aspiration gets for this criterion would be modified on the basis of how many communities decided to adopt this aspiration.

232. Finally, as occurred in the communities, the eight first columns must be multiplied by the last criterion (capacity of territorial area to resolve it). Those aspirations that get a score of zero should be taken to the Municipal Planning Council.

233. Aspirations that are deemed to be the responsibility of the municipality should be studied and prioritized in the same way, without taking into consideration the criterion of "Capacity to resolve" in the points table, just as we did in the communities. The objective is to allow the Municipal Planning Council to take into consideration the opinions of the territorial areas when prioritizing municipal level aspirations.

TERRITORIAL PLANNING AND BUDGETARY TEAM

Activity 3. Coming up with list of prioritized aspirations.

234. Once the work of the Council is done, the Territorial Planning and Budgetary Team should come up with two lists: one with the aspirations that the territorial area can resolve; and one with those aspirations that fall within the responsibilities of the municipality.

TERRITORIAL ASSEMBLY

Activity 4. Approving the list of prioritized aspirations.

235. The lists of prioritized aspirations should be presented to the Territorial Planning Assembly for approval and be made publicly available on a mass scale and readily accessible to everyone.

236. Just as occurred in the Community Planning Assemblies, once the list of prioritized aspirations have been approved, an explanation should be given of the following steps to come and an invitation should be extended to anyone interested in becoming part of the working groups set up by the Territorial Planning Council to explore alternative proposals and elaborate corresponding projects.

237. The list of municipal level aspirations should be presented to the Municipal Planning Council for subsequent study.

CHAPTER V.
METHODOLOGY FOR EXPLORING ALTERNATIVE COURSES OF ACTION (THIRD STEP)

238. This is an activity that should be carried out by the working groups set up by the corresponding Planning Council (Community, Territorial or Municipal) and its results should be collectively analyzed in the respective plenary.

1. ACTIVITIES

PLANNING COUNCILS

Activity 1. (Working groups) Exploring alternative courses of action.

239. Using the prioritized lists of aspirations approved by the Community Planning Assembly, the thematic working groups set up by the Planning Council should be broadened out to include those people from the community who want to participate. They should meet to study the alternative courses of action that could be put forward for realizing all those aspirations that scored higher than zero. They should study all the aspirations in their area that the community,

the territorial area or the municipality have some capacity to resolve, starting with the aspirations that received the highest scores within their area.

240. When exploring the alternative courses of action it is particularly important to study them carefully to detect if some of them will require complementary actions to be successful. One of the worst errors in planning is to think about an action without keeping in mind that to reach the corresponding aspiration it is necessary to carry out other complementary actions.

241. For example, if a community decides to build a soccer field, it is necessary to foresee the need to mobilize interest among youths to participate; or if a community decides to promote a shift in what farmers cultivate to improve their quality of life, it will be necessary to keep in mind the need to prepare distribution networks, and the means to industrialize and commercialize the new products. That is, if the aspiration is to improve the quality of life in a rural area and the community has decided to substitute traditional crops for other more profitable ones, it would demand the development of three very different actions: one, a mobilization to motivate peasants; two, the creation of infrastructure needed to provide the necessary inputs (seeds, payments scheme) for the new crops; and, three, the creation of the necessary infrastructure for the industrialization, distribution and commercialization of those new products. These three actions are linked: to carry out one or two of them while forgetting the other would lead to failure. We would have peasants without infrastructures or infrastructure without peasants, but we would not have achieved the objective. And the economic effort would have been useless, with people's demoralization rising.

242. On the other hand, to explore the alternative course of action that could help realize a particular aspiration, it is important to consider the previous analyzes made in terms of available material and human resources, cost and impact of each proposal on the population, and the capacity of the community to carry out the project and then maintain it over time.

243. As we said in Volume I[11] of this book, we need to analyze each aspiration and reflect, firstly, on what we can do in general to realize this aspiration and, secondly, how we should implement these alternative courses of action, highlighting the various activities that need to be undertaken and taking special care to think of even the smallest detail to ensure that we are successful in achieving our objective. It is possible, as we will see when looking at the example of alternative 3 further below, that after studying each aspiration certain alternatives may emerge whose execution would require the efforts of higher levels. In these cases, the alternative courses of action along with their corresponding aspirations should be put forward as demands to the corresponding higher council.

244. Each group should write down their results on a large sheet of paper.

Activity 2. *(Plenary) Analyzing the results of the previous activity.*

245. Once each group has finished this task, a Plenary involving all those who participated in the working groups should be held and each group should present their results at it. Those present should analyze the results, and potentially complement or correct them. The work sheets should be stuck up on the wall of the meeting room so that everyone can see all of them. This material will be very important for the next step: coming up with projects.

246. After revising the various alternative courses of action, the Plenary should come up with a summarized list that includes: the aspirations they hope to achieve with their respective scores, the different alternative courses of action, and where they will be carried out. Moreover, for community projects, it is worth identifying if they are part of the Immediate Action Plan and in what phase this plan is at (see example further below).

---

11. See paragraphs 313 to 320.

247. On the basis of this list, we will need to prepare one that contains all those alternative courses of action that are the responsibility of a higher level. These should be presented to the corresponding higher level Council for their potential planning and execution.

248. Furthermore, the Planning Council should come up with a second list that includes those alternatives that could affect other communities or territorial areas if they were to be implemented, for example: the creation of a rubbish tip in a zone that borders another community right next to where they want to build a park; or setting up a network for potable water distribution, which could be more effective if various communities worked on it together. These alternatives should also be presented to the corresponding Planning Council at the higher level so that it can hold negotiations among the impacted communities.

2. EXAMPLES OF ALTERNATIVE COURSES OF ACTION AND ACTIVITIES

249. Below are some examples of what we are talking about. (We have chosen once again the example of the community that we mention in the Chapter IV)

ASPIRATION 1: **CREATING ACTIVITIES AND SPACES FOR HEALTHY RECREATION FOR YOUNG PEOPLE AND THE POPULATION IN GENERAL.**

Creating activities and spaces for healthy recreation for young people, and the population more generally, is one of the most deeply felt aspirations of the community because, as we saw in Table 1 in Chapter I (obstacles, problems, strengths and opportunities) there is an absence of initiatives and spaces for recreation, which has led to a rise in alcoholism. At the same time, there is a space that could be fixed up and people are willing to volunteer for this task. Based on this diagnosis, we should now look at what alternative courses of action exist, and which of them is the most viable and consistent with our aims and resources.

Alternative courses of action:
Alternative 1. Transform an abandoned open-air cinema into a plaza.
Alternative 2. Create a place where children can watch kid's television and videos.
Alternative 3. Hold sports competitions.
Alternative 4. Fix up a football field.

After putting forward various alternative solutions, it is evident that they all complement each other and can be implemented given the available human and material resources. For reasons of space, we will only analyze some of them.

Alternative 1. Transform an abandoned open-air cinema into a plaza.

Activities
- Name someone responsible for the project.
- Call a meeting to start planning the work involved.
- Find the necessary tools (machete, paint, cement, sand, etc.).
- Find materials for the plaza (seeds, park benches, garden boxes, gravel, etc.).
- Source food to provide volunteers with lunch.
- Once finished, name a group of people responsible for its ongoing maintenance.
- Make posters to announce the activity.
- Make announcements over community radio.
- Negotiate the handing over of materials with the mayor's office.
- Hand out lunches to volunteers.
- Clean the field
- Plant trees and flowers
- Put gravel on the walk paths
- Install park benches
- Paint a wall white in order to be able to project videos on it at night.

Activities related to its maintenance
- Organize a roster of volunteers willing to look out for people causing damage to the plaza.
- Plan out what gardening will be needed (watering, planting new flowers, etc.).
- Etc.

Summary of alternative course of action N° 1

Aspiration	Provide activites an spaces for healthy recreation for youth and the population in general.
Score	51
Action to be taken	Transform the abandoned open-air cinema into a small plaza.
Place	Street 13, corner with Street 4
Notes	Will become part of the Immediate Action Plan (First Phase)

Alternative 2. Create a space where children can watch television and videos.

Activities related to preparing the space and maintenance
- Designate someone responsible.
- Find a space to hold the activity.
- Bring over a large television that is currently being underused in an office.
- Find pertinent audiovisual materials.
- Create a rotating team of volunteers who will look after the projection of videos.
- Create a roster for regularly cleaning the space, including any associated costs.
- Announce the existence of the project to the community.
- Make sure the space is suited for its purpose.
- Check there are multiple electrical outlets, lights, chairs, etc.

Summary of alternative course of action No 2

Aspiration	Provide activites and spaces for healthy recreation for youth and the population in general.
Score	51
Action to be taken	Create a space where children can watch television and videos
Place	Cultural Center on Street 8, n° 324
Note	Will become part of the Immediate Action Plan (First Phase)

ASPIRATION 2: **YOUNG PEOPLE SHOULD PARTICIPATE IN SPORT TO AVOID FAILING INTO THE PITFALLS OF DRUG ADDICTION OR ALCOHOLISM**

When we carried out a diagnosis in regards to this aspiration (see Table I in Chapter IV, existing situation...) we saw that the community had no sports fields or the necessary equipment. There was little consciousness in the community regarding the importance of sports, but nevertheless there was interest on the part of young people to play sports. Moreover, a vacant area that could be used for sports is available. Based on this diagnosis we should now look at what alternative courses of action exist and which of them are the most viable and pertinent according to our aims and resources.

Alternative courses of action:
Alternative 1. Build a sports complex with fields and swimming pool.
Alternative 2. Fix up a vacant lot to convert it into a football training space.
Alternative 3. Set up a group of sports promoters to encourage sports in the community.
Alternative 4. Set up boys, girls and youth football teams in the territory.
Alternative 5. Establish sports competitions
Alternative 6. Carry out a campaign in schools and the media explaining the importance of playing sports

After proposing various alternative solutions, it is evident that it is impossible to build a sports complex with the available resources; however it is possible to carry out the other initiatives, which all complement each other and can be achieved using the available material and human resources in the community. Below, we will only analyze some of the proposals for questions of space.

Alternative 1. Set up a team of sports promoters

Activities:
- Hold a meeting of the sports and education working committee to select promoters.
- Set a date for the first promoters meeting.
- Nominate someone to coordinate the group.
- Program activities for the promoters.
- Program regular meetings of the group to analyze results and set new plans.
- Invite people to the meeting.
- Call those who have been selected.
- Organize the meeting space and agenda for the meeting.

Summary of alternative course of action No 1

Aspiration	Young people should participate in sport to avoid failing into the pitfalls of drug addiction or alcoholism
Score	42
Action to be taken	Set up a team of sports promoters
Place	No specific location
Note	Will become part of the Immediate Action Plan (First Phase)

Alternative 2. Set up boys, girls and youth football teams

Activities:
- Nominate someone to coordinate.
- Draw up a pamphlet that explains the objectives sought and make copies of it.
- Organize a calendar of visits to schools with the principals.
- Nominate those responsible for this task.
- Find the required sports equipment.
- Visit schools.
- Distribute the pamphlet.
- Set up teams on each street.
- Organize a competition draw for the teams.
- Nominate those responsible for being coachs, referees, etc.
- Plan the use of the playing field.

In this case, the construction of a sports complex with fields and swimming pool, which is out of the reach of the community, should be included in the list of demands given to higher up entities together with the other aspirations that obtained a score of zero during the prioritization process.

Summary of alternative course of action N° 2

Aspiration	Young people should participate in sport to avoid failing into the pitfalls of drug addiction or alcoholism
Score	42
Action to be taken	Set up boys, girls and youth football teams
Place	Schools
Note	Will become part of the Immediate Action Plan (First Phase)

ASPIRATION 3: **BEING ABLE TO GO OUT AT NIGHT WITH OUT FEAR OF BEING ROBBED**

When we carried out a diagnosis regarding this aspiration (see Table I in Chapter I) we saw just how affected the community is by the constant robberies that occur, especially at night, because the streets are poorly lit due to the lack of bulbs for the street lights. The state however has offered to exchange bulbs for scrap metal. There is a lot of scrap metal and, at the same time, a willingness on the part of the people to volunteer to collect it. Based on this diagnosis, we should look at what alternative courses of action exist and which of those are most viable and consistent with our aims and resources.

Alternative courses of action:

Alternative 1. Ask the state for bulbs.
Alternative 2. Collect scrap metal and exchange it for bulbs.
Alternative 3. Set up a safety and defense committee comprised of local residents and organize night patrols.
Alternative 4. Work directly with those youth who have gone off the rails.
Alternative 5. Establish a police station in the community or nearby.

After proposing these alternative courses of action, Alternative 1 is deemed to be unviable because the state does not have the necessary financial resources. Alternative 5 falls outside the capabilities of the community and is therefore included in the list of demands to be given to higher up institutions as occurred with the previous aspiration. The other proposals are all seen to complement each other and achievable with the available human and material resources. Below, we will only look at two of the alternatives because of questions of space.

Alternative 3. Set up a safety and defense working committee.

Activities
- Nominate someone to coordinate.
- Call a meeting of those interested in the issue.
- Draw up a roster.
- Create a system to raise the alarm when problems arise
- Obtain torches, whistles, etc.
- Decide upon points where patrols can swap over.
- Sign attendance book.

Summary alternative course of action N°3

Aspiration	Being able to go out at night with out fear of being robbed
Score	39
Action to be taken	Set up a safety and defense working committee
Place	Cultural Center
Note	Will become part of the Immediate Action Plan (First Phase)

Alternative 4. Work directly with youth that have gone off the rails and their parents or closest relatives.

Activities
- Nominate someone to coordinate.
- Update or carry out a census regarding this issue.
- Organize visits to the respective households.
- Call a meeting with the youth and their parents/relatives.
- Contract them to help with cleaning and looking after green spaces in the community.
- Visit households.
- Find a meeting space.
- Sign them up for a football team, music classes, etc.

Summary of alternative course of action N° 4.

Aspiration	Being able to go out at night with out fear of being robbed
Score	39
Action to be taken	Work directly with youth that have gone off the rails and their parents or closest relative.
Place	Community
Note	Will become part of the Immediate Action Plan (First Phase)

CHAPTER VI.
PROJECTS

1. GENERAL CONSIDERATIONS REGARDING PROJECTS

1) DEFINITION OF A PROJECT

250. By project we are referring to a document that sets out a series of programmed activities and tasks that will allow a community to realize one of their aspirations. This description should be accompanied by the necessary technical information for its execution and a calculation of its cost.

2) PROJECTS AND ALTERNATIVE PROPOSALS

251. The number of projects will depend on how proposals for realizing aspirations are grouped together.

252. We have seen that it is possible to come up with various proposals for realizing the same aspiration. In some cases we will have to opt for one of them, on other occasions they might be complementary and, as such, we might find that we need to come up with more than one project for the same aspiration.

253. For example, to improve safety in a community, three different proposals could be put forward:

(a) Improve street lighting by replacing broken or used light bulbs;
(b) Set up volunteer groups to patrol the streets and chase away criminals; and
(c) Establish a police station in the community to help speed up the response time of the police when a crime is committed, thereby eliminating the current delay.

254. The first two proposals could be taken up by the community. The third, however, would have to be taken to the level of government (territorial area or municipal) that is responsible for this area. This community initiative could end up becoming a more ambitious project that takes in the whole municipality: the decentralization of police stations.

255. The first two proposals are complementary as executing one facilitates the execution of the other: better street lighting would aid the work of the volunteer patrols, while the presence of the latter could reduce the number of lights currently being broken as a result of youth throwing rocks at them.

256. However, as they are quite different proposals in terms of their characteristics – the first involves assuming an economic burden in the form of buying bulbs while the second depends almost exclusive on volunteer labor – it seems better to separate them into two projects.

257. We may also find that we have certain projects for the same aspiration that have to be completed before others or are specifically complementary to each other, as we pointed out previously (see paragraphs 240 and 241). To take another example, five proposals could be put forward for promoting sports among children and adolescents:

(a) Set up a group of sports promoters involving better known athletes that live or have lived in the community;
(b) Carry out a promotional campaign for sports in schools and learning centers;
(c) Set up youth and school-based football teams;
(d) Stage youth and school sporting competitions; and
(e) Convert an abandoned lot into a football field.

258. Evidently, it will not be possible to stage sporting competitions (d) if the first three proposals (a, b and c) are not carried out first. As such, it is possible to view all four as part of a more general project to promote the development of youth and school sporting competitions.

259. That is, generally speaking, when certain proposals are prerequisites for others, have similar characteristics, and are the responsibility of the same team, they should be grouped together as parts or phases of a project or sub-project within the same project, as would be the case with the first four proposals in our example.

260. Regarding the last proposal (e), it is evident that all the previous effort would turn out to be worthless if there were no spaces available to play sports. But because this proposal has its own characteristics and requires special effort in the form of contributions from the community in terms of materials and volunteer labor, it would be best to keep it as an independent project that can be carried out concurrently with the other proposals.

261. In general terms, if certain proposals are dependent on others, have similar characteristics and fall under the responsibility of the same team, we can say they are one project or sub-projects within the same project, as is the case with the first four proposals in our example.

262. This is just our suggestion. There may be times where, for reasons of transparency, it is preferable to identity each sub-project as an independent project within the overall plan. The community should decide this on the basis of their needs and the characteristics of the proposals that have been studied, while always ensuring the smooth running of the process. We should avoid endless debates that can slow down the realization of aspirations.

3) INFRASTRUCTURE PROJECTS AND SERVICE PROVISION PROJECTS

263. When we are talking about projects, it is worthwhile differentiating between infrastructure projects and service provision projects. In general, infrastructure projects (repairing street lighting, building a stadium) involve one-off actions, while service provision projects require continuous actions (staging of sporting competitions, provision of education classes, medical attention to the community).

264. From the economic point of view, this distinction can be very important in terms of distributing the cost between the budget for running costs and the investment budget:

Running costs budget:

- Cost of service provision projects (minus initial investment, if any)
- Cost of maintaining infrastructure projects, if any

Investment budget:
- Cost of the infrastructure projects (minus maintenance costs, if any)
- Initial investments in the service provision projects (if any)

265. As we have said, it is possible to distinguish between different types of projects according to the objectives set. This classification can be useful for assigning resources based on what objectives have been prioritized, as we will see in Chapters VII and IX.

266. But it is important to point out that this classification is merely a point of reference and that projects rarely tend to be strictly delineated; rather they contain elements from different areas. For example, a cultural project can at the same time be a social project, and vice versa. That is why we do not recommend spending lots of time on useless debates classifying projects on the basis of their objectives if this classification will not be used later on in the process.

a) Social projects

267. Social projects are those that contemplate the satisfaction of basic needs and attend to vulnerable populations living in extreme poverty or that require primary attention. For example: street kids, the homeless, women with at-risk pregnancies, elderly people who have been abandoned, those in critical poverty.

268. Social projects are also those that aim at satisfying the needs or strengthening the potentialities of each community; that is, those that seek to promote those community values that strengthen the sense of belonging to the community. For example: communal houses, multiple-use sports fields, health clinics, schools and other educational centers, police stations, community care centers, recreational parks, locations for collection and recycling of rubbish, and other projects that protect the environment.

b) Socio-productive projects

269. Socio-productive projects are those that generate goods and services to satisfy community needs. They should be sustainable over time, and be framed within the concept of internal development. The ideal situation would be to create productive networks that help with the development of the solidarity economy. These projects could be self-managed or co-managed. State resources are generally used to get these projects running.

c) Social infrastructure projects

270. Social infrastructure and equipment projects are those involving the construction of infrastructure required for basic services (water distribution, electricity, roads, drains, etc.) and the provision of equipment required for the correct functioning of particular public services.

d) Housing projects

271. Projects involving the construction of new homes as well as the remodeling of existing homes fall under this label.

e) Cultural projects

272. Projects that seek to ensure full access to culture, in the broad and complete sense of the term, fall under this label. For example: promotion and celebration of traditional festivals, artistic endeavors (music, dance, theater, oral narration, puppetry, plastic arts), traditional and contemporary literature, artisan works, popular technology, culinary art, traditional medicine, new political culture, new values, new forms of communication (Infocenters, community television and radio), conservation of cultural patrimony, etc.

5) NECESSITY OF TECHNICAL SUPPORT FOR SOME PROJECTS

273. There will be projects that are more or less complex, depending on the type and scale of the proposal.

274. It is possible that many of the community's projects will be relatively simple and can be designed by people in the community. For example: paint a school or fix up a room where children can come to watch cartoons on television.

275. But depending on the resources available, communities may also occasionally take on more complex projects that require the participation of specialists.

276. This might include a project to build social housing or the construction of a school or bridge.

277. In terms of territorial area and municipal projects, we imagine that the immense majority of them will be technically quite complex.

278. Designing these projects will require the collaboration of qualified technical personnel, whether volunteers from the community or experts provided by state institutions, who have experience in executing such projects and who have up-to-date knowledge regarding the activities that need to be carried out.

279. For example, a project for social housing will necessarily involve architects, engineers and site managers to determine the technical characteristics of the project, such as design drawings, amount of cement needed, types of material required, etc. This does not mean the community cannot provide its own labor during the construction process. The money saved through the use of volunteer labor can go towards building more homes.

280. For housing projects, qualified personnel should be provided by the municipal entity responsible for housing. More complex infrastructure projects should be designed by the municipal entity responsible for public works. Productive agricultural projects should be designed with the support of state institutions overseeing agricultural development.

281. It is also possible to rely on qualified volunteer personnel.

2. DESCRIPTION OF COMPONENTS THAT MAKE UP A PROJECT

1). A PRIOR CLARIFICATION REGARDING MATERIAL AND HUMAN RESOURCES

282. Before turning to analyze the different components that should be present in all projects, let's look at what we mean by human and material resources.

a) Human resources

283. When, for example, transforming an abandoned site into a plaza for the community to use, we need to work out the amount of labor required. This will involve calculating how many gardeners, bricklayers, welders, painters, among others, will be needed and how many hours of work will be required for each activity to build the plaza.

284. Separately from this, we need to consider the amount of labor required for maintaining the plaza, that is, people who, on a rotational basis, will be needed to supervise to avoid damages to the plaza, and the hours of gardening or cleaning needed each year to avoid the plaza deteriorating.

285. We should see if the community is willing to provide volunteer labor in both cases.

286. Therefore, we need to distinguish between paid and voluntary labor. This first will be paid a certain amount of money; the second will not.

287. It is important to quantify voluntary labor to make it visible to the community. Under capitalism, the only labor that counts is that which is paid for: neither voluntary work nor women's work in the home is considered labor. By making it visible, we can publicly recognize the level of generosity and spirit of collaboration of the community and educate people in the humanist and solidarian values that characterize the new society we want to build. We should count the hours of voluntary labor done each day, and by each person, without differentiating between the labor of a professional and the labor of a layperson. We should value all labor the same. At the end of the project, we will know how many hours of voluntary labor were donated to a particular project and how much was donated by each person.

b) *Material resources*

288. It is also important to know what tools and materials are available for each activity, distinguishing between those that need to be bought (cement, pipes, planks, brooms, hammers) and those that need to be hired (a truck, etc.).

2) TECHNICAL DESCRIPTION

289. The first component we need to consider is a technical description of our objective. This description can be very straightforward for simple projects. In terms of improving street lighting, we need: a map of the community identifying existing lampposts, those that need repairs or a change of light bulb and, if necessary, where new lampposts need be installed.

290. More complex projects, or those we could define as "technical projects" (public works, building homes or factories, etc.) require a much more complicated technical description and, therefore, as we mentioned before, should be drafted with the help of qualified personnel: engineers, architects, etc.

291. That is why, for these projects, we suggest during the first phase coming up with what we have called a "project idea" (a general outline that enables a rough estimation of the costs). Only once the list of projects that will become part of the development plan has been approved should a "technical project" be developed, with all the effort that entails.

292. A general outline can be facilitated by the fact that generic estimations exist for many large projects (cost per square meter for building a home, cost of one meter of road, etc.). This will help with estimating the cost of the project without having to first come up with a specific technical project. Logically, these estimations should be adapted to the type of project that is envisaged (single family home, prefabricated home, brick buildings, etc.).

293. It is important that the process is not left exclusively in the hands of experts, even though technical aspects clearly dominate during this phase of designing the project. Experts do not always take into consideration people's desires and wants. That is why it is important to set up mixed working groups[24], one of whose fundamental functions is, precisely, designing projects. In this way, we avoid the possibility that, in the absence of any other directions, experts mechanically apply formulas without taking into consideration the real needs of the population the project is meant to serve.

294. Furthermore, the affected population often knows more about local aspects that experts may not notice but that could impede or facilitate the execution of the project.

---

24. Mixed working groups are working groups comprised of members of the planning council, volunteer or institutional-based experts and interested people from the community.

295. Below will we look at what should be included in a technical description for a project to transform a vacant lot into a plaza. Obviously, the purpose of this example is to simply show the format of the tables required for this purpose. This is a made up scenario, with made up figures. The resources used in the project and their costs (in an imaginary currency we have called the peso) have no bearing on reality.

(a) A sketch of the future plaza indicating paths, play areas, benches to sit on, lampposts, trees (including what species), flower beds, watering system, etc. We are dealing here with a basic sketch. It does not have to be a perfectly drawn plan, it is enough to draw it free hand. But it is important to include all the elements that will be part of the plaza.
(b) A first table which should contain all the elements foreseen in the future plan, and which identifies their characteristics and quantities needed.
(c) A second table outlining the material resources that will be required: cement, gravel, paint, etc.
(d) A third table outlining the tools and instruments of labor that will be required.

296. For example, a sketch of the plaza could look like this:

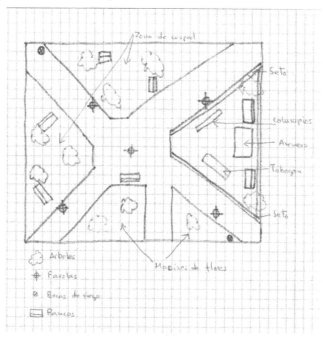

297. Below is what the tables might look like:

Table 1. Elements that make up the plaza

Element	Quantity	Units	Provided by
Lampposts	5	Units	Municipal authorities
Water storage units for irrigation	2	Units	Municipal authorities
Benches	7	Units	Buy
Infant's toboggan	1	Units	Buy
Three seater children's swing	1	Units	Buy
Sandpit	1	Unit	Buy
Trees	11	Units	Buy
Hedges	20	Linear meters	Buy
Grass	50	Square meters	Buy
Flower beds	20	Units	Buy

Table 2. Materials needed to build plaza

Materials	Quantity	Unit	Provided by
Gravel for paths	5	Cubic meters	Buy
Cement	10	Bags	Buy
Sand	5	Bags	Buy
Paint to delineate paths	10	Gallons	Buy
Rocks to delineate paths	1	Cubic meters	Buy

Table 3. Tools and machinery

Tool	Quantity	Unit	Provided by
Shovels	15	Units	Free
Picks	5	Units	Free
Mattocks	10	Units	Free
Rakes	5	Units	Free
Large hammers	5	Units	Free
Wheelbarrows	5	Units	Free
Containers	2	Units	Municipal authorities
Cement mixer	1	Units	Hire
Bricklayers' pallets	10	Units	Free
Paintbrushes	20	Units	Buy
Truck to transport materials	1	Units	Hire

298. If the technical description outlines **what** we want to do, during the second phase we need to set out **when and how** we want to do it in a program of activities. It should include a timeline of activities and tasks that need to be carried out to implement the project and set out who is responsible for each of these.

299. The timeline for infrastructure projects should lay out all the activities that have to be carried out, in as much detail as possible. That is, for each task it should set out the time and human and material resources needed to carry it out.

300. The timeline for service provision projects should set out a timeline or work program indicating the hours within which the service will be available, the places it will be made available, the people assigned to each shift and the person responsible for each shift.

301. In both cases, the team should build upon the work already carried out when exploring alternative courses of action, but carefully revising the list of activities to see if anything was left out in the previous phase. It is worth remembering that many activities require prior organization that should be taken into consideration and therefore be reflected in the timeline, in order to not forget about them and ensure the project is carried out successfully.

302. Furthermore, we have to remember that for any project there is always a preparatory phase in which the project team needs to distribute responsibilities, under the coordination of the project manager.

303. This preparatory phase should include the activities that each person has to carry out to ensure that the following activities can occur (organize campaign to recruit volunteers, purchase or hire necessary materials and tools, get a commitment from the municipal authorities that they will fulfill their promises, etc.).

304. Below is an example of what a possible timeline for a plaza could look like.

Table 4. Timeline

Week	Day	Activity	Prior activity	Key necessities
Preparatory phase	Initial project	Meeting to designate people responsible for managing the project Organizing and carrying out a collection among residents to help finance the project Recruiting and organizing volunteers Organizing food for the workers Negotiating with municipal authorities where containers, lampposts and water outlets should go Negotiating the purchase and hiring of materials, tools and transport; Maintenance		
	Few days prior	Each person responsible for a particular area carries out their corresponding activities to ensure that the necessary resources are available prior to beginning the project.		
Week 1	Friday	Place containers Buy food for 40 lunches		Design and erect signs announcing need for volunteers

Week	Day	Activity	Prior activity	Key necessities
		Recruit volunteers		Play ads on community radio
	Saturday Sunday	1st Clean up of area (2 days)	Municipal authorities install containers	20 people for 2 days (5 hours) voluntary work Shovels Picks Wheelbarrows 40 lunches
Week 2	Friday	Buy food for 40 lunches Recruit volunteers		Design and erect signs announcing need for volunteers Play ads on community radio
	Saturday	2nd Preparing installation of electricity and water (1 day)	1st	20 people for 2 days (5 hours) voluntary work Shovels
	Sunday	3rd Mark out paths and play zone (1 day)	2nd	Picks Wheelbarrows Mattocks 40 lunches
Week 3	Wednesday	4th Collection of materials from municipality (1 day)	2nd	Transport from municipality
	Thursday Friday	5th Install lampposts and sprinklers (2 days)	4th & 2nd	Materials and personnel from municipality
	Friday	6th Collection of materials (seeds, trees) (1 day) Buy food for 40 lunches Recruit volunteers	3rd	Hire truck (5 hours) 10 people for 3 hours voluntary work unloading. Design and erect signs announcing need for volunteers Play ads on community radio
	Saturday Sunday	7th Plant seedlings and trees (2 days)	5th & 6th	20 people for 2 days (5 hours) voluntary work, 5 of them in the garden Shovels, Mattock, rakes 40 lunches
Week 4	Friday	8th Collection of materials (benches, cement etc.) (1 day) Buy food for 40 lunches Recruit volunteers	5th	Hire truck (5 hours) 10 people for 3 hours voluntary work unloading Design and erect signs announcing need for volunteers Play ads on community radio

Week	Day	Activity	Prior activity	Key necessities
	Saturday	9th Lay down grass (1 day)	6th & 7th	20 people for 1 days (5 hours) voluntary work, including 5 gardeners Wheelbarrows Mattocks, rakes. 20 lunches
	Sunday	10th Install infrastructure (benches) (1 day)	5th & 8th	20 people for 1 days (5 hours) voluntary work, including 10 bricklayers Shovels Picks Wheelbarrows Bricklayers pallets, cement mixer (8 hours) 20 lunches
Week 5	Friday	11th Collection of materials (kid's equipment and gravel, rock and paint for paths) (1 day) Buy food for 60 lunches Recruit volunteers	5th	Hire truck (5 hours) 10 people for 3 hours voluntary work unloading Design and erect signs announcing need for volunteers Play ads on community radio
	Saturday	12th Install infrastructure (Kid's playing equipment) (1 day)	5th & 11th	20 people for 1 days' (5 hours) volunteer work, including 10 bricklayers Shovels Picks Wheelbarrows Bricklayers pallet Cement mixer (8 hours) 20 lunches
	Sunday	13th Install paths (1 day)	5th, 7th, 9th, 10th, 11th & 12th	40 people for 1 days (5 hours) voluntary work Shovels, Wheelbarrows Paintbrushes (20) 40 lunches

305. There are techniques such as the critical road method or PERT that can allow us to work out the minimum necessary time for implementing a project. We will need to use these for more complex projects that involve different teams and where it is important to take into account the order in which different activities are carried out so as to avoid delays or dysfunctions. This would

not be the case for the plaza project nor for the immense majority of projects at the community or territorial area level. But we should keep it in mind for certain community and territorial area projects and the majority of municipal projects.

4) CALCULATING COSTS

306. Once we have worked out the what and the how, we can calculate the cost of the project. This will depend on the amount of work, materials and equipment that each activity requires.

307. That is, the cost will depend on the type of activities and tasks required to achieve the objective sought and the time it will take to do so.

308. If we have correctly drawn up the technical description and timeline, we should be able to accurately work out the cost of each activity and task.

309. We can use the table we drew up for the timeline for our purposes, eliminating the first, second and fourth columns and adding two new columns: one that reflects the costs per unit of each material in each activity and another with the total corresponding cost.

310. 331. 649. This will leave us with a table looking like this:

Table 5. Cost of materials for activities

Activity	Key necessities	Cost per unit	Total cost
1st Clean up of area (2 days)	20 people/5 hours/2 days volunteer work	Voluntary (200 hours)	0
		Free	0
	Shovels	Free	0
	Picks	Free	0
	Wheelbarrows	Free	0
	40 lunches	$3,00	120
2nd Preparing installation of electricity and water (1 day)	20 people/5 hours/ 2 days volunteer work	Voluntary (200 hours)	0
	Shovels	Free	0
3rd Mark out paths and kid's play areas (1 day)	Picks	Free	0
	Mattocks	Free	0
	Wheelbarrows	Free	0
	40 lunches	$3,00	120
4th Collection of materials from municipality (1 day)	Transport from municipal offices	Municipal authorities	0
5th Installation of lampposts and sprinklers (2 days)	Material and personnel from municipality	Municipal authorities	0
6th Collection of material (trees, seeds) (1 day)	Truck hire (5 hours)	$20/hour	100
	10 people/3 hours voluntary labor unloading	Voluntary (30 hours)	0
7th Plant seedlings and trees (2 days)	20 people/5 hours/2 days voluntary work, including 5 gardeners	Voluntary (200 hours)	0
		Free	0
	Shovels	Free	0
	Mattocks	Free	0
	Rakes	Free	0

Activity	Key necessities	Cost per unit	Total cost
	40 lunches	$3,00	120
8th Collection of materials (benches, cement etc.)(1 day)	Truck hire (5 hours) 10 people/3 hours voluntary work unloading	$20/hour Voluntary (30 hours)	100 0
9th Lay down grass. (1 day)	20 people/5 hours/1 day voluntary work, including 5 gardeners Mattocks Rakes Wheelbarrow 20 lunches	Voluntary (100 hours) Free Free Free $3,00	0 0 0 0 60
10th Installation of infrastructure (benches) (1 day)	20 people/8 hours voluntary labor, including 10 bricklayers Shovels Picks Wheelbarrows Bricklayers pallet Cement mixer (8 hours) 20 lunches	Voluntary (160 hours) Free Free Free Free $5/hour $3,00	0 0 0 0 0 40 60
11th Collection of materials (children's play equipment and gravel, rocks and paint for paths) (1 day)	Truck hire (5 hours) 10 people/3 hours voluntary labor unloading	20/hour Voluntary (30 hours)	100 0
12th Installation of infrastructure (children's play equipment) (1 day)	20 people/8 hours voluntary work, including 10 bricklayers Shovels Picks Wheelbarrows Bricklayers pallet Cement mixer (8 hours) 20 lunches	Voluntary (160 hours) Free Free Free Free $5/hour $3,00	0 0 0 0 0 40 60
13th Install paths (1 day)	40 people/5 hours volunteer work Shovels Wheelbarrows Paintbrushes (20) 40 lunches	Voluntary (200 hours) Free Free $1 /unit $3,00	0 0 0 20 120

311. In our example, we have assumed that all labor has been volunteered and that simple tools (shovels, wheelbarrows, paintbrushes, etc.) have been supplied for free by the volunteers themselves and a small construction company in the community.

312. That is why they appear as having zero cost in the fourth column. However, it is also worthwhile estimating what this might have cost in order to calculate the total value that the community can save by carrying out this project on its own.

313. By adding up the total cost of each resource in the different activities, and of the inputs and elements required to carry it out, we can come up with an estimation of the cost of the project. In the table that we will use for this stage, it will not be necessary to maintain the same breakdown that we used in the technical description and timeline we have already come up with.

314. Below is Table 6, with a made-up example of how we might calculate the cost of rehabilitating a plaza.

315. In the column for labor, we should make clear how many hours of voluntary labor will be contributed, in order to estimate what this will mean for the community. Supposing that all labor is voluntary, we would be looking at 1310 hours of voluntary labor that the community is saving money on. On the other hand, we should include under human resources the costs of lunches provided to volunteer workers as a minimum compensation for their efforts.

316. The sum of all items will allow us to know the real total cost of the project. But, as we are also interested in knowing what the cost would have been if we did not have the volunteer labor we rely on together with other free contributions, we should add the estimated value of these contributions and subtract any costs currently associated with them (in this case, the lunches for volunteer workers, which would not be necessary if they are being paid).

Table 6: Calculation of cost of project to rehabilitate plaza (made-up figures).

	Required resources			Cost analysis		
Items	Specific description	Unit of measurement	Quantity	Cost per unit	Total cost	Subtotal for item
Human resources	Bricklayers	Hour per person				
	Painters	Hour per person	1310	$0.00	$0.00	$660.00
	Gardeners	Hour per person				
	Lunches	Quantity	220	$3.00	$660.00	
Materials and supplies	Cement	Sack	10	$16.00	$160.00	
	Sand	Sack	5	$2.00	$10.00	
	Gravel	Cubic meter	5	$20.00	$100.00	$570.00
	Paint	Gallon	10	$30.00	$300.00	

	Required resources			Cost analysis		
Items	Specific description	Unit of measurement	Quantity	Cost per unit	Total cost	Subtotal for item
Nursery	Decorative stones	Cubic meter	1	$25.00	$25.00	$1,325.00
	Tree saplings	Unit	11	$50.00	$550.00	
	Hedges	Per meter	20	$15.00	$300.00	
	Grass	Meter square	50	$5.00	$250.00	
	Large flowers	Unit	20	$10.00	$200.00	
Furniture	Park benches	Unit	7	$50.00	$350.00	$550.00
	Slide	Unit	1	$75.00	$75.00	
	Swing	Unit	1	$75.00	$75.00	
	Sandpit	Unit	1	$50.00	$50.00	
Contracted services	Hire truck	Hour	20	$15.00	$300.00	$380.00
	Hired cement mixer	Hour	16	$5.00	$80.00	
Equipment and tools	Paint brushes	Quantity	20	$1.00	$20.00	$20.00
	Other tools	Quantity		$0.00	$0.00	
Other costs						$100.00
Total real cost						$3,605.00
Volunteer labor		Hour per person	1310	$2.00	$2,620.00	
Hire of tools		Overall cost	300	$1.00	$300.00	
Total free contributions						$2,920.00
Costs associated with free contributions (lunches for volunteers)						-$660.00
Total theoretical cost (value) of project						$6,865.00

317. Having done our calculations, we can see that the project will cost $3605, but that if it was not for the volunteer labor, the cost would have been $6225 – a big difference. The 1310 hours of voluntary labor represented a saving of $2620. If we add to this the estimated value of the contributions in terms of free use of tools, the cost would have been $6865, or 65% higher.

318. With these calculations, we have sought to make visible something that capitalism, interested only in real costs and profits, is not interested in revealing, because it means nothing to it. We are making visible the value of the efforts of solidarity and collaboration of the neighbors.

319. For projects that will take a certain period of time to complete, it would be worthwhile coming up with a payments calendar, in accordance with the overall timeline, in order to know what the financial needs will be in the long term.

320. In our example of the plaza, there would be no reason to come up with such a timeline, as all the payments will be made within a very short timeframe. But if the project had of been a more complex one, that lasted several weeks or months, and we needed to come up with an income calendar, it would be very useful to know how much money we would need to invest each week.

321. Let us suppose that we want to finance our project by taking up a collection among the families that make up the community (360) of roughly $10 a family. Because we do not want them to have to pay the whole amount at once (residents survive on very tight budgets), we will come up with a payments calendar to know when and how much money we need to cover costs involved in the project. In this example, we could suppose that payment for the nursery, saplings, seeds, and park bench could be delayed by 90 days. All the rest would have to be paid for at the time of purchase or hire. With this information we can come up with the following payments calendar shown on Table 7. We have not included those costs valued at less than $100 and that do not have a set purchase date.

Table 7. Payments calendar

Week	Concept	Value	Date of purchase	Date of payment	Total for week
1	Lunches	$120	15/06/2016	15/06/2016 Friday	$120
2	Lunches	$120	22/06/2016	22/06/2016 Friday	$120
3	Truck hire	$100	29/06/2016	29/06/2016 Friday	$220
	Lunches	$120	29/06/2016	29/06/2016 Friday	
4	Construction materials	$270	05/07/2016	05/07/2016 Thursday	$530
	Truck hire	$100	06/07/2016	06/07/2016 Friday	
	Lunches	$120	06/07/2015	06/07/2015 Friday	
	Hire of cement mixer	$40	08/07/2016	08/07/2015 Domingo	
5	Paint and paintbrushes	$320	12/07/2016	12/07/2016 Thursday	$840
	Children's toys	$200	12/07/2016	12/07/2016	

Week	Concept	Value	Date of purchase	Date of payment	Total for week
				Thursday	
	Truck hire	$100	13/07/2015	13/07/2015 Friday	
	Lunches	$180	13/07/2015	13/07/2015 Friday	
	Hire of cement mixer	$40	14/07/2016	14/07/2016 Saturday	
Total payments during period of project completion					$1,790
Delayed	Nursery	$1,325	28/06/2016	28/09/2016	$1,325
	Park benches	$350	05/07/2016	05/10/2016	$350
Total delayed payments					$1,675
Total payments					$3,505

322. This calendar tells us that in the first three weeks, payments will be largely irrelevant – mainly the purchase of lunches – while most payments will be concentrated in the last two weeks. Moreover, we have to foresee that three months later we will have to make some important payments.

6) FINANCE PLAN

a) Linked financing and unlink financing

323. Once we know the cost of a project, we need to explain how we will finance it. The most common situation is where costs are covered by funds from the overall Development Plan, but there may be situations in which, for various reasons, a part or all of the funding could come from other sources that condition their contribution to the realization of that concrete project. Consider, for example, an infrastructure project in which the state or a state agency or an NGO has committed itself to covering all or some of the costs of a project. In this case, as the funds are tied to a certain project, we refer to this as **linked** financing, and it should be explained as such in the finance plan we come up with.

324. We might even have a situation where a community, territorial area or municipality has decided to assume the costs of a concrete project that will be financed with funds orientated exclusively to that project; those funds won't be part of the funds available for the plan. In that case we could also say that the project has linked financing, because if that project is not carried out those funds will not be able to be dedicated to other projects. In our example of the square, we can see that the project is going to be completely financed by a collection among families in the community specifically carried out with that goal in mind. If the project is ultimately not carried out, then there will not be a collection of money for that purpose, so there won't be money to be applied to another project. Therefore the remodeling of the square has linked financing.

325. If, on the contrary, it had been proposed to do a general collection among families to totally or partially fund the Investment Plan (for example, to finance the Immediate Action Plan), and then to

use part of this money for the project of remodeling of the square, we would then be talking about **unlinked financing**.

326. It is important to distinguish between linked financing and financing that is not linked. In the case of projects that do not rely on linked financing, they are financed on the basis of resources available for the plan. Therefore, if a project is not carried out or is postponed, the resources assigned to it can be made available for other projects within the plan. On the other hand, if the funding is linked to a certain project, those funds will only be available for the realization of that project.

327. Logically, a project can be financed through a combination of linked and unlinked financing: an entity can commit to financing 50% of a certain project, while the community, the territorial area or the municipality contribute the other 50% from its investment budget. In this case, 50% of financing will be linked (it won't be received if the project is not carried out) and 50% will not be linked (it would be available for other projects if that one is not carried out or it is postponed to a later year).

b) Credit financing

328. It may be the case that parts of the funds for the plan come in the form of loans. That is, the community receives financing that it commits to repaying within a certain timeframe, with or without interest. This is the most common form of financing of socio-productive projects (which through their income can repay the capital and interest). But the community can also ask for loans to deal with other types of projects, whose costs require it be paid within a short timeframe – a loan means the community can pay it back in smaller installments over time.

329. If part of the plan is to be financed via loans, these loans, together with the loaning institution and conditions placed on them (deadlines and forms of repayment, interest, etc.) should be clearly identified. In Chapter VIII, we will deal with forms of financing. For now we want to insist on our recommendation that this form of financing only be used in cases where it is strictly required.

c) Net necessary financing

330. Net necessary financing is the difference between the foreseen cost and the financing linked to the project. As there are different types of financing, we should make note of the type of financing being used alongside the corresponding item. And we should specify its amount, where it comes from and the conditions for obtaining it, if there are any.

d) Income calendar

331. In cases of projects where it is necessary to come up with a **payment calendar**, this financing plan should also incorporate an **income calendar** to ensure payments can be made.

332. In our example, we have already said that we will finance the project through a collection among families in the community. Now, with the information from the payments calendar we can come up with a calendar for collections that will allow families to contribute via small payments that coincide with times when funds are needed. For example: as shown on Table 8.

Table 8. Example of distribution of collection

Date	Amount/family	Total	Accumulated total
14 06 2016	$1.00	$360	$360
21 06 2016	$1.00	$360	$720
28 06 2016	$1.00	$360	$1,080
04 07 2016	$1.00	$360	$1,440
11 07 2016	$1.00	$360	$1,800
01 08 2016	$1.00	$360	$2,160
22 08 2016	$1.00	$360	$2,520
12 09 2016	$1.00	$360	$2,880
03 10 2016	$1.00	$360	$3,240
24 10 2016	$1.05	$378	$3,618

7) MAINTENANCE COSTS

333. It is also worth quantifying in another table the annual cost of maintenance for the project (in our example, a plaza), differentiating between contributions involving voluntary labor and paid labor for more complex tasks (repairing lights, fumigating plants), as well as the cost of possible inputs (water, electricity, etc.).

334. In terms of human resources, we should include those people who volunteer on a roster basis for the necessary tasks of patrolling to ensure the plaza is not destroyed. We also need to consider the hours of work spent by the gardeners or cleaners required for the upkeep of the plaza.

335. Although determining maintenance costs may not be so relevant for small projects, it is for larger ones. Sometimes the resources needed to finance maintenance on an annual basis can be expensive and it could mean that the amount of funds available for new projects in the following years is reduced.

336. In Chapter IX, where we will explain how to come up with a community plan, we will explore the impact of maintenance costs on a community's capacity to invest.

337. Lastly, with projects that have a high maintenance cost, it is worthwhile specifying within the project how it is envisaged that this cost will be paid for: if it will come from Community Council financing, via charging users a fee[25], or a hybrid system. The method chosen will often depend on the characteristics of the project. Charging an entry fee to use a public pool is possible and reasonable, but no one would attempt to charge for access to a plaza.

338. The best way to make this explicit is to distinguish between:

(a) Maintenance costs: spending required to maintain the public work or service and avoid its deterioration;

(b) Generated income: income from charging for use of a specific installation or as a result of a productive activity; and

(c) Net cost of maintenance: the difference between the maintenance costs and income generated.

---

25. Fee refers to the amount that users are charged for use of a public service.

339. We want to insist on the importance of taking maintenance costs into consideration for all cost calculations given that often, in many countries, efforts are made to build public works that improve people's living conditions, but it is often forgotten that after carrying out the project, it is necessary to maintain it. After a few years, due to neglect or forgetfulness, the public work can deteriorate to the point were the situation returns to square one.

3. PROJECT DOCUMENTATION

340. It is important to note that coming up with projects should not be seen as simply a matter of filling out different documents. All projects demand reflection, calculations and studies at each step of the methodology we have outlined. The information contained in the forms should be a synthesis of this reflection.

1) SUMMARY TABLE CONTAINING INFORMATION FOR PROJECTS

341. Once a project has been adopted, the most relevant information should be put into a summary table drawn up in accordance with a previously agreed upon format.

342. A copy of this table should always serve as a basic outline of the complete project. It should include: a technical description, timeline tables and estimated costs.

343. Other copies of this table can be used to present or disseminate the results among the people. In any case, to ensure the transparency of the process, all project documents should be made available to any interested persons.

344. The summary table should include the following information:

a) Identify the project

345. It is important to locate the project in time and space, and point out who is responsible for it. That is why it should indicate:
▪ Project name
▪ Date of adoption
▪ Responsible entities
▪ People responsible for presenting it
▪ Type of project (socio-productive, infrastructure, etc., if this is considered necessary)
▪ Thematic area it belongs to (Health, Education, Recreation, etc.).

346. The name is important for being able to identify it. It should be a short and attractive name that describes it in a simple manner.

b) Project description

347. Here is where a short and simple summary and characterization of the project goes.

c) Justification

348. Here we should explain the motivation for coming up with the project.

d) Objective

349. Here we should outline the aim the community is seeking with the project. It answers the question: what is it we want to achieve?

e) Social impact

350. Here we should specify, in a precise manner, who will benefit from the project in a direct and indirect manner. Beneficiaries should be classified by age, gender, health conditions, level of assistance, work conditions, living in at-risk situation (physical, social, psychological) and others.

351. A separate box should include the points obtained by the aspiration the project is seeking to respond to.

f) Investment plan

352. We should include the total cost (without including volunteer contributions of labor, inputs and equipment) and the payment calendar, if relevant.

g) Volunteer contributions

353. It is important to include an estimation of the costs that the community will save as a result of the volunteer contributions made by neighbors (voluntary work, lending of tools, donation of materials, etc.) and what the project would have cost if it was not able to count on these. This information, while not having any economic impact does have an important moral value that should never be forgotten.

h) Financing Plan

354. This should indicate where funds to finance the project are expected to come from, and in the case of linked financing, the amount, origins and conditions should be included, along with an income calendar, where this is deemed necessary.

i) Timeline

355. This should outline how long the project is expect to take, distinguishing between the key stages (design, preparation, collection of materials, carrying out the project, etc.)

j) Maintenance Plan

356. The Maintenance Plan should indicate the periodic costs that will need to be covered to avoid the deterioration of the public work (paint, gardener, etc.) and clearly specify any commitments undertaken when the project was initiated by the community (voluntary or paid labor, small purchases, etc.) and other institutions (supply of replacement parts, maintenance of services, etc.).

k) Economic forecasts

357. If maintenance costs are expected to be fully or partially covered by income that the project might generate, it should be specified how much this is expected to be. In this case the net maintenance cost should also be included, which, as we have already noted, is the difference between maintenance costs and generated income.

358. When we are dealing with projects that generate income, as is the case of productive projects, we should:
(a) Forecast the income expected to be generated
(b) The future viability of the project
(c) When it is expect that the project could become self-sustaining, and if this will never be the case, the reasons that justify carrying it out even though it will not become self sustaining.

359. Although this section might seem of secondary importance when it comes to smaller projects, or projects of a social or cultural character, it is especially relevant for socio-productive projects given that we need to know if they will be genuinely viable before we initiate them, and in those case where they are not, the reasons why it they are deemed necessary to go ahead with them despite this fact.

360. Let us have a look on Table 9 where you can find a summary table for our example of a plaza.

Table 9. Example of summary table of plaza project

Project	Rehabilitation of plaza behind market
Responsible entities	Community of Guadalupe Territorial Area Los Llanos Municipality of Las Lagunas
Date of adoption	15 May, 2016
Presented by	Working Group 5
Type of Project	Social
Thematic Area	Culture and Recreation
Justification	With a small investment and volunteer labor by neighbors, we can eliminate a site that has been overrun with rubbish and crime and improve the lives of neighbors.
Objective	Provide spaces for recreation in the community. Respond to the aspiration of the community that the community of Guadalupe have access to activities and spaces for healthy recreation.
Social impact	Benefits all neighbors and in particular children and youth and will have indirect benefits for mothers concerned about their sons and daughters.
Aspiration points	27
Investment Plan	Purchase of inputs (cement, gravel, paint) .... $570 Purchase of furniture (park benches, swings, slide)................................. $550 Purchase of plants and trees .... $1325 5 lanterns and 2 sprinklers (Mayor's office) .... $0 Total for inputs .... $3015 Hire of truck (three trips) and mixer .... $380 Hire of equipment (shovels, picks, rakes (provided for free)........................ $0 Total for services .... $380 Labor (volunteer labor)... $0 Lunch for volunteers .... $660 Total labor costs .... $660 Other costs (unforeseen)... .... $100 TOTAL INVESTMENT .... $3605 The mayor's office has confirmed that it will provide the lanterns and sprinklers and can do so whenever needed.

	Two local companies and some workers themselves have agreed to do some work for free. There are people willing to do volunteer work. The theoretical cost of the project would have been $5865
Volunteer contributions	Volunteer labor .... $2620 Equipment hire .... $300 Total for volunteer contributions .... $2920 Minus costs associated with free contributions .... $660 Total savings due to volunteer contributions...................................... $2260 Volunteer contributions represent 38.5% of the theoretical cost of the project
Financing	The project will be financed by a collection among the 360 families in the community who will contribute $10.05 each, in 10 installments over three months, totaling $3605 We are dealing with linked financing as the project will be directly financed by the community itself.
Timeline	1.Clean up of site ....2 days 2.Preparation of site ....1 day 3.Marking out walkways and play .... 1 day 4.Installation of electricity and water supplies ....1 day 5.Installation of lanterns and sprinklers... 2 days 6.Collection of supplies and materials .... 3 days 7.Planting hedges and trees ....2 days 8.Laying grass. .... 1 day 9.Installing park benches and other furniture............ .... 2 days 10.Fixing up paths... ... 1 day All activities will be carried out on weekends to make use of volunteer labor, except for the collection of materials which will occur the Friday before activities 7, 9 and 10 begin, and the installation of lanterns and sprinklers that could be done on workdays after activity 4 is done and before activity 7 begins. The project will be completed within five weeks. The key is punctuality in the execution of activities 6, 4 and 5, and in particular making sure that the last of these does not depend on the community.
Maintenance Plan	Annual cost Preservation and replacement of plants (watering, pruning...) $150

	Cost of electricity and water.. $100
	Repair and replacement of damaged material (light bulbs)............................ $50
	Security patrols by volunteer mothers $0
	Annual cost of maintenance ....…........ $300
	There is no forecast to generate income, meaning the net annual cost for maintenance for the plaza after initial construction is $300
Person responsible	Coordinator: Luisa Pérez

3. METHODOLOGY

361. Once we have a definitive list of alternative courses of action, the Council working groups – whether at the community, territorial area or municipal level – should come up with corresponding projects, on the basis of the work previously carried out when analyzing alternatives.

362. The essential steps for carrying out this task are similar for all three levels and only vary in their complexity, in the sense that certain projects may be more complex and may require more technical support.

PLANNING COUNCIL

Activity 1. (Working groups) Design projects

363. After exploring different proposals, the working groups should meet and begin converting them into projects. Although the time dedicated to this task will vary depending on the number of projects and their complexity, we are certain that it cannot be done in a single meeting. This means that a number of meetings will need to be held.

364. If the working group is big enough, we recommend setting up smaller groups comprised of those who know the most about each thematic area to help speed up the process. Each group can then simultaneously work on different projects or aspects of the same project.

365. Nevertheless, once these smaller groups have finished their work, all members of the working group should vote on approving the projects before presenting them to the Plenary.

366. Each project should be the result of a serious and thorough study and discussion regarding what we want to achieve, how to achieve it and what human (labor) and material (instruments and objects of labor) resources are needed to achieve the objective.

367. We have to consider everything to ensure that the execution of the project goes off without a hitch.

368. Recall that planning means thinking before acting, thereby avoiding improvisation, which can put at risk the objective we want to achieve.

369. Former Venezuelan President Hugo Chavez, quoting Venezuelan independence fighter Simon Bolivar, repeatedly said that battles are won or lost in the details.

CHAPTER VII. ESTABLISHING BUDGETARY AND SECTOR-BASED PRIORITIES

1. INTRODUCTION

a) What we mean by budget

370. Budget refers to a forecasted calculation of income and expenditure or costs of a person or entity during a determined period of time (generally one year) or for carrying out a specific activity (carrying out a project, for example).

371. There are domestic budgets which families use to work out the income they expect to obtain during a period of time and the expenditure they will have to make so that they fall within the forecasted income, while also seeing if it is possible to buy household electronic goods (for example) or to save up for a holiday.

372. A well-organized family functions on a budget, that is, it knows exactly what amount of money the household will receive each month, and based on this the family can plan out its spending.

Family budget

Income (money it has)	Expenditure or costs (money it spends)
Salaries Remittances Subsidies Other income	Food Water Electricity (plus other utilities e.g. gas) Rent Education of children Transport Clothing Others

373. Costs generally refer to spending on the following items: food, electricity, gas, rent or mortgage, water, transport, clothing, school materials, furniture, household electronic goods. If, for example, remittances decline due to an economic crisis, the family tends to have to reduce costs and must decide what it will spend less on.

374. In the economic sphere, all companies come up with more or less complex budgets for the same reasons. But here the most important thing is being able to forecast the results (profits or losses) of its overall activity and detect in time any deviations (particularly negative ones) from these forecasts.

375. With even more reason, public institutions (states, provincial governments, municipalities, public agencies, etc.) should come up with income and expenditure budgets that not only direct the actions of the institutions, but also serve as a guide for citizens to know what each institution is doing throughout the year.

376. As such, the amount for each line item in the expenditure budget can serve as an indication of the institutions' priorities for the year (for example, if a mayor's office is going to spend more on education or police). The income budget normally reflects the fiscal pressure that the population must assume to maintain the activities of this institution.

377. That is why the approval of these kinds of budgets occurs within a very strict, formal regime. In the case of state budgets, it has to be approved by the corresponding parliament, and

in the other institutions by its maximum representative organ (Municipal Council in the case of municipalities, Provincial Parliament in the provinces, or federal states).

378. Moreover, tradition dictates that limitations are placed on expenditure budgets (the executive cannot spend more than what is authorized in the budget, either in an overall sense and for each item) and the income part of the budget serves more as a guide, given it is not possible to know with precision, a year before, how much taxes will be collected.

379. Budget approval is so important that parliamentary democracy itself emerged in England as a result of the demand of the nobility and bourgeoisie to control what the King could spend and how he financed it.

b) The budget as an instrument of the Plan

380. We have said that an institution's expenditure budget is important because it allows us to know what its priorities will be during the period covered by the budget and, in the case of decentralized participatory planning, the funds available to carry out our development plans.

▪*Running costs and capital costs*

381. The expenditure budget can be divided into two main columns: running costs and capital costs. Running costs refers to expenditures that the institution dedicates to maintaining services it provides and to maintaining the institution itself. Capital costs refer to the part of the budget earmarked for public investment (construction of hospitals, schools, purchase of buses, etc.) and repayment on loans previously taken out.

382. Capital costs relating to loan repayments are objective facts that are very difficult to modify as they result from commitments that have been previously undertaken. This is not the case with investment costs: these are a result of political choices – how much is spent and on what is a decision that someone must make and reflects certain priorities.

383. As the budget designation to investment costs represents precisely the funds available to implement the projects that emerge out of our aspirations, determining its amount and, if possible, increasing it, constitutes one of the objectives of participatory planning.

384. As the overall amount of costs is limited to the foreseeable income, how much we can invest depends on how much of the budget is spent on running costs.

385. At the same time, the bulk of running costs have line items that are difficult to modify (rents, salaries, supplies). Undoubtedly, running costs could be reduced – through wage reductions, cost saving measures, elimination of rents, etc. – but these measures have very high social and political costs.

386. We have to take into consideration that a very large part of these running costs responds to the need to maintain the existing level of services provided to the population.

387. To provide services such as education, healthcare, drinking water, rubbish collection, road maintenance, street lighting, etc., we need to designate a significant part of available budget resources to them. These costs are rigid because if you do not provide the necessary resources, these services are affected. The relative weight of this type of expenditure can only be reduced over the mid-to-long term if services become more efficient and their costs diminish.

388. The other alternative, increasing income, presupposes either an increase in fiscal pressure, increasing or creating new taxes or taking out loans (directly from financial institutions or via the sale of public bonds), with the knowledge that what is not paid now will have to be paid in following years, reducing the funds for other costs.

389. We can see that the autonomy to make decisions in terms of budgetary matters is relatively limited, but even so there is always room to decide to expand investment spending or improve

service provision, decisions that, when it comes to participatory planning, should be the focus of a prior debate not only among experts or political leaders but among the population as a whole.

- *Breakdown of cost by objective or thematic area*

390. Normally the expenditure budget, once divided into running costs and capital costs, is further divided along the lines of a) the economic breakdown of costs (salaries, supplies, purchase of goods and services, financial cost and existing subsidies) and b) the entity responsible for managing these funds (ministries for state budgets, respective municipal departments for municipal budgets).

391. Although this distinction has important practical effects (knowing "on what" money is spent and "who" is doing it), we think it is more important to know "why" it is being spent. That is, what is the objective being sought every time money is spent.

392. We can try to directly establish the different objectives being sought, or rather, to simplify, determine specific thematic area and sub-areas (Education: primary, secondary, professional, university) associated with concrete objectives.

393. In any case, this breakdown, which affects both running costs and investment costs, allows us to visualize, on the basis of the amount destined to each objective, the priorities of those responsible. Prioritizing education over security, or vice versa, is the result of political choices.

C) INCOME BUDGET

394. The income budget also reflects determined priorities: the decision to reduce fiscal pressure despite the risk of having less funds, for example, is a political decision that reflects a certain set of priorities. On the other hand, asking the population to make a greater fiscal contribution in order to be able to carry out certain investments cannot simply be the result of a technical study; rather it has to reflect a political decision that in our case should be the result of an open debate among all citizens.

2. COMING UP WITH BUDGET PRIORITIES

395. We have seen that a public institution's budget is not simply a technical document; it is the result of political decisions that have established a certain set of priorities.

396. Moreover, the budget is a vital instrument in the planning process, given that it reflects **how much** will be invested in each budget, and **in what** and **for whom** this investment will be made.

397. The participatory planning process therefore cannot ignore the budget.

398. That is why every year, to begin the planning process, a debate must be opened up at all levels to approve budget allocations for investment and running costs, and their distribution among the different sectors.

399. We are talking here about a debate that will differ greatly depending on whether we are dealing with a community, territorial or municipal budget.

400. In the case of community budgets, we are dealing with very simple budgets because, as we said in the first part, while communities can and should take over the implementation of small projects with a great impact on the daily lives of people, the decentralization of responsibilities and services should be fundamentally directed towards the territorial areas, as the ideal spaces for self-government.

401. Community budgets are essentially investment budgets with small allocations made to maintenance costs for prior investments and for the general cost of maintaining the structures of the Community Council itself.

402. As we will see, here the debate on budget priorities can be reduced to setting a target for the total amount of income that the community hopes to obtain and how much it will set aside for maintaining existing projects and Council running costs,

403. At the level of the territorial area, the level of decentralization of responsibilities and resources that has occurred will determine the complexity of the budget. If this has occurred to a larger extent, the budget allocation for providing decentralized services will be larger and it will be more important to determine what is set aside for new investments so that Territorial Budget and Planning Teams can come up with a budget proposal1 to present for evaluation at the first annual meeting of the Territorial Area Assembly, even before the debate on aspirations begins.

404. Logically, at the municipal level, it is important to know how much in funds will be left for municipal investment, after allocating resources to communities and territorial areas, prior to the process of coming up with a Municipal Plan.

405. That is why the debate on the financial capacity of territorial areas and municipality to undertake an investment plan should be the first step in the decentralized participatory planning process and should start in the communities in order to then move up to the territorial area and finally the Municipal Planning Council and Assembly.

406. It is also worthwhile ensuring that the debate on budget priorities is not limited to discussing the distribution of spending on running and investment costs.

407. As we have said before, it is true that a large part of running costs can be considered as not subject to alteration. In the short term it will be very difficult to reduce the amount of funds allocated to providing services without generating resentment among the people.

408. But it is very useful if citizens involved in the participatory planning process have the chance to know and discuss the budget allocations for the different services being provided so that they can decide on priorities that may turn out to be different compared with how funds are currently being distributed.

409. This could allow for more funds to be directed toward services that are deemed to be a priority and, in the contrary case, when it is necessary to reduce costs, ensure that any reduction has the minimum possible effect on priority areas.

410. We recommend preparing a table where each row corresponds to a sector or subsector (the level of breakdown depends on the capacity to define objectives) and that there be columns to include: an indicator of the existing situation in each sector or subsector (for example, rate of school drop outs); the objective being sought; and a breakdown of expenditure in terms of salaries, rent, purchase of supplies and subsidies, if they exist. An additional column should reflect the total running costs initially assigned to this sector.

---

1. We are talking about a proposal that collects estimations of total forecast income, a breakdown of running costs divided into objectives or sectors (Education, Health, Urban development, Security, etc.) capital costs that have already been committed to (interest and loan repayments, as well as investment commitments assumed in previous years) and the amount available for new investments.

411. These costs could simply reflect what happened the previous year or what the Municipal Budget and Planning Cabinet is proposing, or, in the relevant cases, what the equivalent teams in the territorial area are proposing.

412. Once aspirations have been discussed and prioritized, this table can serve to initiate debates in Planning Councils and Assemblies over which sectors or subsectors are currently receiving enough funds and where spending should increase or decrease.

413. We have to consider that these priorities may not exactly coincide with the sector-based priorities that emerge from the sector-based groups and that are part of the list of priority aspirations: there may be a sector whose services are considered to be satisfactory and whose performance explains why no new aspirations have emerged, but which everyone believes need to be maintained or improved.

414. The Territorial and Municipal Budget and Planning Teams should take the results of this debate into consideration when coming up with their budget proposals.

3. COMING UP WITH SECTOR-BASED PRIORITIES

415. As we have seen, it is possible that certain limitations may be applied to our investment budget as part of helping us reach our objective.

416. In the previous chapter – where we dealt with projects – we noted that these can be classified according to the objectives sought. We are talking here about social, cultural, social enterprise, infrastructure and housing projects.

417. It is possible that there may be a desire to allocate a minimum percentage of the investment budget to certain types of projects (for example, allocating at least 30% of the investment budget to social enterprise projects). On the other hand, certain limits on the percentage of the investment budget allocated to other types of projects may also be sought (for example, to limit funding for cultural projects to a maximum of 10% of all funds).

418. These limitations might be the result of pre-established guidelines set out in national plans or the results of debates in the corresponding Planning Council. In any case, they should be known and be debated in the corresponding Assemblies.

419. It's worth noting that even if these guidelines were not imposed by a superior body, it would still be worthwhile for the Council to decide to adopt them before coming up with projects, as they can help steer focus away from a particular issue towards others.

420. Undoubtedly it is possible to broaden out this breakdown and, for example, within the social projects distinguish between projects in the area of health, education, security or the environment, to be even more concrete in terms of the limitations we are talking about.

421. Nevertheless, it is advisable to avoid a situation where so much detail ends up making the process of coming up with and prioritizing aspirations practically meaningless.

422. Although these limitations only need to be applied when coming up with investment plans at the different levels, we recommend that the debate on them occur at each level at the start of the process.

423. This can be very useful for directing any increase in income towards priority areas, or where necessary to reduce costs, to do so in a way to ensure that priority areas are least affected.

424. This second debate can simultaneously occur in the communities, territorial areas and municipality.

4. METHODOLOGY

425. We have seen three aspects of the budget that should be a focus of the participatory process:

(a) Determining the financial capacities for investments (amount of investment spending)
(b) Setting limitations, if there are to be any, among different types of projects on the basis of their objectives.
(c) Determining priorities among services or sectors covered by the municipality and the territorial areas.

426. The first two aspects above – (a) and (b) – should be established at the start of the process.

427. Regarding the third aspect, we have to distinguish between two phases:
(a) Determining the objectives or thematic areas and sub-areas that the running costs budget will be broken down into at the municipal and territorial area levels, something that should occur at the start of the process.
(b) Determining priorities for these objectives or thematic areas and sub-areas in the budget, which can be done once the process has advanced and a diagnosis of the situation has been done.

428. In the first year, the first two aspects and the first phase of the third will no doubt begin as a proposal from the superior level of local government, in this case the Mayor's office. In the following years, the proposal is more likely to come out of the deliberations of the Municipal Planning Council.

429. For this, we propose the following methodology:

CABINET AND TERRITORIAL BUDGET AND PLANNING TEAMS[2]

Activity 1. Determining the basis for establishing sector-based budget priorities

430. The Budget and Planning Cabinet and the territorial technical teams, at their corresponding levels, prepare the following proposals:
(a) Based on forecast income, a proposal for the percentage to be allocated to funding investments in the plan.
(b) Proposal for minimum and maximum limits based on type of investment.
(c) Proposed table that breaks down the services funded in the budget according to objectives or areas and sub-areas.

COMMUNITY PLANNING ASSEMBLIES

Activity 2. Debate and approval of the sector-based and budget priorities

431. In each community, the first meeting of the Assembly should approve or modify these proposals. Modifications must be reasonable and a special quorum can be set to ensure that all agreements are representative (the respective Community Planning Council can be in charge of taking note of the arguments made during the Assembly).

TERRITORIAL AREA PLANNING COUNCILS

Activity 3. Debate regarding proposals to modify the framework for establishing sector-based and budget priorities

432. 63. Where proposed modifications have come from the communities, the Territorial Area Planning Council must study them, see if they are compatible with each other and, lastly, in relation to the existing framework of the territorial budget, prepare a document modifying or reaffirming the initial proposal and presenting it for approval to the Territorial Planning Assembly.

433. Regarding the proposals of modification of the priorities on Municipal level, it should prepare a similar document to remit it to the Municipal Planning Council.

TERRITORIAL AREA PLANNING ASSEMBLIES

Activity 4. Debate and approve the framework for establishing sector-based and budget priorities

---

2. In following years, the corresponding Territorial and Municipal Planning Councils should do this.

434. The Territorial Area Planning Assembly should debate and approve the framework for establishing budget and territorial sector-based priorities.

MUNICIPAL PLANNING COUNCIL

Activity 5. Debate proposed modifications to the framework for establishing sector-based and budget priorities

435. Finally, if modifications have been proposed, the Municipal Planning Council should debate them in the same way that the Territorial Area Councils did and prepare a document that modifies or reaffirms the proposed framework, which should then be presented for approval to the Municipal Planning Assembly.

CHAPTER VIII. PRIOR TASKS TO BE CARRIED OUT BY THE PLANNING AND BUDGET TEAMS

INTRODUCTION

436. The projects that the different Working Groups come up with will constitute the central core of the Development Plan. But to integrate these projects into the plan and to write it up, we need to carry out a serious of prior tasks that, in some cases, could be undertaken during the process of coming up with projects, but that will only be completed once that phase is over, when all the projects and project-ideas are finished.

437. These prior tasks include the following:
(1) Prepare a summary-document of the multi-year development plan that describes the characteristics that, according to residents, the community, territorial area or municipality should ideally have (the dream); details of the aspirations that help make this dream take concrete form and the objectives that would be achieved if they come to fruition; and the strengths, obstacles, opportunities and threats that have been found in relation to these aspirations (diagnostic).
(2) Draft a single list of all the projects that the Working Groups from the corresponding council have come up with.
(3) Study the resources available for financing projects, taking into consideration the entire execution (including funds to be obtained from other sources).
(4) Draft a proposed budget for the year.

438. The body responsible for carrying out these tasks at the municipal level is the Planning and Budget Cabinet; in the territorial areas, it is the responsibility of the Territorial Planning Teams; and in the communities, it falls to the corresponding Community Planning Team. To simplify things, from now on we will refer to all of these three types of teams as planning and budget teams.

FIRST TASK: PREPARE A SUMMARY-DOCUMENT OF THE MULTI-YEAR DEVELOPMENT PLAN

439. Once the alternative proposals have been distributed to the different Working Groups within each Council, the corresponding Planning and Budget Team should prepare a summary-document of the Plan for the corresponding community, territorial area and municipality, respectively.

440. The summary-document represents the formal framework within which all the activities of the Development Plan should occur. It should reflect the conclusions that have been reached at each level, during the different steps taken in the process of coming up with the plan.

1) DESCRIPTION OF THE CHARACTERISTICS OF THE COMMUNITY WE WANT AND THE CONCRETE FORM THEY TAKE IN CERTAIN ASPIRATIONS

441. In Chapter V of Volume I, we noted that within the participatory planning process, the first step consisted of understanding the reality from which we are starting and the society we want to see.

442. The Planning Teams should draft a short summary of the conclusions from the diagnostic investigation regarding the community, the territorial area or the municipality, that the corresponding Planning Council came to and that were approved by the respective Assemblies.

443. Then a prioritized list of aspirations approved by the Assembly should be gathered.

444. One way of expressing the main themes that residents are interested in is to group aspirations by thematic area or sub-area and assign each of them a score determined by the sum of the points that each aspirations within it obtained.

445. This will help us illustrate what the real priority areas are.

2) DIAGNOSIS

446. Based on the information collected in the database and ensuing debates in the corresponding Planning Assembly and the Planning Council itself, a short summary description should be written of the most relevant strengths, obstacles, threats and opportunities that exist in relation to the aspirations collected.

447. We are not talking here about an exhaustive report, just a short summary that describes the situation we are starting from in relation to the situation we aspire to.

3) OBJECTIVES TO ACHIEVE WITH EACH ASPIRATION

448. It is not enough to come up with aspirations, we need to, as much as possible, come up with quantifiable objectives that are to be achieved once the aspirations have been concretized, in order to measure results and see whether the plan is being fulfilled.

449. For example, the aspiration that we all have dignified housing can be translated into a quantifiable objective such as, that within x years the percentage of homes in a bad state will be reduced to zero, taking as our starting point the fact that half the population currently lives in inadequate housing.

450. When translating an aspiration into a quantifiable objective, we need to consider the genuine possibilities of achieving them. It is not reasonable to expect that we can reduce the percentage of homes in a bad state to zero in one year, or even in the four years of a Development Plan

451. Ideally, we should set objectives that are slightly above our expectations, meaning that we will be have to make an extra effort if we want to reach them.

452. In the case of inadequate housing, we could set as an objective of the Development Plan to reduce the percentage of such housing by half in the four years covered by the plan. For example, if there are 80 homes in a bad state to start with, we should aim to reduce the number to 40 by the end of the 4-year period, fixing or replacing 10 homes a year.

453. In other cases, we could set objectives that suppose the complete satisfaction of a particular aspiration.

454. It is also true that there are aspirations that are difficult to quantify. In these cases, we have to look for indicators that, even if indirectly, allow us to see if an aspiration has been fulfilled. The impact that artists working with children has can be measured by the number of artists involved, by the percentage of children that have participated or by the number of sessions held. But perhaps a better indicator of results would be the demand for places for children to be able to participate, and if these have been met completely or to what level.

455. Although the indicator in some cases can be precise, as is the case for example of the aspiration of spaces for healthy recreation (build a small plaza, a small sports field, a space for children to view kid's programs, etc.) it is useful to also look at indirect indicators of achievement of our objectives such as the evolution of levels of alcoholism or drug addiction during the execution of the plan.

II. SECOND TASK: PREPARE A SINGLE LIST OF PROJECTS

456. In Chapter VI we saw how each project that the Working Groups came up with was written up in a document and a summary table that, once completed, was to be given to the Planning and Budget Team. These should be used for coming up with the single list of projects, which in turn will be used for coming up with the Development Plan.

457. This list can only be completed once the documentation for the last project has been completed and handed in. However, as the Planning Team receives projects and checks them for errors (and if any are found sends them back to the corresponding Working Groups to be fixed), they can begin preparing the list of projects in order to reduce the time between when the final project is handed in and the Council Plenary is held to discuss the Plan.

458. Moreover, in the communities, it would be worthwhile for the Community Planning Team to be working on the projects that do not require funds or whose financing is linked to the project itself. This is because they represent the basis for coming up with the first list of projects for the first phase of the Immediate Action Plan, which can be approved and initiated even before the Development Plan, the Annual Investment Plan and the Community Budget are approved.

459. The list of projects should contain a table where alongside the name of each project the following information can be found in successive columns. To illustrate this we have taken the example of the small plaza that we looked at in detail in Chapter VI.

1) EXAMPLE OF INFORMATION THAT EACH PROJECT SHOULD CONTAIN

(1) **Name of project: Rehabilitation of a small plaza inside the market.**
(2) **Type of project: Social, public infrastructure.**
(3) **Thematic area: Culture and recreation.**
(4) **Score for the aspiration that it is trying to satisfy: 27 points.**
(5) **Cost: $3605 (not including labor and inputs that have been volunteered for free).**
(6) **Linked financing (if there is any): $3605.**
(7) **Required net financing: $0.**
(8) **Cost of annual maintenance: $300.**
(9) **Forecast income from the project: $0.**
(10) **Net cost of maintenance: $300.**

460. To facilitate future calculations, it is worth adding a column that reflects accumulated net financing for projects from available funds.

461. Similarly, it would be good to create an additional column for observations, to indicate the modifications in the project that might occur, as we will see shortly.

2) HOW DO WE ARRANGE THE PROJECTS IN THE LIST?

462. The list should arrange the projects according to the score obtained by the aspiration that the project corresponds to. When two or more projects correspond to the same aspiration, the order will be determined by the cost: from cheapest to most expensive.

463. The same cost criteria should be applied in cases where the aspirations of different projects obtained the same score.

464. For complex projects that require various phases, each phase should be viewed as a stand-alone project, with a score corresponding to its aspiration.

465. Let's look at the list of projects in the community we have been using as an example.

466. In this scenario, we will collect the first 24 projects, even if there tends to be many more.

467. We have ordered them according to their score, in decreasing order and, where projects have the same score, from cheapest to most expensive.

468. According to what we have said above, the four phases that make up the project to organize sport competitions should be included as stand-alone projects, all with the same score (see Chapter VI).

469. We have also included a project for improving homes that are in a bad state, which is a project with four phases (one each year). Each phase has been included as a distinct project, although with the same score.(See Table 1 in the next page)

Table 1. List of projects in order of score and corresponding

PROJECT	Score	Type of project		Thematic area	Cost	Tied funding	Required funding	Net required funding	Maintenance cost	Expected income	Net maintenance cost
1 Transform landfill site into plaza	51	Infrastructure	Public works	Culture and Recreation	3,605	3,605	0	0.00	300		300
2 Create infants video club	51	Social	Services	Culture and Recreation	100		100	100.00	100		100
3 Artists working with children	39	Social	Services	Culture and Recreation	50		50	150.00	50		50
4 Fix up space for ambulatory	39	Social	Public works	Sanitation	4,000		4,000	4,150.00	150		150
5 Organize night security committee	39	Social	Services	Security	50		50	4,200.00	20		20
6 Improve lighting in the streets	39	Infrastructure	Public works	Security	600		600	4,800.00	100		100
7 Hold sports competition phase 1: create groups of sports promotors	36	Social	Services	Education and Sport	0		0	4,800.00	0		0
8 Hold sports competitions phase 2: Carry out campaign to promote sport	36	Social	Public works	Education and Sport	50		50	4,850.00	0		0
9 Hold sports competition phase 3: Set up school and youth football teams	36	Social	Services	Education and Sport	300		300	5,150.00	60		60
10 Hold sports competitions phase 4: stage competitions	36	Social	Services	Education and Sport	0		0	5,150.00	0		0
11 Recondition football field	36	Infrastructure	Public works	Education and Sport	500		500	5,650.00	150	150	0
12 Improve rubbish collection	35	Infrastructure	Public works	Environment	400		400	6,050.00	50		50
13 Create space for popular music concerts	34	Social	Public works	Culture and Recreation	500		500	6,550.00	0		0
14 Remove illegal waste dump	33	Infrastructure	Public works	Environment	180		180	6,730.00	0		0
15 Put a roof over the bus stop	30	Infrastructure	Public works	Housing and town planning	600		600	7,330.00	0		0
16 Fix up space for public library	29	Social	Public works	Culture and Recreation	1,000		1,000	8,330.00	150		150
17 Improve homes in bad state phase 1	28	Housing	Public works	Housing and town planning	10,000	10,000	0	8,330.00	400	400	0
18 Improve homes in bad state phase 2	28	Housing	Public works	Housing and town planning	10,000	10,000	0	8,330.00	400	400	0
19 Improve homes in bad state phase 3	28	Housing	Public works	Housing and town planning	10,000	10,000	0	8,330.00	400	400	0
20 Improve homes in bad state phase 4	28	Housing	Public works	Housing and town planning	10,000	10,000	0	8,330.00	400	400	0
21 Opening wells and create channels in rural area	28	Infrastructure	Public works	Environment	1,250		1,250	9,580.00	30		30
22 Shed to process tobacco	26	Productive	Public works	Sustainable economy	3,000		3,000	12,580.00	150	150	0
23 Create women's sewing cooperative	24	Productive	Public works	Sustainable economy	4,500	3,000	1,500	14,080.00	0	150	0
24 Fix up social center	23	Social	Public works	Culture and Recreation	900		900	14,980.00	100		100

470. Moreover, let's suppose that the state housing agency has committed itself to financing improvement works once a community has presented its project. This would mean the project would have linked financing available to the value of the forecast costs.

471. Regarding the social enterprise project for a women's sewing cooperative, we have spoken with an NGO that is willing to finance two-thirds of the costs of the project, which means there is linked financing available to cover two-thirds of the total project cost.

472. Finally, let's recall that we will be organizing a collection to cover the cost of improving the plaza, meaning that linked financing will cover the total cost of the project.

473. As such, column 6 will include the cost for each project; the seventh will include the required net funding to come from the overall plan; and column 8, the accumulated required net funding.

474. Regarding maintenance costs, we have anticipated that for the project for dilapidated homes, it will be the beneficiaries who cover the maintenance costs, meaning the net maintenance cost is zero.

475. The same is true for the social enterprise project to build a shed to process tobacco, because the farmers who benefit from the project should assume the maintenance costs.

476. We also expect the maintenance costs for the reconditioned football field can be covered by a small sum paid by spectators who attend games (entry fee). This means that income should cover maintenance costs.

477. All projects must include maintenance costs that correspond to the year they are initiated within their cost. For example, in the case of the artists working with children, a project that costs nothing to initiate, we should include the cost of maintaining the project during the first year as part of the costs of the project.

478. You will see that in the accumulated cost we have not counted the costs covered by linked financing, given that this is supposed to come once the specific project it is linked to has been approved, and will not affect the budgets of the projects that have been presented.

3) PROJECTS FOR THE FIRST PHASE OF THE IMMEDIATE ACTION PLAN

479. In our case study community, we can see that there are very few projects that do not need financing or have linked financing that covers the cost of the project: those that fit within these categories are project 1 (transform landfill site into plaza with tied funding); 7 (create groups of sports promoters); 10 (stage sports competitions) and 17 (first phase of improving dilapidated homes).

480. We could also consider three other projects that are low-cost ($50) to be essentially zero cost projects. These include project 3 (Artists working with children); 5 (Organize night security committee) and 8 (Carry out a campaign for sports).

481. These are projects that can be approved by the Planning Assembly while the other projects are still being drawn up, because their execution will not use up resources from the Development Plan. Moreover, the simple fact of starting them early can generate more enthusiasm by showing residents that "things are happening and not just being talked about."

482. Nevertheless, their inclusion in the first phase of the Development Plan cannot be done in a mechanical manner: given that project 10 requires project 9 to be executed first (set up school and youth football teams), which does have a cost, it should be put aside. The inclusion of project 17 (improve homes) will depend on the time required to come up with a proper technical project and the conditions imposed by the state agency to approve the release of the linked funds.

483. The Community Planning Team should prepare a list with the remaining selected projects that will make up the first phase of the Immediate Action Plan.

Table 2. Projects included in first phase of Immediate Action Plan

	PROJECT	Score	Type of project		Thematic area	Cost	Tied funding	Required funding	Net required funding		Observations
1	Transform landfill site into plaza	51	Infrastructure	Public works	Culture and Recreation	3,605	3,605	0	300		
3	Artists working with children	39	Social	Services	Culture and Recreation	50		50	50		
5	Organize night security committee	39	Social	Services	Security	50		50	20		
7	Hold sports competition phase 1: create groups of sports promotors	36	Social	Services	Education and Sport	0		0	0		
8	Hold sports competitions phase 2: Carry out campaign to promote sport	36	Social	Public works	Education and Sport	50		50	0		

484. The Council should therefore momentarily interrupt its work to discuss and approve this first phase of the Immediate Action Plan and present it to the Community Planning Assembly for ratification.

485. Once approved by the Assembly, the execution of the first phase of the Immediate Action Plan should start without delay. The Council should assign some of its members so that they take the responsibility of the oversight and control of the projects included in the first phase, while the rest of the members are reincorporated into the Mixed Working Groups to continue coming up with the remaining projects.

486. For its part, the Community Planning Team should modify the initial list of projects, putting at the top those included in the first phase of the Immediate Action Plan (while respecting the order according to aspiration score).

487. 52. As a result of these modifications, the final list of projects contained in Table 1 would now look like this: (See Table 3 in the next page)

III. THIRD TASK: CARRY OUT STUDY OF AVAILABLE RESOURCES

1. ESTIMATION OF RESOURCES

488. As we explained in Chapter VII, during the preparatory phase of the planning process the corresponding Technical Planning and Budget Teams should come up with an estimate of the available resources for the community, territorial area or municipality to implement their respective Development Plans. These estimates should be studied by the respective Planning Council and approved by the respective Planning Assembly in order to establish budget priorities.

489. Nevertheless, while the Working Groups are drawing up projects, the corresponding Planning and Budget Team should make an effort to make these estimates and the conditions for obtaining additional resources a reality. Moreover, they should come up with an income calendar that is as precise as possible for each year of the Plan.

Table 3. List of projects taking into consideration first phase of Immediate Action Plan

#	PROJECT	Score	Type of project		Thematic area	Cost	Tied funding	Required funding	Net required funding	Maintenance cost	Expected income	Net maintenance cost	Observations
1	Transform landfill site into plaza	51	Infrastructure	Public works	Culture and Recreation	3.605	3.605	0	0,00	300		300	Phase 1 Immediate Action Plan
3	Artists working with children	39	Social	Services	Culture and Recreation	50		50	50,00	50		50	Phase 1 Immediate Action Plan
5	Organize night security committee	39	Social	Services	Security	50		50	100,00	20		20	Phase 1 Immediate Action Plan
7	Hold sports competition phase 1: create groups of sports promoters	36	Social	Services	Education and Sport	0		0	100,00	0		0	Phase 1 Immediate Action Plan
8	Hold sports competitions phase 2: Carry out campaign to promote sport	36	Social	Public works	Education and Sport	50		50	150,00	0		0	Phase 1 Immediate Action Plan
2	Create infants video club	51	Social	Services	Culture and Recreation	100		100	250,00	100		100	
4	Fix up space for ambulatory	39	Social	Public works	Sanitation	4.000		4.000	4.250,00	150		150	
6	Improve lighting in the streets	39	Infrastructure	Public works	Security	600		600	4.850,00	100		100	
9	Hold sports competition phase 3: Set up school and youth football teams	36	Social	Services	Education and Sport	300		300	5.150,00	60		60	
10	Hold sports competitions phase 4: stage competitions	36	Social	Services	Education and Sport	0		0	5.150,00	0		0	
11	Recondition football field	36	Infrastructure	Public works	Education and Sport	500		500	5.650,00	150	150	0	
12	Improve rubbish collection	35	Infrastructure	Public works	Environment	400		400	6.050,00	50		50	
13	Create space for popular music concerts	34	Social	Public works	Culture and Recreation	500		500	6.550,00	0		0	
14	Remove illegal waste dump	33	Infrastructure	Public works	Environment	180		180	6.730,00	0		0	
15	Put a roof over the bus stop	30	Infrastructure	Public works	Housing and town planning	600		600	7.330,00	0		0	
16	Fix up space for public library	29	Social	Public works	Culture and Recreation	1.000		1.000	8.330,00	150		150	
17	Improve dilapidated homes phase 1	28	Housing	Public works	Housing and town planning	10.000	10.000	0	8.330,00	400	400	0	
18	Improve dilapidated homes phase 2	28	Housing	Public works	Housing and town planning	10.000	10.000	0	0,00	400	400	0	
19	Improve dilapidated homes phase 3	28	Housing	Public works	Housing and town planning	10.000	10.000	0	8.330,00	400	400	0	
20	Improve dilapidated homes phase 4	28	Housing	Public works	Housing and town planning	10.000	10.000	0	8.330,00	400	400	0	
21	Opening wells and create channels in rural area	28	Infrastructure	Public works	Environment	1.250		1.250	9.580,00	30		30	
22	Shed to process tobacco	26	Productive	Public works	Sustainable economy	3.000	3.000	3.000	3.000,00	150	150	0	
23	Create women's sewing cooperative	24	Productive	Public works	Sustainable economy	4.500	3.000	1.500	11.080,00	0	150	0	
24	Fix up social center	23	Social	Public works	Culture and Recreation	900		900	11.980,00	100		100	

490. If possible, we recommend setting up a small group within the team made up of those with the best qualifications – due to experience or training – to focus on studying sources of financing for this and the next task, while the rest of the team is working on the first and second task. The Planning Team as a whole should nevertheless approve any conclusions reached.

491. This is a difficult task that can only be completed once all the projects that the Working Groups come up with and the sources of financing are known.

492. We want to insist on the importance of being as imaginative as possible when it comes to finding resources within the municipality, territorial area or community, and not waiting for resources to come from outside.

1) AVAILABLE FINANCIAL RESOURCES

493. When studying what available resources there are, we need to distinguish between financial resources and other types (volunteer labor, materials, etc.). Of the financial resources that may be available, we need to distinguish between:

a) Own resources

494. In a community this could be from a collection carried out among families or possible income derived from community projects. In the territorial area and particularly at the municipal level, it is common for these resources to come from taxes and fees that the municipality or territorial area collect, in cases where these have been totally or partially decentralized.

b) Resources assigned from outside

495. This refers to funds transferred from higher up entities to finance the Plan. It could be the case that the Mayor's office or the territorial areas have set aside funds to finance small community projects. Or that, while municipal taxes remained centralized for reasons of efficiency and equity, a part of the funds collected are transferred to territorial areas to cover running costs and finance its respective Plan. Similarly, the national state or province may have specific funds set aside for this purpose.

c) Outside resources that are expected to be obtained once the plan is approved

496. The transfer of capital we referred to above can be conditioned, on occasions, on the presentation of the Plan by the community, territorial area or municipality. In this case, it should be included in the same column.

d) Other resources that remain uncertain

497. Finally, there are resources that are under negotiation or depend on finalizing agreements whose results are not yet definitively known. This will often be the case with funds from NGOs or international organizations.

498. We need to establish a certain scale based on the probability of gaining access to these resources: we can almost certainly rely on resources from group a) and b); in terms of group c) the resources are not entirely secure for various reasons – they may not arrive or the amount may differ from what was originally anticipated; for group d) there is no guarantee that the resources will arrive.

499. In the same way, it is important to know the origins of financial resources: if they are funds that originated from the municipality, provincial government, national state, independent agencies, etc., in order to know the level of financial dependency of the Plan on other entitles.

e) Linked and unlinked financial resources

500. Moreover, it is important that within each type of resource we distinguish between those whose availability is linked to a specific project, which in Chapter VI we called linked financing, and those that are not.

501. Why the distinction?

502. Because in the first case, linked financing can only be included as income in the Plan once the project itself has been included. If the project is postponed or we decide to not go ahead with it, we cannot count on these resources.

f) Credit financing

503. If part of the Plan will be financed via loans, then we need to identify the lending agency and the conditions of the loan (timeframe and form of repayment, interest, etc.). In Chapter VI we spoke about this type of financing. Further down, starting at paragraph 527, we will delve deeper into this concept. Here we want to insist on our recommendation that this form of financing only be used when strictly required. We should not forget that asking for a loan implies that a more or less important part of our funds in the following years will have to be directed towards meeting obligations imposed by the loans, such as repayments and interest payments.

2) INCOME CALENDAR

504. Finally, we need to come up with an income calendar that reflects the moments at which each source of financial resources becomes available. We do not need to set exact dates, but we do need to at least define the periods (month, trimester, semester) when we expect to receive the resources and, in any case, the year, in order to be able to know with certainty and precision the available resources for each annual investment plan within the Multi-Year Development Plan.

505. The method for coming up with this calendar will differ according to whether we are dealing with the community's own resources or resources that are transferred from the territorial area, municipality or state. In the first case, we can know with precision the moment the funds become available; in the second case, it will depend on the fiscal and budgetary norms in place in the country. If we are dealing with funds from NGOs or international organizations, this will depend on the norms by which the entity is regulated.

506. All of this might seem extremely complex. In practice, while it may require a serious and detailed study, it does not need to be very complicated, particularly when we consider that, in the case of the community, we are talking about a small amount of funds.

507. In the case of the territorial areas and the municipality, there should be experts within the Planning and Budget Team with experience in this type of task.

3) EXAMPLES OF INCOMES

508. Let's consider for example a small community in which the planning team has concluded that they have access to the following resources:
Own resources: The community has collected $4500 annually from raffles, voluntary donations, contributions from small companies in the community, etc.
Outside resources: The budget forecasts that the municipality will assign $10,000 annually to finance the Annual Community Plan once it is approved.

509. Once the Planning Team receives the documentation for the various projects that the Working Groups have come up with, we find that the following linked financing is available for specific projects:
Community linked financing: $3605 to finance the construction of a plaza via a voluntary collection carried out among neighbors.
Outside linked financing:
State: The State Housing Agency has committed to contributing $10,000 annually to rehabilitate dilapidated homes in the community.
International: The Sustainable Economy Working Group was in contact with an NGO that has committed itself to contributing two-thirds of the cost of a project to create a women's sewing cooperative ($3000 in total).

510. There are no other foreseeable sources of funds. Nevertheless, foreseeing the possibilities of delays in receiving certain funds, the Planning Team has been in touch with a public bank that has agreed to provide them with a loan, if necessary, with a very favorable interest rate.

511. In terms of the income calendar for non-linked financing, the Planning Team believes that community resources will be available from July 1 each year, while municipal resources will become available from January 1, the year after the budget has been approved.

512. The calendar for receiving linked financing will depend on when work begins on the projects the funds are linked to.

513. According to these calculations, the community will have available $14,500 annually to fund its Development Plan, not including any linked financing. However, as we will see below, there are other costs that add up to $2500 a year, meaning that the funds available for the Plan are actually $12,000 a year. This sum could be reduced further if there is an increase in the funds set aside to cover annual maintenance costs.

514. As a consequence, in the first year we will have $12,000 available for the Plan (plus any linked financing) and in the following years, if there is no modification in the amount of funds received, this amount will fall due to the need to cover maintenance costs. In practice, however, this will not be the case: it is normal that in the first year the community will find it hard to identify potential sources of financing, but as they gain experience they will find new sources of financing and make better use of those they already known exist. It is therefore likely that available financing will rise as the Plan progresses.

2. CALCULATE GENERAL AND RUNNING COSTS

515. As not all available resources can be used for the Development Plan, the Planning Team that came up with the forecast income has to also come up with an estimation of what we would call running costs, that is, costs that the community, territorial area or municipality will incur that do not correspond to specific projects.

1) IN THE COMMUNITIES

516. In the communities, we have to subtract what we call **general or running costs** from estimated financial resources, to determine available funds to finance projects.

517. That is why it is important at this stage to make an effort to tighten as much as possible the expenditure line item in order to increase the capacity for investment in the community.

518. Among general costs we can distinguish:

▪ *Operational or functioning costs*

519. **Functioning or operational costs** include: payment of basic services (electricity, water, telephone, sewerage), office materials and equipment, office rent, transport and parking costs and all material and services costs that enable the Working Group to carry out their role.

520. Even though, as we have said before, we believe that the work of the Community Planning Council should be *ad honorem*, it may be the case that in some communities, if they have taken on more complex tasks, it may be necessary to rely on some paid personnel. This cost should be included in this line item.

▪ *Administration costs*

521. Administration costs refer to costs incurred when doing transactions, activities and tasks that are required to achieve certain objectives that do not fall within certain projects. For example, to obtain a large television to install in the community meeting space, or to explain to a state organ why they should finance a larger project. These tasks also involve costs such as, for example,

transport costs to go where is required, or the cost of transporting the television. This is why it is important that the community is able to rely on its own resources.

■ *Service provision*

522. This refers to costs that may be incurred by a community if it has taken on the provision of a certain service (for example, rubbish collection).

523. This would include, for example, the wages for personnel to provide the service.

■ *Maintenance costs*

524. Maintenance costs refers to costs incurred when maintaining a public works or community service, for example, looking after a garden in the plaza, repairing the television used for infant recreation if it breaks down, etc.

■ *Social action costs*

525. As we are trying to build solidarian communities, it is important to promote the creation of a community fund to attend to urgent social needs such as emergencies and health problems that cannot be covered by those affected due to their precarious socio-economic situation.

526. To all these costs – which can be viewed as running costs – we should add, on a needs-be-basis, two types of costs that correspond to capital costs but that are not part of the investment plan:

■ *Financial costs*

527. **Credit** refers to a financial operation in which a person (creditor) lends a set amount of money to another person (debtor), who commits to returning the money over time or by a set deadline, in accordance with the conditions established as part of the loan.

528. **Amortization of capital** refers to the complete or partial repayment of the loan.

529. We also have to consider that when we obtain a loan, together with paying back the money lent, that is, repaying the capital, we have to pay a certain amount of additional money as compensation of being leant the money. This additional sum is called interest.

530. Only the interest should appear in this line item. The **amortization of capital** should go under the following line item: repayment of credit.

■ *Repayment of credit*

531. Refers to the amortizations, anticipated for the period in question, of the capital obtained in the form of a loan.

■ *Fund for unforeseen costs*

532. Depending on the complexity of the community, it would also be useful to reserve a small part of available funds for dealing with potential unforeseen costs.

2) IN TERRITORIAL AREAS AND THE MUNICIPALITY

533. In the territorial areas and the municipality, determining these costs is much more complex because one of government's essential functions is to routinely provide services to citizens, such as education, health care, sanitation, security, etc.

534. It's true that a very significant part of this cost is carried over as a result of decisions made in previous years: the cost of teachers wages will depend on how many are currently employed and will only vary if, depending on the budget priorities expressed by citizens, their wages are modified or the number of teachers rises or falls.

535. In a majority of countries, there are protocols for calculating running costs, which public administrations need to abide by and that generally refer to an economic classification and to an expenditure management body.

536. Despite this, we want to insist on the importance of working not only "on what" is money going to be spent and "why", but above all, on the "for what" of the cost. That is, the objectives or sectors that will be attended to with these costs.

537. For this purpose, it would be useful to come up with a budget outline, described in the previous chapter, in which, after debate in the Assemblies and Councils, budget priorities are set, so that the planning and budget team can set out a forecast of costs.

FOURTH TASK: COME UP WITH A PROPOSED BUDGET

538. Finally, once the list of projects (Task 2) is complete, and once we have a financial forecast that relates directly to the projects we have come up with, including an estimation of income and costs (Task 3), the specialized group of the Planning Team should prepare a proposed budget, that takes into consideration the fact that even the smallest community can have costs outside those directed tied to projects, as we have seen, and which could reduce the community's capacity for investment.

1. THE ECONOMIC STRUCTURE OF THE BUDGET

539. In the majority of countries, legal norms set out what the structure of the budget of a public entity must be like. Community, territorial area and municipal budgets will have to comply with these norms.

540. Nevertheless, for our example of what the structure of a budget might look like, we will take as given that these norms do not exist or at least do not apply to the community or territorial area.

1) INCOME BUDGET

541. In the income budget, it is worth distinguishing between:

a) Fiscal income

542. This is income obtained due to its condition as a public institution from a corresponding entity. That is, its capacity to impose on citizens certain obligatory payments.

543. This includes taxes, both direct and indirect, collected by the entity, fees and other public charges, etc.

544. While in the municipalities this type of income can be the most important source of revenue, in the territorial areas its importance will depend on the level of decentralization of responsibilities in terms of financial matters. It is very likely that communities will not be able to count on this type of income.

b) One's own or private income

545. This refers to income that the entity generates through its own activities in the private sector, without taking into consideration its condition as a public entity: this can come about through voluntary collections, income from raffles, lotteries, etc. or as a result of carrying out certain economic activities and rent derived from properties it owns (rent from properties, rent from farming or forestry concessions, etc.). We could also conveniently disaggregate under here possible financial income from interests from current accounts or community deposits.

546. Unlike the previous case, these costs, that tend to be residual at the municipal level, can be very important in the case of the community, as they are the main source of resources for these, apart from the funds transferred from other institutions (municipal, territorial area, etc.).

c) Transfers and current subsidies

547. This refers to money transferred from other institutions and public or private entities to the community, territorial area or municipality, and which are designated to finance general running costs of the entity.

548. In this line item, it is worth noting the origins of the funds: municipal, state, international, public or private.

d) Sale of public patrimony

549. This is income derived from the sale of public patrimony that belongs to the entity (buildings, land, etc.). It includes the sale of material goods it owns such as vehicles, machines, etc.

e) Transference of capital

550. This refers to the transference of money from other institutions and public or private entities, designated to finance capital investment or cover other capital costs (amortization of loans, for example).

f) Variation in financial assets and liabilities

551. This line item should include, where they exist, the amount of loans or credit to be received during the period.

552. Similarly, where they exist, the repayment of partial amortization of loans to other entities or individuals, including the sale of bonds and public or private shares.

553. This line item should also disaggregate loans according to their origin, differentiating between public entities, private loans (from banks or other entities) and international loans.

2) COSTS AND EXPENDITURE BUDGET

554. The **costs and expenditure budget** refers to the ordered presentation of costs and anticipated investment in the projects that are to be carried out during the year.

555. The economic content of the cost should be classified as follows:

a) Personnel costs

556. This line item should conveniently disaggregate the costs of salaries, social security payments, etc.

b) Purchase of goods and services

557. This includes all running costs in terms of goods and services that are required for the activities of the entity. This includes the purchase of non-inventory goods (office materials, etc.) and payment of services and provision (rent, provision of electricity, water, repairs, etc.)

c) Financial costs

558. The financial costs line item only appears if the entity has financed one of its activities or projects through a loan. This should include the interest paid for the loan.

d) Current transfers

559. This includes regular or recurring costs, that may be conditional or not, such as pensions, periodic social aid or transfers to other entities for the maintenance of regular activities. It is particularly important to disaggregate anticipated social costs.

f) Investment costs

560. This refers to projects the entity hopes to carry out. It is important to group projects by sector.

g) Capital transfers

561. This includes costs involved in payments, conditioned or otherwise, to other entities or individuals, to carry out investments or the amortization of loans.

h) Variations in financial assets and liabilities

562. This line item should reflect the amortization of capital of loans received. The granting of loans to other entities or individuals, or the purchase of bonds and public or private shares should also be included.

i) Fund for unforeseen costs

563. It is worthwhile reserving a percentage of the expenditures budget for covering potential unforeseen costs.

564. The four first line items correspond to what we call the Running Costs Budget. The following three line items form part of the Capital Budget, and the last is a stand-alone line item, but could be included in the latter.

2. EXPENDITURE BUDGET ACCORDING TO OBJECTIVES

565. As we have said before, it is worthwhile disaggregating the expenditures budget according to the objectives sought so that we know where costs in each one of the line items of the economic structure are destined.

566. If we use the budget outline we have previously spoken about, we will have a clear and simple presentation of the "on what" and "for what" for each expenditure made.

1) THE COMMUNITY EXPENDITURE BUDGET

567. However, in small communities, it is possible that we may not even need to come up with this type of instrument, and a more simple expenditure budget, where line items correspond to the types of expenditure we spoke about when looking at resources, will suffice:

568. Line items could be:

a) Operational or functioning costs

569. This should include a disaggregation of operational costs.

b) Administration costs

570. This should include administration costs.

c) Service provision

571. This should reflect costs incurred from service provision. If various services are provided, they should be grouped into the thematic areas the Council has organized, and within each we should disaggregate personnel costs and purchase and services costs.

d) Maintenance costs

572. This should only include costs of maintaining public works that have already been carried out. It is worthwhile disaggregating maintenance costs along the lines of thematic areas.

e) Social action costs

573. The community should decide if this line item should be created and how much is dedicated to it.

f) Financial costs

574. Where they exist

g) Project costs

575. Without a doubt the most important costs are those relating to the projects the community hopes to carry out.

576. Given that at this stage of coming up with a proposed budget we still do not know which projects will be carried out during the year, this line item will represent the difference between total anticipated income and the sum of the remaining costs, the so-called general costs.

577. If certain maximum and minimum limits have been set on investment in certain sectors due to instructions from higher up entities or by agreement of the community, these limits should be reflected here.

h) Loan repayment

578. This line item should indicate the amortization of capital of loans, if any exist.

579. The first six line items correspond to what we have called the Running Costs Budget. The last two form part of the Capital Budget or Investment Budget.

2. OTHER ASPECTS

a) Linked income and expenditure

580. We have said that there is a type of income that is linked to a specific project and that cannot be included in the budget until there is certainty that the project will go ahead within the period covered by the budget. That is why, once established, the Annual Plan will have to modify the proposed Budget, incorporating in the income budget a line item corresponding to linked financing for projects included in the Annual Plan.

b) Budgetary forecasts for subsequent years

581. As the Community Development Plan spans several years, it is necessary to make a forecast of costs that, putting aside projects, the community needs to cover during the subsequent years of the plan. It is also worthwhile anticipated income that is expected to come in during those years, in order to know approximately what the community's capacity to finance projects will be over the duration of the plan.

582. Similarly, in the territorial areas and municipality, we should make a forecast of resources that will be available in the following years to be able to continue financing the Investment Plan.

583. Obviously, there are costs, such as maintenance, that cannot be incorporated until we know which projects will be carried out during the first year.

3) AN EXAMPLE TO EXPLAIN THESE CONCEPTS

584. To explain these concepts, we will look at an example of what an income and expenditure budget for the small community we described above could look like. (See Table 4 next page)

585. In this case, as well as spending on electricity, telephone, water, etc., and a line item of $1200 for social action costs, we have assumed that the Planning Team will set aside $50 to cover any interest on bank loans they may need to take if there are any delays in receiving funds.

586. As we will see, at this state, the proposed budget does not include linked financing. This will only be incorporated once we know the details of the Annual Plan.

587. In terms of estimating the capacity for investment in projects for the following years, the Planning Team in our example believes that general costs, with the exception of maintenance costs, will remain the same. This means that the community's investment capacity will only be

affected by any potential increase in maintenance costs due to the implementation of projects laid out in the plan.

Table 4. Proposed community budget (not including tied funds)

Income budget			14,500
Own income		4,500	
Voluntary collections	*1,500*		
Raffles and lotteries	*2,.000*		
Others	*1,000*		
Transferences and subsidies		10,000	
From the municipality	*10,000*		
Credits and Loans		0	
Expenditure budget			**14,500**
Functioning costs		1,150	
Electricity and water	*300*		
Telephone	*200*		
Office materials	*600*		
Transport and parking	*50*		
Administration costs		100	
Travel costs	*100*		
Financial costs		50	
Interest payments on loan	*50*		
Service provision		0	
Maintenance costs		0	
Social actions costs		1,200	
Expenditure on projects		12,000	
Loan repayments		0	

CHAPTER IX. FORMULATING PLANS I.

GENERAL ASPECTS

588. Once we have come up with the projects and project-ideas[3], and the Planning and Budget Teams have the documentation ready for each level (see Chapter VIII), the respective Planning Council should hold a plenary session to prepare proposals for the Development Plan, the First Annual Plan and the Budget. The community level should also discuss the Immediate Action Plan.

589. We should make sure that it is not only the councilors who participate in the meeting; we should also include members of the Mixed Working Groups that have participated in coming up with the projects (particularly any experts or technicians) and the Planning and Budget Team itself.

590. This plenary session of the Planning Council, which can last up to two days, is the most important moment of the planning process. That is why we recommend that it be open to any interested person to attend. If there is not a large enough meeting space, then efforts should be made to find a way to allow others to follow the debate occurring in the meeting (for example, by broadcasting it on a screen outside).

591. However, to avoid endless discussion and maintain a level of order, we believe that speaking rights should only be given to Council members, a representative of each of the Working Groups and members of the Planning and Budget Team.

592. We should make sure that all councilors receive at least the summary tables of all the projects presented and a list of projects that the Planning and Budgetary Team have come up with, well before the plenary session is held.

593. Furthermore, complete documentation for each project and any documentation the Planning and Budget Team has come up with should be made available for consultation to any interested person. We should also make sure it is accessible on the day of the meeting, in case it needs to be consulted during the debate.

594. We also recommend that the list of projects be compiled on a spreadsheet that can be projected on a large screen so that it can be modified as the meeting progresses, in accordance with the results of the debates, as we will see when we study the distribution of projects for each year.

---

3 Remember that a project-idea is a general outline of a project that includes an estimation of costs, but whose complete technical description has been left aside to be dealt with later due to its complexity and to avoid unnecessary work. From now on, when we talk about projects, we are referring to both projects and project-ideas.

II. WORK PHASES

595. The work of the Planning Council is divided into six phases:
(1) **Review of the proposed Budget.**
(2) **Overall review of the projects that the Working Groups have come up with.**
(3) **Distribution of projects across the different years.**
(4) **Selection of projects to comprise the Immediate Action Plan (at the community level).**
(5) **Formalization of proposed Development Plan, Annual Plan and Budget, by the Planning and Budget Team (and Immediate Action Plan at the community level).**
(6) **Approval of the proposed Development Plan, Annual Plan and Budget, by the Planning and Budget Team (and Immediate Action Plan at the community level).**

596. The results of the work carried out by the Planning Council should be put to a vote of the corresponding Planning Assembly.

597. It is worth noting that these phases correspond to the first year of coming up with a Development Plan. In the following years, it will be simpler, as it will be limited to studying new projects that have been incorporated as a result of new aspirations that have emerged as the Development Plan has been implemented. It will also involve updating the Development Plan and Annual Investment Plan for the second year, including taking note of any new projects, any deviations that have been detected in the projects undertaken so far, and any modifications in the initial income forecasts.

598. In terms of the Budget we recommend that special efforts be made each year to thoroughly revise budget priorities and the objectives sought, taking into consideration an evaluation of the implementation of the previous year's budget. We should not simply repeat the numbers in the previous year's budget line items if experience shows that we need to make changes.

1. REVIEW OF PROPOSED BUDGET

599. Each year's budget will determine the amount to be invested that year. That is why the first task of the Planning Council is to study and approve the proposed provisional yearly Budget that the Planning and Budget Team has come up with, and the budget forecasts for the following years.

600. However, this review should not be limited to discussing investment forecasts. The Council should also take a position on budget priorities on matters of running costs for the proposed budget and determine whether they are in line with what was previously agreed upon (See Chapter VII).

PLANNING COUNCIL

Activity 1. (Plenary) Review proposed budget

601. The Planning and Budget Team presents the proposed Budget they have come up with (see Chapter VIII) and succinctly explains how they have arrived at these figures.

602. A round of discussion is opened up for people to ask for clarifications or to formulate ideas or suggestions for possible modifications.

603. Following debate, the Council approves or modifies the proposed Budget that establishes the capacity to finance projects for the year.

604. The same is done with the budget forecasts for the following year, which could reduce the capacity to finance projects.

2. OVERALL REVIEW OF PROJECTS THAT THE WORKING GROUPS HAVE COME UP WITH

605. Previously, the Planning Council had been divided into Working Groups to elaborate different projects (see Chapter VI) on the basis of the various alternative proposals put forward.

In this phase, the Council as a whole should look at all the projects and review them before moving forward.

Activity 2. (Plenary) Summary presentation of each project

606. Each Working Group should present a summary of its projects to the plenary, in the order in which they appear on the list of projects. They should concisely explain the solutions they have adopted and any calculations.

607. At the end of the presentation of each project, discussion should be opened up to allow people to ask for clarifications or formulate ideas or suggestions for the project.

608. In those communities where the first phase of the Immediate Action Plan is already underway, the projects included in this phase that have already been discussed and approved will appear first.

3. DISTRIBUTION OF PROJECTS OVER THE YEARS

609. When we referred to the First Step of the planning process in Volume I – coming up with desired changes – we recommended letting the imagination run wild and thinking about the society we want to live in[4]. It was on the basis of this that we suggested coming up with an initial list of aspirations. We think that it is important that, at this moment in the process, we do not limit ourselves solely to those projects that seem most viable.

610. But reality also tells us that resources are always limited, and given that we cannot do everything at once, we need to establish an order in which we will try to make these projects a reality.

611. This moment, when we are establishing a timeline for carrying out projects, is the most important plenary session. The debate therefore has to be open, to collect ideas and suggestions from those present, and structured, to avoid endless discussions, interruptions and repetition.

Activity 3. (Plenary) Distribution of available funds over the different years

612. With the list of projects that the Planning and Budget Team has come up with, ordered according to the score of the corresponding aspiration in descending order[5], and knowing what funds are available (proposed Budget) for each year of the Development Plan, we can begin to assign projects to the different years covered by the plan. We should start with those that correspond to the first year, until there are no more funds available for that year, and then move on to the following year.

---

4. See Volume I, paragraphs 59 and 277-284.

5. For those communities that agreed to carry out the first phase of their Immediate Action Plan, those projects included in the plan and that also need to be included in the first Annual Investment Plan, should be listed first.

613. Logically, in the case of projects that contain multiple phases, each phase will have to be distributed across different years.

614. It is also possible that we may come across very complex and expensive projects that might use up a disproportionate amount of the resources available for that year. In this case, we should consult with the team that came up with the project to see if the project can be broken down into multiple phases that can be executed over various years. Breaking down an expensive project like this can free up resources to carry out a number of other smaller projects during that same year.

615. It is even possible to include some projects that will not be finished within the timeframe of the Plan. In these cases, they will have to be included and completed in the following Development Plan; otherwise more funds will need to be found from elsewhere.

616. An easy way to carry out these calculations is to indicate the funds available for the first year at the top of the column corresponding to this period. As projects are incorporated, the accumulated funds that each project represents can be indicated in this column (see Table 1, column: "Necessary accumulated funds").

617. We should recall that financing linked to a specific project will not be incorporated in the table as available financing, nor should it be considered when calculating the accumulated cost of projects.

618. The last project to be included in the first year will be one whose costs are roughly equal to the remaining funds left for the year.

619. It might be the case that, even though there are funds to finance another project, the cost of the following project on the list surpasses the available funds. If this occurs, the project should be substituted for a project further down the list that can be financed with what funds are left. The more expensive project would then be held over to the next year.

620. We should recall that in our case study of a community, the study carried out by the Planning Team (see Chapter VIII, paragraph 513 and Table 4) found that the community could designate $12,000 to the first year of the Development Plan (not including linked financing for certain projects). However, over the following years, part of this money would have to be spent on maintenance costs for projects already undertaken, meaning that the amount for investment in new projects will fall unless new financing sources are found.

621. To make it easier, we will suppose in our example that no new financing sources will be found (even though the opposite is usually the case). As such, we will have $12,000 available in the first year (plus linked financing); in the following years this amount will fall due to the need to cover new maintenance costs.

622. As the community we are using as an example has already approved and begun undertaking projects included in the first phase of the Immediate Action Plan, these projects will go first on the list because, logically, they should be included in the first year of the Plan.

623. As we will see in Table 1, the project to improve dilapidated homes has been broken down into different phases and spread out over the four years. Similarly, the cost of project 22 (Shed to process tobacco) has an investment cost ($3000) that exceeds the amount of funds available that far down the list, meaning that the following two projects (23 and 24), which require much less funds, have been bumped up.

624. In the table, the anticipated investment for the first year is $11,980, while available financing total $12,000 for the year. These means that we need to come up with a very cheap project to make use of the remaining $20. If this is not possible, we can leave this sum as a reserve for any

unforeseen costs or use it to improve some of the approved projects. In any case, it is important to never surpass the total available funds[6].

625. In this way, we have distributed all of our projects across the four years of the plan.

626. Table 1 outlines the distribution per year of the list of projects:(See Table 1 next page)

PLANNING COUNCIL

Activity 4. (Plenary) Review distribution per year taking into consideration sector-based priorities

627. It is important to note that although this distribution of projects may appear simple, it can be modified if the Council deems it necessary.

628. First, it is highly likely, as we indicated in Chapter VII, that certain restrictions[7] or "priority sectors" will have been approved at the start of the process in terms of the amount of money that should be set aside for particular projects (either a limit that should not be surpassed or a minimum set percentage of the overall annual budget that has to be met).

629. This might mean that, in order to favor certain areas that are considered of strategic interest, a set amount of money is set aside for it, for example, 30% of available funds for social enterprise projects while social projects should not use up more than 40% of available funds.

630. In this case, when we get down the list to a social project whose cost would surpass the limit fixed for such projects, we would have to shift it and any similar project after it to the following year in order to make way for other types of projects.

631. Similarly, if by the time we get to the end of the list of projects for the year we notice that we have not reached our 30% target for social enterprise projects, we will have to shift some projects that obtained a higher score to the following year in order to make way for this type of project.

632. Using our example, we will suppose that there is a general agreement that at least 30% of available funds should go to social enterprise projects. Given that in our example, there is only one social enterprise project in the first year (Create women's sewing cooperative), whose cost is $1500 and represents 12.5% of available funds, we will need to bring forward the next social enterprise project. This means that other projects with a higher score will have to be shifted to the following year. In our example, projects 16 (Fix up space for public library), with an anticipated investment of $1000; 21 (Open wells and create canals in rural area), with a forecast investment of $1250, and 24 (Fix up social center), with an anticipated investment of $900, will have to be shifted to the second year to leave space for the construction of a shed to process tobacco, with an anticipated investment of $3000, during the first year. By doing this, the sum of both social enterprise projects for the year ($4500) will comply with the requisite of setting aside more than 30% of available funds for such projects ($4500 over $12,000 represents 37.5%)

---

6. We could however include projects whose financing is not secure because they are dependent on receiving additional financing. We should make it clear that the go ahead for these projects is conditioned on receiving this financing.

7 Alternatively, it is possible that these restrictions are the results of guidelines or instructions coming from higher entities.

Table 1. Distribution per year of projects

#	PROJECT	Score	Type of project		Thematic area	Cost	Tied funding	Required funding	Net required funding	Maintenance cost	Expected income	Net maintenance cost	Observations
	Funds available for 1st year								**12.000**	**1.660**	**550**	**1.110**	
1	Transform landfill site into plaza	51	Infrastructure	Public works	Culture and Recreation	3.605	3.605	0	0,00	300		300	Phase 1 Immediate Action Plan
3	Artists working with children	39	Social	Services	Culture and Recreation	50		50	50,00	50		50	Phase 1 Immediate Action Plan
5	Organize night security committee	39	Social	Services	Security	50		50	100,00	20		20	Phase 1 Immediate Action Plan
7	Hold sports competition phase 1: create groups of sports promoters	36	Social	Services	Education and Sport	0		0	100,00	0		0	Phase 1 Immediate Action Plan
8	Hold sports competitions phase 2: Carry out campaign to promote sport	36	Social	Public works	Education and Sport	50		50	150,00	0		0	Phase 1 Immediate Action Plan
2	Create infants video club	51	Social	Services	Culture and Recreation	100		100	250,00	100		100	
4	Fix up space for ambulatory	39	Social	Public works	Sanitation	4.000		4.000	4.250,00	150		150	
6	Improve lighting in the streets	39	Infrastructure	Public works	Security	600		600	4.850,00	100		100	
9	Hold sports competition phase 3: Set up school and youth football teams	36	Social	Services	Education and Sport	300		300	5.150,00	60		60	
10	Hold sports competitions phase 4: stage competitions	36	Social	Services	Education and Sport	0		0	5.150,00	0		0	
11	Recondition football field	36	Infrastructure	Public works	Education and Sport	500		500	5.650,00	150	150	0	
12	Improve rubbish collection	35	Infrastructure	Public works	Environment	400		400	6.050,00	50		50	
13	Create space for popular music concerts	34	Social	Public works	Culture and Recreation	500		500	6.550,00	0		0	
14	Remove illegal waste dump	33	Infrastructure	Public works	Environment	180		180	6.730,00	0		0	
15	Put a roof over the bus stop	30	Infrastructure	Public works	Housing and town planning	600		600	7.330,00	0		0	
16	Fix up space for public library	29	Social	Public works	Culture and Recreation	1.000		1.000	8.330,00	150		150	
17	Improve dilapidated homes phase 1	28	Housing	Public works	Housing and town planning	10.000	10.000	0	8.330,00	400	400	0	
21	Opening wells and create channels in rural area	28	Infrastructure	Public works	Environment	1.250		1.250	9.580,00	30		30	
23	Create women's sewing cooperative	24	Productive	Public works	Sustainable economy	4.500	3.000	1.500	11.080,00	0		0	
24	Fix up social center	23	Social	Public works	Culture and Recreation	900		900	11.980,00	100		100	
	Funds available for 2nd year								**10.890**				
18	Improve dilapidated homes phase 2	28	Housing	Public works	Housing and town planning	10.000	10.000	0	0,00	400	400	0	
22	Shed to process tobacco	26	Productive	Public works	Sustainable economy	3.000		3.000	3.000,00	150	150	0	
	Funds available for 3nd year								**10.890**				
19	Improve dilapidated homes phase 3	28	Housing	Public works	Housing and town planning	10.000	10.000	0	8.330,00	400	400	0	
	Funds available for 4th year								**10.890**				
20	Improve dilapidated homes phase 4	28	Housing	Public works	Housing and town planning	10.000	10.000	0	8.330,00	400	400	0	

633. A similar process will have to be undertaken if certain guidelines for spending exist for projects related to Health, Education, Communication, etc.

634. Table 2 shows what the new distribution of projects per year will look like following these modifications.

635. As you can see, when we modify the projects included in the first year, we also modify the amount of funds available for the second year, as total anticipated maintenance costs drop.

PLANNING COUNCIL

Activity 5. (Plenary) Review distribution taking into consideration if certain projects are preconditioned on the implementation of others

636. It may also be the case that a project has as a precondition the implementation of another one (key project). In this case, the key project will have to be brought forward, independent of the score it obtained, to ensure that the other project can be carried out.

637. In our example, we can see that, due to its high cost, the reconditioning of the football field was placed after the four phases of the complex project of staging sports competitions. However, in order to carry out phase four (stage sports competitions), we need the football field to be reconditioned.

638. As such, we should shift this project (N° 11) to before the last phase of the project to organize sports competitions (N° 10), because the former is a precondition for the latter.

639. In this case, the change will only affect the order of priorities, but not our investment capacity for the first year, meaning that the distribution per year of projects does not change. If bringing forward a project that is a requisite for others had taken us over our investment capacity for the year, we would have to shift some projects with higher scores to the following year, as we did above, to avoid going beyond our investment capacity.

640. The table for distribution per year will now look like this: (See Tables 2 and 3 next pages)

PLANNING COUNCIL

Activity 6. (Plenary) Review distribution to attend to emergencies and come up with definitive list

641. After all these modifications, the list should undergo a final review. As the score given to each aspiration is the result of evaluating different criteria (urgency, population affected, impact on certain sectors, etc.), it is possible that some aspirations, despite being quite urgent, may obtain a lower score than other much less urgent ones, perhaps because the number of people affected is very small.

642. For this reason, the plenary should look at the urgency of the projects that have been pushed back to later years (or left out of the Development Plan due to lack of funds) and see if a delay in any off these projects could have grave consequences, even if they only benefit a small sector.

643. If this is the case, the Planning Council should look at ways to bring these projects forward, even if it means delaying others with a higher score but that are less urgent.

644. In our example, the doctor from the health clinic has noted that although the drinking water well in the rural area will only affect a small number of families, the situation is very serious and there is a risk of a pandemic among children, meaning urgent action has to be taken.

Table 2. Distribution per year of projects (taking restrictions into consideration)

PROJECT	Score	Type of project		Thematic area	Cost	Tied funding	Required funding	Net required funding	Maintenance cost	Expected income	Net maintenance cost	Observations
Funds available for 1st year								**12.000**	**1.660**	**550**	**1.110**	
1 Transform landfill site into plaza	51	Infrastructure	Public works	Culture and Recreation	3.605	3.605	0	0,00	300		300	Phase 1 Immediate Action Plan
3 Artists working with children	39	Social	Services	Culture and Recreation	50		50	50,00	50		50	Phase 1 Immediate Action Plan
5 Organize night security committee	39	Social	Services	Security	50		50	100,00	20		20	Phase 1 Immediate Action Plan
7 Hold sports competition phase 1: create groups of sports promoters	36	Social	Services	Education and Sport	0		0	100,00	0		0	Phase 1 Immediate Action Plan
8 Hold sports competitions phase 2: Carry out campaign to promote sport	36	Social	Public works	Education and Sport	50		50	150,00	0		0	Phase 1 Immediate Action Plan
2 Create infants video club	51	Social	Services	Culture and Recreation	100		100	250,00	100		100	
4 Fix up space for ambulatory	39	Social	Public works	Sanitation	4.000		4.000	4.250,00	150		150	
6 Improve lighting in the streets	39	Infrastructure	Public works	Security	600		600	4.850,00	100		100	
9 Hold sports competition phase 3: Set up school and youth football teams	36	Social	Services	Education and Sport	300		300	5.150,00	60		60	
10 Hold sports competitions phase 4: stage competitions	36	Social	Services	Education and Sport	0		0	5.150,00	0		0	
11 Recondition football field	36	Infrastructure	Public works	Education and Sport	500		500	5.650,00	150	150	0	
12 Improve rubbish collection	35	Infrastructure	Public works	Environment	400		400	6.050,00	50		50	
13 Create space for popular music concerts	34	Social	Public works	Culture and Recreation	500		500	6.550,00	0		0	
14 Remove illegal waste dump	33	Infrastructure	Public works	Environment	180		180	6.730,00	0		0	
15 Put a roof over the bus stop	30	Infrastructure	Public works	Housing and town planning	600		600	7.330,00	0		0	
17 Improve dilapidated homes phase 1	28	Housing	Public works	Housing and town planning	10.000	10.000	0	7.330,00	400	400	0	
22 Shed to process tobacco	26	Productive	Public works	Sustainable economy	3.000		3.000	10.330,00	0		0	Sector-based priority
23 Create women's sewing cooperative	24	Productive	Public works	Sustainable economy	4.500	3.000	1.500	11.830,00	0		0	
Funds available for 2nd year								**11.170**				
16 Fix up space for public library	29	Social	Public works	Culture and Recreation	1.000		1.000	1.000,00	150		150	
18 Improve dilapidated homes phase 2	28	Housing	Public works	Housing and town planning	10.000	10.000	0	1.000,00	400	400	0	
21 Opening wells and create channels in rural area	28	Infrastructure	Public works	Environment	1.250		1.250	2.250,00	30		30	
24 Fix up social center	23	Social	Public works	Culture and Recreation	900		900	3.150,00	100		100	
Funds available for 3rd year								**10.890**				
19 Improve dilapidated homes phase 3	28	Housing	Public works	Housing and town planning	10.000	10.000	0	1.000,00	400	400	0	
Funds available for 4th year								**10.890**				
20 Improve dilapidated homes phase 4	28	Housing	Public works	Housing and town planning	10.000	10.000	0	1.000,00	400	400	0	

Table 3. Distribution per year of projects (taking into consideration limitations and preconditions)

#	PROJECT	Score	Type of project		Thematic area	Cost	Tied funding	Required funding	Net required funding	Maintenance cost	Expected income	Net maintenance cost	Observations
	Funds available for 1st year								**12.000**	**1.660**	**550**	**1.110**	
1	Transform landfill site into plaza	51	Infrastructure	Public works	Culture and Recreation	3.605	3.605	0	0,00	300		300	Phase 1 Immediate Action Plan
3	Artists working with children	39	Social	Services	Culture and Recreation	50		50	50,00	50		50	Phase 1 Immediate Action Plan
5	Organize night security committee	39	Social	Services	Security	50		50	100,00	20		20	Phase 1 Immediate Action Plan
7	Hold sports competition phase 1: create groups of sports promoters	36	Social	Services	Education and Sport	0		0	100,00	0		0	Phase 1 Immediate Action Plan
8	Hold sports competitions phase 2: Carry out campaign to promote sport	36	Social	Public works	Education and Sport	50		50	150,00	0		0	Phase 1 Immediate Action Plan
2	Create infants video club	51	Social	Services	Culture and Recreation	100		100	250,00	100		100	
4	Fix up space for ambulatory	39	Social	Public works	Sanitation	4.000		4.000	4.250,00	150		150	
6	Improve lighting in the streets	39	Infrastructure	Public works	Security	600		600	4.850,00	100		100	
9	Hold sports competition phase 3: Set up school and youth football teams	36	Social	Services	Education and Sport	300		300	5.150,00	60		60	
11	Recondition football field	36	Infrastructure	Public works	Education and Sport	500		500	5.650,00	150	150	0	Prerequisite for 10
10	Hold sports competitions phase 4: stage competitions	36	Social	Services	Education and Sport	0		0	5.650,00	0		0	
12	Improve rubbish collection	35	Infrastructure	Public works	Environment	400		400	6.050,00	50		50	
13	Create space for popular music concerts	34	Social	Public works	Culture and Recreation	500		500	6.550,00	0		0	
14	Remove illegal waste dump	33	Infrastructure	Public works	Environment	180		180	6.730,00	0		0	
15	Put a roof over the bus stop	30	Infrastructure	Public works	Housing and town planning	600		600	7.330,00	0		0	
17	Improve homes in bad state phase 1	28	Housing	Public works	Housing and town planning	10.000	10.000	0	7.330,00	400	400	0	
22	Shed to process tobacco	26	Productive	Public works	Sustainable economy	3.000		3.000	10.330,00	150	150	0	Sector-based priority
23	Create women's sewing cooperative	24	Productive	Public works	Sustainable economy	4.500	3.000	1.500	11.830,00	0		0	
	Funds available for 2nd year								**11.170**				
16	Fix up space for public library	29	Social	Public works	Culture and Recreation	1.000		1.000	1.000,00	150		150	
18	Improve homes in bad state phase 2	28	Housing	Public works	Housing and town planning	10.000	10.000	0	1.000,00	400	400	0	
21	Opening wells and create channels in rural area	28	Infrastructure	Public works	Environment	1.250		1.250	2.250,00	30		30	
24	Fix up social center	23	Social	Public works	Culture and Recreation	900		900	3.150,00	100		100	
	Funds available for 3rd year								**10.890**				
19	Improve homes in bad state phase 3	28	Housing	Public works	Housing and town planning	10.000	10.000	0	1.000,00	400	400	0	
	Funds available for 4th year								**10.890**				
20	Improve homes in bad state phase 4	28	Housing	Public works	Housing and town planning	10.000	10.000	0	1.000,00	400	400	0	

645. Following a debate, the Planning Council concludes that, while the beneficiaries may be few (hence the low score), the criterion of solidarity should take priority. Therefore the Council agrees to give maximum priority to the well.

646. This would require another modification to the distribution per year, pushing back another two projects to the second year: project 13 (Create space for concerts for popular music) and project 15 (Put a roofed shelter over the bus stop).

647. In the end, the distribution per year of projects will look like Table 4.(See next page)

648. It is worthwhile marking, as we have, the projects whose order has been modified and indicating in the observations column the reason why.

649. This system for distributing different projects across the years of the Development Plan can be very useful when working at the level of communities and even territorial areas. But the debate cannot be limited to analyzing a list of projects when we are dealing with Plans on a larger scale (municipality, regions, states or nation), where we are including as objectives the realization of significant socio-economic transformations. It has to take into consideration other factors that the technical teams should submit for the consideration of the Planning Council during the debate.

650. If the municipality has contemplated undertaking various big impact social enterprise projects, it would be worth considering not only if there are prerequisite projects that need to be undertaken prior to completion, but also if undertaking these projects requires carrying out other projects that were not initially contemplated (for example, improving the network for agrarian product conservation for the agro-food industry) and the possible impact on other sectors (impact on increased traffic along existing roadways as a result of the creation of an industry.)

651. Furthermore, in these cases, the description of the dream in the socio-economic sphere should be made tangible in the form of quantifiable structural objectives that allow us to determine the overall impact of the plan on the existing social enterprise structure.

652. We are clearly dealing with tasks that go beyond the objective of this book and these should be taken up by planning experts, always respecting the principle of transparency, the forms of popular representation and ensuring that citizens in general can clearly see the real impact of the objectives being sought.

4. SELECTION OF PROJECTS THAT MAKE UP THE IMMEDIATE ACTION PLAN (AT THE COMMUNITY LEVEL).

653. In Chapter IV of Volume I, we noted that in the case of communities, we need to come up with an Immediate Action Plan comprised of projects from the Annual Plan that do not require external funding. In this way, as soon as the plan is approved, these projects can begin to be implemented immediately, as the community has all the resources they need for the job.

654. In Chapter VIII of the current volume we explained the usefulness of having a first phase of the Immediate Action Plan, including those community projects that can be resolved with the resources of local neighbors or those that can be obtained through donations or collections linked to specific projects; that is, projects whose implementation does not have an impact on the resources available for the overall community Development Plan. These projects could even be initiated before coming up with and approving the Immediate Action Plan itself.

655. Once the definitive list of projects has been drawn up, the plenary should select which ones to include in the Immediate Action Plan out of the projects in the Annual Investment Plan.

Table 4. Distribution per year of projects (definitive)

PROJECT	Score	Type of project		Thematic area	Cost	Tied funding	Required funding	Net required funding	Maintenance cost	Expected income	Net maintenance cost	Observations
Funds available for 1st year								**12.000**	**1.660**	**550**	**1.110**	
1 Transform landfill site into plaza	51	Infrastructure	Public works	Culture and Recreation	3.605	3.605	0	0,00	300		300	Phase 1 Immediate Action Plan
3 Artists working with children	39	Social	Services	Culture and Recreation	50		50	50,00	50		50	Phase 1 Immediate Action Plan
5 Organize night security committee	39	Social	Services	Security	50		50	100,00	20		20	Phase 1 Immediate Action Plan
7 Hold sports competition phase 1: create groups of sports promoters	36	Social	Services	Education and Sport	0		0	100,00	0		0	Phase 1 Immediate Action Plan
8 Hold sports competitions phase 2: Carry out campaign to promote Sport	36	Social	Public works	Education and Sport	50		50	150,00	0		0	Phase 1 Immediate Action Plan
2 Create infants video club	51	Social	Services	Culture and Recreation	100		100	250,00	100		100	
4 Fix up space for ambulatory	39	Social	Public works	Sanitation	4.000		4.000	4.250,00	150		150	
6 Improve lighting in the streets	39	Infrastructure	Public works	Security	600		600	4.850,00	100		100	
9 Hold sports competition phase 3: Set up school and youth football teams	36	Social	Services	Education and Sport	300		300	5.150,00	60		60	
11 Recondition football field	36	Infrastructure	Public works	Education and Sport	500		500	5.650,00	150	150	0	Prerequisite for 10
10 Hold sports competitions phase 4: stage competitions	36	Social	Services	Education and Sport	0		0	5.650,00	0		0	
12 Improve rubbish collection	35	Infrastructure	Public works	Environment	400		400	6.050,00	50		50	
14 Remove illegal waste dump	33	Infrastructure	Public works	Environment	180		180	6.230,00	0		0	
17 Improve homes in bad state phase 1	28	Housing	Public works	Housing and town planning	10.000	10.000	0	6.230,00	400	400	0	
21 Opening wells and create channels in rural area	28	Infrastructure	Public works	Environment	1.250		1.250	7.480,00	30		30	Urgent solidarity
22 Shed to process tobacco	26	Productive	Public works	Sustainable economy	3.000		3.000	10.480,00	150	150	0	Secot-based priority
23 Create women's sewing cooperative	24	Productive	Public works	Sustainable economy	4.500	3.000	1.500	11.980,00	0	150	0	
Funds available for 2nd year								**11.170**				
13 Create space for popular music concerts	34	Social	Public works	Culture and Recreation	500		500	500,00	0		0	
15 Put a roof over the bus stop	30	Infrastructure	Public works	Housing and town planning	600		600	1.100,00	0		0	
16 Fix up space for public library	29	Social	Public works	Culture and Recreation	1.000		1.000	2.100,00	150		150	
18 Improve homes in bad state phase 2	28	Housing	Public works	Housing and town planning	10.000	10.000	0	2.100,00	400	400	0	
24 Fix up social center	23	Social	Public works	Culture and Recreation	900		900	3.000,00	100		100	
Funds available for 3rd year								**10.890**				
19 Improve homes in bad state phase 3	28	Housing	Public works	Housing and town planning	10.000	10.000	0	2.100,00	400	400	0	
Funds available for 4th year								**10.890**				
20 Improve homes in bad state phase 4	28	Housing	Public works	Housing and town planning	10.000	10.000	0	2.100,00	400	400	0	

Activity 7. (Plenary) Selection of projects that will make up the Immediate Action Plan

656. Knowing what resources the community can count on (financial and other types), we can begin selecting projects according to the order established in the Annual Plan, where the first ones in the list are the projects included in the first phase of the Immediate Action Plan. We should analyze what projects can be executed just with these resources. If a project surpasses the available financial capacity, we should jump ahead to the next one.

657. This order of inclusion does not necessarily determine the order of implementation. At this point in the process, it is preferable to start with the simplest projects that can be most quickly carried out, as a way of strengthening the confidence of the community in its capacity to confront numerous problems with its own means.

658. In our example, we know that the community has an initial amount of $2000 that could be used to finance the Immediate Action Plan.

659. Therefore, going through the list that corresponds to the first year of the plan, we can make the following estimations:

660. The first five projects are the ones we have already put at the top of the list for the Annual Plan and that make up the first phase of the Immediate Action Plan.

661. Attending to the urgency of project 21 (open wells and canals), which was discussed when approving the Annual Plan, means it should also be included, even though it will use up more than half of the available funds.

662. Once project 2 (Create a children's infant video club), which is seventh on the list, is included we can see that the necessary accumulated funds already totals $1500, meaning we will have to skip the next two projects (4 and 6) because their costs ($4000 and $600) surpass the available funds ($500). This means we get to project 9 (Set up football teams) whose cost ($300) will leave us with $200 to finance another project. Looking at the following projects we can see that 10 (Stage sporting competitions) has no cost and 14 (Remove illegal landfill), whose cost is $180, both total less than the $200 remaining.

663. Table 5 (See next page) shows the selection of projects for the Immediate Action Plan (in grey)

664. It turns out that projects 7, 8, 9 and 10, which have been included in the Immediate Action Plan correspond to the phases of the project to organize sports competitions, which in turn are subordinated to the reconditioning of the football field (project 11), which has not been included. This means that projects 7, 8 and 9 will be useless if project 11 is not completed first.

665. Given this, the Plenary should debate what the best solution is: it could choose to not remove the illegal waste dump and reorder the projects involved in organizing sports competitions to delay the purchase of equipment for the different teams (jerseys, shorts, balls, etc.) which costs $300 and is part of phase 3 (Set up school and youth teams). In this scenario, the competitions would have to start with provisional equipment supplied by the players until municipal funds arrived. This would also mean that the football field could be reconditioned with the $500 that is still available after the creation of an infants video club.

666. But it could also choose to not hold the sports competitions and instead include improvements to rubbish collection ($400) within the Immediate Action Plan, and even seek out additional funds (just $80 more) to remove the illegal waste dump, which costs $180, thereby solving two environmental problems.

Table 5. Immediate Action Plan (studied projects)

PROJECT	Score	Type of project		Thematic area	Cost	Tied funding	Required funding	Net required funding	Maintenance cost	Expected income	Net maintenance cost
Funds available for 1st year								2,000	1,560	700	860
1 Transform landfill site into plaza	51	Infrastructure	Public works	Culture and Recreation	3,605	3,605	0	0	300		300
3 Artists working with children	39	Social	Servicios	Culture and Recreation	50		50	50	50		50
5 Organize night security committee	39	Social	Servicios	Security	50		50	100	20		20
7 Hold sports competition phase 1: create groups of sports promoters	36	Social	Servicios	Education and Sport	0		0	100	0		0
8 Hold sports competitions phase 2: Carry out campaign to promote sport	36	Social	Public works	Education and Sport	50		50	150	0		0
21 Opening wells and create canals in rural area	28	Infrastructure	Public works	Environment	1,250		1,250	1,400	30		30
2 Create infants video club	51	Social	Service	Culture and Recreation	100		100	1,500	100		100
9 Hold sports competition phase 3: Set up school and youth football teams	36	Social	Service	Education and Sport	300		300	1,800	60		60
10 Hold sports competitions phase 4: stage competitions	36	Social	Servicios	Education and Sport	0		0	7,080	0		0
14 Remove illegal waste dump	33	Infrastructure	Public works	Environment	180		180	1,980	0		0
4 Fix up space for ambulatory	39	Social	Public works	Sanitation	4,000		4,000	5,980	150		150
6 Improve lighting in the streets	39	Infrastructure	Public works	Security	600		600	6,580	100		100
11 Recondition football field	36	Infrastructure	Public works	Education and Sport	500		500	7,080	150	150	0
12 Improve rubbish collection	35	Infrastructure	Public works	Environment	400		400	7,480	50		50
17 Improve dilapidated homes phase 1	28	Housing	Public works	Housing and town planning	10,000	10,000	0	7,480	400	400	0
22 Shed to process tobacco	26	Productive	Public works	Sustainable economy	3,000		3,000	10,480	150	150	0
23 Create women's sewing cooperative	24	Productive	Public works	Sustainable economy	4,500	3,000	1,500	11,980	0		0

667. As we have previously noted, even though the selection of projects for the Immediate Action Plan has as its starting point a set of objective criteria, this cannot be seen as a purely mechanical process. The Council must always debate and take into consideration other factors when choosing projects to include.

668. Let us suppose that in our example, the Plenary decides to prioritize sports competitions, while delaying the purchase of equipment for players until the municipal funds arrive (project 9). In this case, the Immediate Action Plan would look like this:

Table 6: Immediate Action Plan (Final)

PROJECT	Score	Type of project		Thematic area	Cost	Tied funding	Required funding	Net required funding	Maintenance cost	Expected income	Net maintenance cost	Observations
First phase								2,000	710	150	560	
1 Transform landfill site into plaza	51	Infrastructure	Public works	Culture and Recreation	3,605	3,605	0	0	300		300	1st phase Immediate Action Plan
3 Artists working with children	39	Social	Services	Culture and Recreation	50		50	50	50		50	1st phase Immediate Action Plan
5 Organize night security committee	39	Social	Services	Security	50		50	100	20		20	1st phase Immediate Action Plan
7 Hold sports competition phase 1: create groups of sports promoters	36	Social	Services	Education and Sport	0		0	100	0		0	1st phase Immediate Action Plan
8 Hold sports competitions phase 2: Carry out campaign to promote sport	36	Social	Public works	Education and Sport	50		50	150	0		0	1st phase Immediate Action Plan
Second phase												
21 Opening wells and create canals in rural area	28	Infrastructure	Public works	Environment	1,250		1,250	1,400	30		30	Urgent solidarity
2 Create infants video club	51	Social	Services	Culture and Recreation	100		100	1,500	100		100	
9 Hold sports competition phase 3: Set up school and youth football teams	36	Social	Services	Education and Sport	300		300	1,500	60		60	See note 1
11 Recondition football field	36	Infrastructure	Public works	Education and Sport	500		500	2,000	150	150	0	Prerequisite for 10
10 Hold sports competitions phase 4: stage competitions	36	Social	Services	Education and Sport	0		0	2,000	0		0	

Note 1: The necessary financing for this project is dependent on receiving municipal funds

5. FORMALIZING THE DIFFERENT PLANS AND BUDGETS AT EACH LEVEL

669. Once we have come up with the definitive list of projects distributed by year and, where appropriate, the Immediate Action Plan, the Plenary should go into recess to allow time for the

Planning Team to come up with formal documents that summarize the Development Plan, the Annual Investment Plan, and the Budget.

PLANNING AND BUDGET TEAM

Activity 8. Formalizing the Plan documents

670. We need to formalize the results of the previous debates into a series of documents. These documents include:

(1) Multi-year Development Plan
(2) Annual Investment Plan
(3) Annual Budget
(4) Immediate Action Plan (at the community level)

(1) MULTI-YEAR DEVELOPMENT PLAN

671. At each level, the Development Plan should incorporate the following documents:
(a) A summary document, as outlined in Chapter VIII which includes a diagnosis of the community, territorial area or municipalitiy, and its aspirations.
(b) The projects included in the Plan, grouped by year and by area and thematic sub-area, with the total costs and a brief explanation of the process followed to come up with these results.
(c) Anticipated financing for the plan.
(d) Any other complementary measures that will be adopted to achieve the objectives set out.
(e) A table with the objectives sought and the expected effects that will be achieved as a result of implementing the plan

672. Annexed to the Development Plan should be the summary-tables for all the projects included within it.

673. Table 7 is an example of how we should synthesize the data from the projects included in the Development Plan (here we are only including data for those we have worked on so far; we would need to also include all the other projects).

674. Table 8 provides an example of a financing plan. (See tables 7 and 8 in next page)

675. As you can see in the line item for non-linked own resources, each year we have subtracted functioning costs and other maintenance costs for projects completed in previous years from the available resources. As such, the sum of available resources decreases as more projects are completed and maintenance costs rise.

(2) ANNUAL INVESTMENT PLAN

676. The Annual Investment Plan is part of the Multi-year Development Plan and includes:
(a) All of the projects to be undertaken during the year, grouped by thematic area and sub-area and the total costs.
(b) Anticipated financing for these projects.
(c) An approximate income calendar and anticipated expenditure calendar.
(d) Any complementary measures that might be adopted to achieve the objectives set out.

677. Annexed to the Annual Investment Plan should be all the documentation corresponding to each project that has been included.

678. In our example, the community's Annual Investment Plan for the first year would look like this: See table 9 next pages

Table 7. Projects included in the Development Plan

Thematic area	Type of project	PROJECT	Score	Year 1	Year 2	Year 3	Year 4	Total Plan	Year 2	Year 3	Year 4
					Forecast Investment				Net Maintenance Costs		
Environment	Infrastructure	Opening wells and create canals in rural area	28	1,250				1,250	30	30	30
Environment	Infrastructure	Improve rubbish collection	35	400				400	50	50	50
Environment	Infrastructure	Remove illegal waste dump	33	180				180	0	0	0
								0			
								0			
		Total Environment	96	1,830	0	0	0	1,830	80	80	80
Culture and Recreation	Social	Artists working with children	39	50				50	50	50	50
Culture and Recreation	Infrastructure	Transform landfill site into plaza	51	3,605				3,605	300	300	300
Culture and Recreation	Social	Create space for popular music concerts	34		500			500	0	0	0
Culture and Recreation	Social	Create infants video club	51	100				100	100	100	100
Culture and Recreation	Social	Fix up space for public library	29		1,000			1,000		150	150
Culture and Recreation	Social	Fix up social center	23		900			900		100	100
								0			
		Total Culture and Recreation	##	3,755	2,400	0	0	6,155	450	700	700
Education and Sport	Social	Create groups of sports promoters	24	0				0	0	0	0
Education and Sport	Social	Carry out campaign to promote sport	24	50				50	0	0	0
Education and Sport	Infrastructure	Recondition football field	24	500				500	0	0	0
Education and Sport	Social	Set up school and youth football teams	24	300				300	60	60	60
Education and Sport	Social	Stage competitions	51	0				0	0	0	0
								0			
								0			
		Total Education and Sport	##	850	0	0	0	850	60	60	60
Housing and town planning	Housing	Improve dilapidated homes	28	10,000	10,000	10,000	10,000	40,000	0	0	0
Housing and town planning	Infrastructure	Put a roof over the bus stop	30		600			600	0	0	0
								0			
		Total Housing and town planning	58	10,000	10,600	10,000	10,000	40,600	0	0	0
Sanitation	Social	Fix up space for ambulatory	39	4,000				4,000	150	150	150
								0			
								0			
		Total Sanitation	39	4,000	0	0	0	4,000	150	150	150
Security	Infrastructure	Improve lighting in the streets	39	600				600		100	100
Security	Social	Organize night security committee	39	50				50	20	20	20
								0			
								0			
		Total Security	78	650	0	0	0	650	20	120	120
Sustainable economy	Productive	Shed to process tobacco	26	3,000				3,000	0	0	0
Sustainable economy	Productive	Create women's sewing cooperative	24	4,500				4,500	0	0	0
								0			
								0			
		Total Sustainable economy	50	7,500	0	0	0	7,500	0	0	0
		Total Community Development Plan	695	28,585	13,000	10,000	10,000	61,585	760	1,110	1,110

Table 8. Financing Plan

Financing	Year 1	Year 2	Year 3	Year 4	Total per line time	Total per chapter	TOTAL GENERAL
Immediately available resources							8.725
- Own resources						8.725	
Linked to plaza	3.605				3.605		
Not linked	2.000	1.140	990	990	5.120		
- Outside resources						0	
Funds assigned from state	0	0	0	0	0		
Others							
Expected resources							80.000
- Non-linked financing						40.000	
Financing from municipality	10.000	10.000	10.000	10.000	40.000		
- Linked financing						40.000	
Financing from Housing Institute	10.000	10.000	10.000	10.000	40.000		
Other resources							3.000
- Non-linked financing							
- Linked financing						3.000	
Contribution from NGO for sewing workshop	3.000				3.000		
TOTAL	28.605	21.140	20.990	20.990	91.725	91.725	91.725

Table 9. Projects included in Annual Plan

Thematic area	Type of project	PROJECT	Score	Year 1
Environment	Infrastructure	Opening wells and create canals in rural area	28	1,250
Environment	Infrastructure	Improve rubbish collection	35	400
Environment	Infrastructure	Remove illegal waste dump	33	180
		Total Environment	**96**	**1,830**
Culture and recreation	Social	Artists working with children	39	50
Culture and recreation	Infrastructure	Transform landfill site into plaza	51	3,605
Culture and recreation	Social	Create infants video club	51	100
		Total Culture and recreation	**141**	**3,755**
Education and Sport	Social	Create groups of sports promoters	24	0
Education and Sport	Social	Carry out campaign to promote sport	24	50
Education and Sport	Infrastructure	Recondition football field	24	500
Education and Sport	Social	Set up school and youth football teams	24	300
Education and Sport	Social	Stage competitions	51	0
		Total Education and Sport	**288**	**850**
Housing and Town Plan	Housing	Improve dilapidated homes	28	10,000
		Total Housing and Town Planning	**28**	**10,000**
Sanitation	Social	Fix up space for ambulatory	39	4,000
		Total Sanitation	**39**	**4,000**
Security	Infrastructure	Improve lighting in the streets	39	600
Security	Social	Organize night security committee	39	50
		Total Security	**78**	**650**
Sustainable economy	Productive	Shed to process tobacco	26	3,000
Sustainable economy	Productive	Create women's sewing cooperative	24	4,500
		Total Sustainable economy	**50**	**7,500**
		Total Annual Plan for 1st Year	**720**	**28,585**

679. And the Financing Plan for the first year will look somewhat like Table 10:

Table 10. Anticipated financing for 1st year

Financing	1st Year	Partial	Total
Immediately available resources			**5,605**
- *Own resources*		*5,605*	
Linked to plaza	3,605		
Not linked	2,000		
- *Outside resources*		*0*	
Funds assigned from state	0		
Others	0		
Expected resources			**20,000**
- *Non-linked financing*		*10,000*	
Funds from municipality	10,000		
- *Linked financing*		*10,000*	
Funds from Housing Institute	10,000		
Other resources			**3,000**
- *Non-linked financing*		*0*	
- *linked financing*		*3,000*	
Contribution from NGO for sewing workshop	3,000		
TOTAL	**28,605**	**28,605**	**28,605**

(3) ANNUAL BUDGET

680. Once we know which projects will be included in the Annual Investment Plan, we have to look over the proposed Budget (see Chapter VIII) that was provisionally approved at the start of this phase, and complete the information, incorporating all anticipated investment and income into the Annual Plan.

681. As we already know which projects we will be investing in during the year, it is worth disaggregating the line items corresponding to projects by thematic area, as a way of gauging the importance of each cost in each area.

682. Furthermore, we should recall that when distributing projects across the different years, we did not use all our funds for the first year. That is, we had some money left, which should be reflected in the budget as a difference between income and anticipated expenditure.

683. To balance income and expenditure, we can put these remaining funds at the bottom of the expenditures (if we decide it can be used for any cost) or within the line item for projects (if we want to use it exclusively to finance investment). In our example, we have decided to go with the latter option.

684. This means that the budgeted line item for projects will be $20 more than the total cost of the projects we have included, as we have added the $20 we had left over.

Table 11. Annual budget

Income budget			**31,105**
Own income		8105	
Voluntary collections	1500		
Raffles and lotteries	2000		
Others	1000		
Collection for plaza	3605		
Transferences and subsidies		23,000	
From municipality	10,000		
From Housing Institute	10,000		
From international NGO	3000		
Credit and loans		0	
Expenditure budget			**31,105**
Functioning costs		1150	
Electricity and water	300		
Telephone	200		
Office materials	600		
Transport and parking	50		
Administration costs		100	
Travel	100		
Financial costs		50	
Interest on loan	50		
Service provision		0	
Maintenance costs		0	
Social Action costs		1200	
Project costs		28605	
Environment	1830		
Culture and Recreation	3755		
Education and Sport	850		
Housing and Town Planning	10,000		
Sanitation	4000		
Security	650		
Sustainable Economy	7500		
Pending	20		
Loan repayment			

685. Documentation for the Immediate Action Plan is simpler: it includes a table with the list of projects included in this Plan and its corresponding phase, together with a brief explanation of the changes made to the original order.

686. If there was a first phase, it would be worthwhile indicating the stage of completion of the projects included.

687. In our example, the table would look like this:

Table 12. Projects included in the Immediate Action Plan

Thematic area	Type of project	PROJECT	Score	Forecast investment	Phase	State of execution
Environment	Infrastructure	Opening wells and create canals in rural area	28	1,250	2nd	Project stage
		Total Environment	**28**	**1,250**		
Culture and recreation	Social	Artists working with children	39	50	1st	Completed
Culture and recreation	Infrastructure	Transform landfill site into plaza	51	3,605	1st	Underway
Culture and recreation	Social	Create infants video club	51	100	2nd	Project stage
		Total Culture and recreation	**141**	**3,755**		
Education and Sport	Social	Create groups of sports promoters	24	0	1st	Completed
Education and Sport	Social	Carry out campaign to promote sport	24	50	1st	Underway
Education and Sport	Infrastructure	Recondition football field	24	500	2nd	Project stage
Education and Sport	Social	Set up school and youth football teams	24 Delayed 300 (1)		2nd	Project stage
Education and Sport	Social	Stage competitions	51	0	2nd	Project stage
		Total Education and Sport	**147**	**550**		
Security	Social	Organize night security committee	39	50	1st	Completed
		Total Security	**39**	**50**		
		Total Immediate Action Plan	**355**	**5,605**		

(1) Players will use their own equipment. The purchase of these ($300) will be delayed until funds arrive from the municipality.

688. And the Financing Plan for the Immediate Action Plan would look like this:

Table 13. Financing of Immediate Action Plan

Resources available from the community	2.000
Collection among neighbours for the small plaza	3.605
TOTAL	**5.605**

6. APPROVING THE PROPOSED DEVELOPMENT PLAN, THE ANNUAL INVESTMENT PLAN AND THE BUDGET

PLANNING COUNCIL

Activity 9. (Plenary) Approving the proposed Development Plan, the Annual Investment Plan, and the Annual Budget (and in the case of the community, the Immediate Action Plan)

689. Once the Planning and Budget Team has prepared the corresponding documents for the Development Plan, the Annual Investment Plan, and the Annual Budget, a Plenary meeting of the Planning Council should be convened to study the documents and give them a final approval.

690. If the Planning Team has done its job well, correctly collecting the previously adopted agreements, this should be a mere formality of ratifying the previous decisions. However, we

recommend closely studying the documents presented to avoid any possible errors that could have consequences later on.

691. Once the proposals are adopted, the documents become the draft Development Plan, Annual Plan, and Budget (and, where relevant, the Immediate Action Plan), which should be submitted for approval to the corresponding Planning Assembly.

PLANNING ASSEMBLY

Activity 10. Final approval of the various Plans and Budget.

692. Once the Plenary has concluded its job, the corresponding Planning Assembly should be convened to submit the documents that the corresponding Planning Council have come up with for final approval.

693. Prior to the meeting of the assembly, it would be worthwhile organizing a broad informational campaign regarding the content of the Plans and Budget. Moreover, all citizens should have access to all documentation related to the process.

7. COMING UP WITH THE GENERAL DEVELOPMENT PLAN, ANNUAL INVESTMENT PLAN, AND CONSOLIDATED BUDGET IN THE TERRITORIAL AREAS AND MUNICIPALITY

694. All the community, territorial and municipal Plans should be brought together into a single document that outlines the anticipated overall investment and that allows us to evaluate the results obtained at the territorial area and municipal levels.

695. We should do the same with the community and territorial budgets, so that we have a single document that outlines the budget required to carry out the activities of all the different public entities present at the territorial area and municipal level.

696. This is a task for the Territorial Planning and Budget Teams and the Municipal Planning and Budget Cabinet.

TERRITORIAL PLANNING TEAMS

Activity 11. Come up with a General Plan and consolidated Budget for the territorial areas

697. As the Community Planning Assemblies approve their respective Plans and Budget, a copy of these should be handed over to the Planning and Budget Team in the corresponding territorial area.

698. With the information provided by the communities, and with the information it has collected in the territorial area, the Territorial Planning and Budget Team should come up with a short summary of the General Development Plan and the General Annual Investment Plan for the area.

699. This summary could include various tables: one that breaks down anticipated investment by thematic area or sector, distinguishing between actions carried out at the territorial area from those planned at the community level.

700. In this way, anticipated investment for the whole of the General Territorial Development Plan would follow a schema similar to Table 14 below:

Table 14. General Territorial Development Plan: Anticipated investment (Model)

Year	Year 1			Year 2			Year 3			Year 4			TOTAL		
Thematic Area	Territorial Area	Communities	Total	Territorial Area	Communities	Total	Territorial Area	Communities	Total	Territorial Area	Communities	Total	Territorial Area	Communities	Total
Environment															
Culture and Recreation															
Sanitation															
Etc															
Total															

701. And the distribution of investment in the Annual Investment Plan should look like this:

Table 15. General Territorial Annual Investment Plan: Anticipated Investment (Model)

Thematic area	Territorial Area	Communities	Total
Environment			
Culture and Recreation			
Sanitation			
Etc.			
Total			

702. It would also be interesting to break down by communities investments included in the General Territorial Development Plan. For this we could use a model table like Table 16, which uses a cell for each community and a final one that indicates the sum for the overall General Development Plan.

Table 16. General Territorial Development Plan: Anticipated investment according to communities Year 1 (Model)

Thematic Area	Community 1	Community 2	Community 3	Etc.	Total
Environment					
Culture and Recreation					
Sanitation					
Etc.					
Total					

703. Finally, a consolidated Budget for the territorial area should outline all the activities foreseen for the territorial area, as well as anticipated income and expenditure (minus any transfers between the territorial area and the communities).

704. Once this documentation is completed, it should be broadly disseminated and a copy should be sent to the Municipal Planning and Budget Cabinet.

MUNICIPAL PLANNING AND BUDGET CABINET

Activity 12. *Come up with a General Plan and consolidated Budget for the Municipality*

705. Once the Territorial Planning and Budget Teams have sent this documentation, the Municipal Planning and Budget Cabinet should come up with equivalent documentation for the municipal level, with the exception that in the table where anticipated investment is broken down by thematic area or sector, we need to distinguish among the three levels: municipal, territorial

area and community.

Table 17. General Municipal Development Plan: Anticipated investment Year 1

Thematic Area	Municipality	Territorial Areas	Communities	Total
Environment				
Culture and Recreation				
Sanitation				
Etc				
Total				

706. The same should be done for the following years. A final table should present all the accumulated totals for the entire Development Plan.

707. Logically, the anticipated investment for the Annual Plan will be the table that corresponds to the first year.

708. Below, a second group of tables outlines the breakdown of anticipated investment by sectors and territorial areas for the territorial area, distinguishing within each area between investment corresponding to the area itself and that which corresponds to the communities within it.

Table 18. General Municipal Development Plan: Anticipated investment by Territorial Areas Year 1. (Model)

	Territorial Area 1			Territorial Area 2			Etc.	TOTAL		
Thematic Area	Territorial Area	Communities	TOTAL AREA	Territorial Area	Communities	TOTAL AREA		Territorial Area	Communities	TOTAL MUNICIPALITY
Environment										
Culture and Recreation										
Sanitation										
Etc.										
Total										

709. The same should be done for the following years. A final table should present the totals for the entire General Municipal Development Plan.

710. Finally, the consolidated Municipal Budget should outline all foreseeable economic activities, for all levels within the municipality, for the different entities that are part of the participatory planning process (including income and expenditures, but excluding transfers between entities).

CHAPTER X: IMPLEMENTATION, OVERSIGHT AND EVALUATION

INTRODUCTION

711. We said in Volume I that "it would make no sense to come up with a plan if it was to only remain on paper". If this happened, all the work we have done would have been in vain. That is why we believe that implementation and participatory processes of oversight and control to ensure it is carried out in the proper manner are an integral part of the participatory planning process.

712. We can complete a task for the sake of completing it, but not do it correctly. For example, we could collect the debris for a house, but if we leave it piled up on the footpath, it will disturb people walking by. It is important that members of the community monitor what happens to ensure this does not occur.

713. We could asphalt a street, but if it is not done properly, the condition of the road can quickly deteriorate. We have to make sure that neighbors are alert to the situation and seek out a person who understands how the job should be done, to inspect it, and to make sure this does not happen

714. We could build a house with steel girders that are not strong enough or that tend to rust quickly, meaning that the house will deteriorate very quickly. We need to check to make sure that the girders used comply with established norms and building codes.

715. Just as the parents in a family should monitor their children's homework, society, and more concretely, the neighbors in a community should exercise some control over the activities carried out in their area. The exercising of this type of control by a social collective is what we mean by social oversight.

716. The lack of organized oversight by the people not only allows corruption and the diversion of resources to occur, it also means that neighbors themselves do not do things as they should be done for the benefit of the whole.

717. In practice, social oversight is perhaps one of the most forgotten elements, and yet at the same time perhaps one of the most fundamental elements, of democratic management. Nothing is gained from deciding particular priorities or obtaining funds for specific projects if the people are not organized to monitor these initiatives, ensure that the resources are used on the project they were assigned to and guarantee that quality control occurs.

718. This control or oversight, carried out by the affected people themselves, is what we call social oversight.

719. Social oversight of public works should begin the moment that the first actions related to the implementation of the project are taken (in cases of complex projects, this will start with the process of contracting for the project) and should not finish once the project itself is complete. Why? Because every public works suffers from a process of wear and tear as time goes by and requires maintenance. That is why it is important to promote neighborhood groups to carry out this task.

720. There is no possibility of social oversight if people do not have access to transparent and appropriate information.

721. Only a well-informed populace can develop a political model of participatory and protagonistic democracy. This entails the broadest possible transparency in regards to the projects being carried out. Citizens should know what is contained in the budget, what public works and services are being carried out, which functionaries and public employees are at their service, how

well they are doing their jobs and how the public resources of the community, municipality or nation are being used.

722. "Black holes" should disappear. The more "confidential" and shrouded in secrecy that information regarding various activities of the public administration is, the more chance there is that illicit acts will be carried out when administering resources that belong to everyone.

723. We need to establish mechanisms for citizens to monitor and evaluate the process of carrying out public works. It is also important to have quantitative and qualitative methods to evaluate the success of the work being done, and, if necessary, to implement contingency plans to resolve any obstacles found along the way. Some believe we should not allow a lot of time to pass before carrying out our evaluations – no more than three months.

724. Given this, below we will outline some criteria which we believe are essential to ensuring the correct implementation of (1) projects and (2) the Plan, as well as an adequate evaluation of its results.

1. IMPLEMENTATION, OVERSIGHT AND FINAL EVALUATION OF PROJECTS

725. As we said in the previous chapter, the central element of the Development Plan is the amount of investment contemplated for all of the projects included within it.

726. When we are talking about a Community Development Plan, and even a Territorial Area Plan, we can say that the sole content of the Plan is investment in projects. However, as a Development Plan begins to cover larger territorial areas (municipality, region and, logically, the nation), the plan will no longer be limited to the sum of investment in projects; it will also include other measures that could affect general regulation, fiscal and budgetary norms, and the development of certain credit instruments.

727. As such, by modifying fiscal norms we can favor or discourage the development of certain activities. For example, it is possible that a Municipal Development Plan could contemplate the (permanent or temporary) elimination or reduction of taxes that affect the development of certain activities. Or it could create or raise taxes that discourage activities deemed to be detrimental to neighbors.

728. It could also modify regulations, and eliminate or simplify red tape, all with the aim of encouraging development in certain activities.

729. Similarly, it could promote the creation of cooperatives by granting interest-free loans, either directly or via a subsidy to cover interests for loans given out by private entities.

730. Enacting these measures is part of implementing the Plan. Therefore they should also be subject to oversight to ensure correct implementation and appropriate results. We should analyze the evolution of any spending as we go along and be alert to any possible deviations in relation to what was intended in the Plan.

731. However, here we will deal exclusively with the implementation, oversight and control of direct investment contemplated in the Plan, which, as we said before, is the central and almost sole element of any Community and Territorial Area Plans.

1) DIRECT INVESTMENT AND FORMS OF EXECUTING

732. Let us recall that direct investment refers to investment carried out by the municipality, the territorial areas or communities using their own funds and under their direction and/or supervision.

733. Executing direct investment can take two forms: direct execution by an entity (Mayor's office or Municipal, Territorial Area or Community Council) that has the responsibility for

carrying out the project; or indirect execution, whereby a responsible council entrusts a third party (a private or public company) with carrying out a project that the Council will finance.[8]

734. The latter form is common for more complex projects, such as building a bridge or hospital, because public entities do not normally have the organization or means to carry out such large-scale projects.

2) DIRECT EXECUTION

735. As we saw in the example of the plaza in Chapter VI, when dealing with direct execution a team working on behalf of the Community Planning Council takes charge of finding tools and means of labor, organizing days of volunteer labor, coordinating different activities, and generally directing the execution of the project.

a) Requirements to take into consideration

736. In this case, it is very important to adopt the principle of collective responsibility when implementing the project. At the same time, we should clearly delineate the responsibilities that each person within the team has, to avoid interferences and conflicts. In this way, every person is responsible for a specific task but is also responsible for the project as a whole, and so therefore must coordinate his or her actions with others.

737. A fundamental principle for overseeing the process of public works from the financial viewpoint is ensuring that every cost incurred is adequately documented (receipts, invoices, etc.) according to existing norms. Only by complying with this principle will we be able to draw up a final balance sheet to present to the inspection agency, where this may be the case, and the corresponding Planning Council and Assembly.

738. It is also important to ensure that if there are any types of regulations (municipal, regional, state) that might affect the project, these are rigorously complied with: if workers are hired, this should be done so on the basis of existing labor laws; required permits should be obtained for relevant projects, etc.

739. If we are going to use volunteer labor, we should ensure that the call is issued as widely as possible. We should not exclude anyone and we should make an effort to make use of the abilities and training of the volunteers, slotting them into roles where they can be of most use for the project.

b) Instruments for social oversight

▪ *Overseeing costs*

---

8 There is a third form, in which the company carrying out the project assumes all or some of the costs and the entity that contracted them commits to paying them back over regular quotas until they have been fully reimbursed, including any possible interest incurred. We are dealing here with financing projects via a loan, in this case indirect and more expensive, but which in some countries has been used intensively as a way to hide the real level of indebtedness of public entities in a context of the privatization and liberalization of public services

740. As well as presenting a balance sheet, which should occur at the end of the project, it is important to monitor accumulated costs as they are incurred in order to detect any possible deviations from the anticipated cost and adopt any necessary measures to rectify this.

741. We can use a table for this purpose, with the anticipated accumulated cost of each phase in one column, and another column for the actual accumulated cost incurred[9], like the one we have below for our plaza example.

Table 19: Accumulated cost

Activity		Anticipated Accumulated Cost		Real Accumulated Cost	
Clean up of site		120	120		
Preparation of installation of electricity and water		60	180		
Marking out paths		60	240		
Installing lights and sprinklers		0	240		
Planting trees, hedges and grass	Nursery	1,325			
	Transport	100			
	Labor	180	1,845		
Installing benches and equipment	Play equipment	550			
	Cement and sand	170			
	Transport	200			
	Tools	80			
	Labor	120	2,965		
Fixing paths	Paint and brushes	400			
	Tools	20			
	Labor	120	3,505[10]		

c) Overseeing the timeline of activities

742. We should also use the timeline of activities included in the project document to compare with the actual progress made in order to determine if delays are occurring and how these partial delays could distort the progress of the project.

743. It could be very useful to come up with a form like the one below where we can follow the intended progress of the project compared with its actual progress.

744. For doing this we have used the same example of the plaza.

9 Note that we are referring to costs that have been incurred, that is we are referring to the moment we have to pay for a purchase or rental. Remember that sometimes we might be able to pay for things afterwards if there is an agreement to pay later or with a loan, which is what happens in our example.

10 There is a difference of $100 in regards to the budget that corresponds to "other costs" of indeterminate character that is there to deal with any unforeseen costs.

Table 20: Timeline of activities for the project

Activity	Weekends									
	1ª		2ª		3ª		4ª		5ª	
Clean up of site	▓									
Preparation for installation of electricity and water			▓							
Marking out paths				▓						
Installing lights y sprinklers					▓					
Planting trees, hedges and grass						▓	▓			
Installing benches and equipment								▓	▓	
Fixing paths										▓

745. We can mark the advances made in the execution of the project on this chart in order to see if we are on track. If the project will take a long time to complete, it would be worthwhile carrying out a balance of each stage in order to be able to detect any problems or deviations early.

■*Records of implementation, at the start and end of the project*

746. It would be good when beginning the project to fill out a "***Proof of implementation***" form to leave a record of when the project was started, as well as doing so on the designation completion date.

747. Similarly, once the project is finished, we should fill out a "***Proof of completion***" form, to leave a record of the fact that the project was successfully completed and that the public work meets the conditions that were initially established.

■*Photographic record*

748. It is also useful to keep a photographic record of the project's progress, with photographs taken at the start and during each stage of the project. For example, in the case of the plaza, we should take photos of the initial state of the site; the situation once it has been cleaned up; the state it is in after the third weekend (when paths have been marked out and trees and hedges planted); after the street lights and sprinklers have been installed; and finally, when the plaza is finished.

■*Public information*

749. Both the proof of implementation and the photographic record should be stuck up on informational noticeboards that indicate when the project started, its designated completion date, its cost and funding sources, and any voluntary labor and contribution of tools and equipment. Photos that illustrate the stages of the project should accompany all of this.

2) INDIRECT EXECUTION

750. As we said, indirect execution means that the responsible entity limits itself to providing the funds for the project while its implementation is handed over to a third party (either a public or private company) which signs a contract, organizes and acquires the necessary labor and material resources, and supervises the implementation of the project.

751. In these cases we have to consider two essential aspects:
a) The granting of the contract to carry out the project
b) The external oversight done by the entity that granted the contract to ensure that the project is carried out correctly.

a) Ways of granting contracts

752. Given we have to entrust a third party with carrying out the project, an important issue is the question of how to select them. This has to be done in the most transparent and objective manner possible to ensure that we obtain the best results for the least cost.

753. We should not forget that one of the sources of corruption in public institutions can be found in the process of granting contracts of these types. Many private companies are willing to pay functionaries and politicians to win contracts that benefit them.

754. Even when there is no direct payment, corruption can exist if the company that is contracted belongs to a friend or family member and is contracted for no other reason than friendship or family connections.

755. Almost every country has norms that set out guidelines for how to grant contracts, generally according to the importance of the contract, to combat corruption, at least formally.

Direct assignment

756. When a project has a small cost but, for various reasons, needs to be carried out by a third party (or we are dealing with small purchases for directly executed projects, such as the inputs we need for the plaza), the entity can enter into a direct relationship with a provider or contractor to acquire the materials or carry out the project.

757. In these cases, it is very important to operate with maximum transparency, explaining the reasons why a particular provider or contractor was used and not another one, and avoiding nepotism and cronyism in the selection process.

Tender for offers

758. When the project is going to be very expensive or we are dealing with an important input, we could demand a system of tender for offers. In this case, the public entity should approach a designated number of contractors or providers (in most countries this ranges from 3 to 5), indicating the characteristics of the project or input and asking about price and any condition that might be imposed.

759. This process is more transparent that the previous one as it allows for an objective comparison among different offers, but as the entity is still ultimately responsible for selecting who will get the contract, the risk of manipulation continues to exist.

760. The typical case of manipulation involves approaching a sole provider or contractor and asking them to find from among their colleagues another four who are willing to put forward more expensive offers so that they are selected. There have even be cases in which the same business owner has registered other companies whose only activity is to tender for the same contracts, but at a much higher price.

761. It is the responsibility of the planning councilors to make sure this is avoided by approaching clearly independent companies, not always approaching the same groups of companies (to avoid situations of "today its my turn, the next one is yours"), and automatically eliminating offers from groups of companies where non-competition pacts have been detected between them.

Public tender

762. To avoid these situations, the best option is public tender in which the project and its characteristics are described with a set of selection criteria and everyone is invited to present proposals within a set timeframe. Once the deadline has passed, the offers are evaluated in order to select the one that is best suited to the quality and price of the project.

763. While this process is the most transparent and objective, it is costly in terms of time (sufficient time has to be allowed to ensure that everyone can prepare their offers) and money (the

call for a public tender and the evaluation process involve costs). This is why we have said that for smaller and less expensive projects we should use one of the aforementioned methods.

764. We recommend, even when legislation does not require it, that the Planning Councils give preference to the tender method, even if in a simplified form, except in cases of projects where because of their immediacy and simplicity, this would unnecessarily delay or add to the cost of the project.

765. A public tender ensures that the council cannot select or limit the companies that make offers. If the evaluation of the different offers is also made public, citizens can find out why a particular contract was given to one company and not another.

766. But even here there are potential forms of manipulation that should be avoided and that councils should look out for: from providing a company with details of a future tender before their rivals to give them a time advantage to introducing conditions among the requisites to participate in the tender that only certain companies can meet, thereby eliminating competitors. We have even seen cases of tenders in which a particular company drafts the selection criteria to be used in the tender so that during the tender process it can present itself as the best option for the project.

▪*Selection criteria.*

767. An essential element of any form of tendering is the selection criteria. The statement of the selection criteria outlines the objectives of the project, its characteristics, the qualities it requires and any technical aspects that could be relevant, such as timeframe.

768. Obviously the complexity of the selection criteria will vary a lot depending on the method used: in a direct assignment, it might be limited to a description of the inputs to be purchased or the public works to carry out, while in a public tender it should contain a detailed description of the project as a whole. In the latter case, we may not include the technical project for the public works; however, it is quite common to include it as a way to ensure that deviations from the original project do not occur.

769. For especially significant projects – a town remodeling, a particular building with a representative character – we may even put the task of coming up with the technical project up for public tender, so that teams of experts can propose solutions to the problems faced.

770. But in every case, it is important to clearly define the objective sought. If it is the supply of inputs, then the exact material and its quality and quantity should be specified; if we are dealing with a public work we should outline its characteristics, its quality level, the materials to be used, etc.

771. With public tenders, there is reason to expect that certain requisites will be set, such as level of solvency of the company, experience with previous similar projects and fiscal state. But we have to be very careful to avoid, as we said before, these requisites becoming barriers to participation for companies that could have done the job better.

772. Although in the capitalist system this is not very common, we could include requisites of a social character, such as mandating the employment of a certain percentage of local labor, respect for collective contracts or establishing wage levels to avoid the super exploitation of workers.

773. Often the criteria include a set limit for the estimated cost (which the offer price cannot exceed) or provide some guidelines (an estimation of the cost is made and each company is free to offer a different price, whether higher or lower). The estimated cost is the one that initially appeared on the approved Investment Plan.

▪*Transparency of the process*

774. Both in a tender for offers and in a public tender, the selection criteria should specify how each criterion will be evaluated and the relative weight of each one of them in the final evaluation. Done in this way, the team that will evaluate the offers will have a clear and pre-established idea of what and how to evaluate.

775. Often the offer price is considered to be the only relevant element and other aspects such as quality, social conditions or timeframe are not taken into consideration, aspects that may be crucial to determining which is the best company to select, even if they may not be the cheapest.

776. It is very important to be careful of what are called "reckless offers", which offer a price that is so low that – if they are selected – they will not be able to comply with. To avoid this we can calculate the median price of the offers received and exclude those that are a certain percentage below this price (it could be 20% or 30%, but it will vary depending on the number of offers received and the absolute cost of the project).

777. In any case, it is vital that even if the selection criteria is drafted by experts, the content is discussed and approved by the Planning Councils and any interested person can view them, because transparency is what will ensure that corruption does not occur.

778. Moreover, when evaluating the offers received, an evaluation team should be set up that is not made up exclusively of experts. It is very important that members of the Planning Council participate in the evaluation, not only to ensure transparency but also because their local knowledge might detect certain aspects in the offer that may not be perceived by experts.

779. Once all the offers have been evaluated, the Council should, once it has heard and debated the explanations given by the evaluation team, approve a company for the contract in a Plenary session.

780. Finally, once the tender process is finished, all the offers received should be made public as well as the value given to each criterion and the name of the selected company. By giving all citizens the possibility to know the details of the evaluation carried out, a blockage is placed in the way of any possible arbitrariness or favoritism.

b) Instruments for social oversight

781. Just as it is important that the process of contracting companies is transparent and overseen socially, once the execution of the project by a contracted company has begun, it is extremely important to ensure that there is social oversight of its implementation. In this case, it is not members of the council or designated people overseeing the project and organizing the collection of inputs and the hiring of a labor force. A company will be doing all these tasks and its possible that the interests of the company – increasing its profit margins by reducing costs – will not coincide with the interests of the Council, which wants the public work to be of the quality indicated in the offer and required by the selection criteria.

782. That is why, immediately after signing the contract with the company, an Oversight Team should be set up to monitor the execution of the project and make sure the company does not diverge from what it promised in its offer.

▪ *Social Oversight Team*

783. The Social Oversight Team should be at least partially comprised of the people who made up the team that evaluated the different offers because they will be the most acquainted with the content of the offer that was selected in terms of what was outlined in the selection criteria.

784. Moreover, some people who were not part of the evaluation team should also be included, as they can contribute an unbiased view of the implementation process (a person who participated in

the selection process may instinctively forgive deviations that could put into question their selection choice).

785. In any case, all members of the Social Oversight Team should be people with prestige within the community and have sufficient knowledge to carry out their task. This is not to say that they must be experts, but they should be able to evaluate results and prove that what has been done is in accordance with the initial proposal. It is very likely that the company that carried out the project will have its own ad hoc experts to oversee and evaluate the project.

▪ *Complying with deadlines*

786. The execution of complex projects should be broken up into stages, with a deadline set for completing each stage. Penalties should be established for non-compliance with deadlines.

787. An essential task of the Social Oversight Team is to ensure that deadlines are met. For this task, it could draft up what is called a "Proof of compliance" with which the team certifies that a stage has been executed within the allotted timeframe and that it has been completed in accordance with what was established in the selection criteria and the company offer.

788. This certificate can be used to justify payments to the company as each stage is completed.

789. Because of this, the Proof of compliance cannot be a merely formal procedure: the Social Oversight Team must thoroughly review what has been done, proving that each specification has been met and demanding explanations if deviations have occurred.

790. A similar table to the one we used in our example for overseeing the timeline for direct executions can be used to program the inspections and proofs of compliance.

791. As well as these planned inspections, the team should carry out surprise inspections to monitor the progress of the project and to detect any possible defects before it is too late.

▪ *Avoid cost deviations*

792. One of the risks with indirect execution is that, once started, the company might request a change in the price that was agreed to, arguing that unforeseen costs have arisen.

793. Without denying the possibility that this might be true in some cases, the Social Oversight Team should be very firm when confronted with such requests and only attend to them when it is clear that unforeseen events have led to a rise in the cost of the project.

794. Some companies deliberately put forward cheaper offers in order to win contracts, with the intention of requesting a price rise once the job has started while citing alleged unforeseen costs. The best way to avoid this is to ensure that, when evaluating offers, no reckless offers have been made.

795. In any case, the Planning Council, based on information provided by the Social Oversight Team, should approve or reject any modification to the agreed upon price.

▪ *Photographic record*

796. As with direct execution, it is worthwhile maintaining a photographic record of the progress of the project (including its initial state). Informational noticeboards with a succession of photos can be set up showing how the project has progressed over time.

4) FINAL EVALUATION OF RESULTS

796a. It is not enough to simply come up with good projects if they only remain as ideas on paper or are not correctly carried out. That is why overseeing and evaluating projects are fundamental tasks. Unfortunately, while there are many more proposals for how to design a project and how to evaluate if it has been carried out correctly, there are very few tools to help evaluate a project's results and, in particular, evaluate how the people who participated in its completion have changed, much less what it means to the people to have actively participated in the planning process in which they had to decide which of the possible projects were selected to be part of the plan.

797. That is why once the project is finished, it is not enough to simply issue a certificate of good faith saying that the project has been completed satisfactorily

798. It is important that the team responsible for the project (in the case of directly executed projects) or the Social Oversight Team (in the case of indirectly executed projects) draw up a balance sheet of the experience that can be useful in the future.

799. We suggest drafting the following documents for this purpose:

a) Verification list of expected results

800. Based on the data included in the original project, we need to make sure that the project, once finished, meets our criteria. It would be useful to come up with a verification list that includes the essential points of the project and then goes point-by-point demonstrating that these have been met.

801. This is particularly important in cases where a contracted company has carried out the project, as we need to effectively demonstrate that the company has complied with its promises.

b) Meeting objectives and impact on the community, territorial area or municipality

802. As the aim of the project was to meet an aspiration that had been broken down into concrete objectives, we must confirm whether these objectives have been reached once the project is finished or almost complete.

803. That is, it is not enough to be able to say that the project was completed satisfactorily. We need to evaluate whether it serves the purpose of achieving the objective that was sought. It would be of no use to build a factory to process maize if the farmers (due to lack of information, training and tools) do not plant maize; or to fix up a plaza that no one ends up using because it is too far from the center of the community.[11]

804. We also have to evaluate the impact the project will have on the community as a whole. This type of evaluation should be done some time after the project is finished, once the results can be seen. The amount of time will depend on the character of the project.

c) Systemization of the experience

----

11. These errors typical occurring when planning is done from above, when experts do not pay attention to the immediate reality and expectations of the people. But they can also occur during planning from below due to a lack of experience or the existence of pressure groups. That is why it is important to not only evaluate the project itself, but its relation to the objective sought, so as to not repeat the same errors. It is bad to act without planning, but so is bad planning.

805. Once we have completed the project, we should prepare a brief balance sheet of the experience, pointing out the difficulties encountered and the ways in which the people overcame them. This could be very important for future experiences.

806. In cases of indirectly executed projects, we should look at how the relationship with the responsible company developed, their level of collaboration with the Social Oversight Team, if they willingly accepted suggestions and observations from the team, if the price they were contracted for had to be modified, if labor conflicts arose, etc.

806. This information could be taken into consideration the next time a new project is put out to tender.

d) Democratic consolidation of the project

807. We believe it is also important that, once a project is finished (for example painting a school or building a children's play area), the corresponding Planning Council organizes a system for maintaining its upkeep (for example, a security patrol made up of neighbors from the community). As we said in Volume I, former mayor of Caroni Clemente Scotto was right when he called this stage of the process: "the democratic consolidation of the project".[12]

2. OVERSIGHT AND CONTROL OF THE PLAN

1) OVERSEEING THE PLAN

a) Permanent oversight

808. Once we have begun to implement a Development Plan, we should permanently monitor the work carried out, in order to check what is working or fix what is not working.

809. The corresponding council should designate a Social Oversight Team for the Plan, whose task is to monitor the progress of the Plan as a whole, on the basis of information that they should receive from the teams responsible for implementing or overseeing each project.

810. We can follow the progress of all the projects using a form like the one we described in paragraph 743 (Table 2), where the first column lists all the projects included in the Plan, indicating the starting and estimated finishing dates. We can mark down the progress of the projects on this form to work out if delays are occurring and propose measures to the Planning Council to rectify the situation, if this is the case.

811. This process of oversight is particularly important for projects that are prerequisites for carrying out other projects. These projects should be placed together on the form to make it easier to visualize any potential problems.

812. At the same time, we should monitor the evolution of the costs incurred, of the funds available in the treasury, and in particular of any irregularity that might occur in terms of anticipated income to make sure that funds are available to make payments as required.

---

12. Volume I, paragraph 338.

813. It would be useful to jot this down on an income and expenditure calendar to show that everything is occurring according to plan.

814. In cases where the Plan, as we said in paragraph 726, includes other direct investments, we should monitor these to make sure that they are occurring, their level of effectiveness, their cost and any possible deviations in order to suggest ways to rectify them.

b) Periodic evaluations

815. Periodically, the Plan Social Oversight Team should present an evaluation of the Plan's progress and, if any deviations are occurring, suggest measures to rectify the situation to the corresponding Planning Council.

816. This should not be a merely formal act. The Council should closely study the evaluation presented and ask, if necessary, for clarifications to those responsible or the Social Oversight team for the specific project, in order to adopt the measures they believe pertinent to ensure the Plan is complied with.

c) Informational transparency

817. Information regarding the progress of the Plan should be accessible to everyone who is interested. It should be uploaded onto a website, posted on informational noticeboards, etc. It is very important that the population knows what is happening and how it is being done.

818. Where important deviations have been detected that could affect the Plan, we should convene the corresponding assembly to inform them of the situation and the measures that have been deemed appropriate to adopt.

2) OVERSEEING THE RESULTS OF THE PLAN

a) Balance sheet of results

819. Each year, the Plan Social Oversight Team should come up with a balance sheet of the results of the Annual Investment Plan, as well as at the conclusion of the Development Plan. The balance sheet should indicate the projects that were satisfactorily completed, those that have not been finished yet and, if there are any, those that could not be started or have been put aside for whatever reason.

820. This balance sheet should include figures for overall investment made, breaking it down by thematic area, indicating what was anticipated in the Plan and explaining and justifying any possible deviations.

821. If the Plan included any other direct investments, it should specify the results obtained and the cost (including the implicit fiscal cost for the income foregone in the case of tax deductions).

822. All of this should allow us to evaluate the overall effort made.

823. Furthermore, as the Plan has a series of objectives in terms of the aspirations that the population came up with at the start of the process, we should analyze if these objectives were met.

824. This task will be easier the more the objectives can be quantified. But even if we are dealing with non-quantifiable objectives, we should try to work out if the objective has been met or at least make sure that we are moving in the right direction.

825. All this information should allow the Planning Council to evaluate the results of the Plan (whether it is an Annual Investment Plan or a Multi-year Development Plan) and work out if modifications need to be made to the subsequent Annual Plans. Any modifications should be discussed and approved by the corresponding Assembly.

826. We should point out that although the definitive balance sheet of the Annual Investment Plan or the Multi-year Development Plan can only be made at the end of the corresponding period for the Plan, it is always necessary to come up with provisional balance sheets (with an estimation of results) a few months prior to the completion of the corresponding Plan, in order to revise or come up with the following Plan before the conclusion of the current one. In this way, once the Annual Investment Plan is completed, we can begin, without delay, the following one. We should also have a Multi-year Development Plan ready before the end of the previous Development Plan.

b) Social balance sheet of the Plan

827. Lastly, the Council should not only monitor the concrete material actions included in the Plan; it should also evaluate the positive and negative effects that the projects are having on the subjective situation of the people. It should not only look at those aspects that are direct or indirect consequences of the Plan but also those that could be the result of the influence of other factors besides the Plan. For example, it should study how relations among residents are evolving, how well the various work committees and community organizations are working together, how the people are perceiving the government's work, where conflicts have arisen, etc. It would be very useful to make flipcharts with all this information in order to visualize the situation of the population as a whole at a specific moment its development, to see how the situation is developing over time and point out critical bottlenecks that have to be overcome, in order to include the lessons learnt in subsequent plans.

APPENDIX I.

EXAMPLES OF FORMS AND TABLES FOR COLLECTING AND CONSOLIDATING INFORMATION INTO A DATABASE

INTRODUCTION

828. As we indicated at the end of Chapter I in this volume, it is important to prepare forms or sheets for collecting the data that will be used to generate a database. The ideal situation would involve having the available IT resources to come up with a simple program that can collect, sort out and make use of the information. But, understanding that there may be communities where this is not possible, we are making available to the reader some examples of forms or sheets that can be filled our manually.

829. In the first model form (Residents, households and levels of participation), which relates to the information that activists should gather during their door-to-door visits (see Volume I, paragraphs 223-4), we have included questions regarding the personal data of residents in a household, ethnic background, level of schooling, employment situation, gender inequality and health issues. We have also included questions regarding the state of their home, its furnishings, etc. Finally, we have included the issue of levels of participation of the residents in the community, something that is rarely broached in these types of forms.

830. Where possible, the age and gender of all residents in the household should be obtained from the municipal census and roll. This step should be taken prior to initiating the process and will be of help in planning out the visits that need to be made door-to-door later on, once we have collected the aspirations, in order to complete the information with direct questions to residents.

831. Furthermore, it is possible that in the case of information regarding more conflictive questions (sexuality, abortion, gangs, etc.) it will be necessary to collect indirect information from neighbors, social workers, etc., as it may be difficult to obtain this information directly.

832. In any case, we should point out that collecting this information door-to-door involves an enormous amount of work for the activists that take up this task and, whether we like it or not, a certain level of intromission into the private affairs of family. That is why, in our example, we have made an effort to limit the number of questions as much as possible and focus on the truly relevant questions, without trying to cover all topics.

833. The second model form can be used to consolidate the information obtained from the first form, via tables that will reflect the overall situation of the community. Only in this way will the efforts exerted in going door-to-door and the information collected be of use and allow us to have an overall view of the whole community.

834. This is a task of the Community Planning Team or the people it has assigned to it in the cases where it has been decided to first consolidate the information collected in the neighborhood areas. Unfortunately, what tends to occur is that forms are collected in a particular place, but effort is not made to consolidate the results. That is why we have insisted so much on this point that might seem so obvious.

835. The tables for consolidating information from the first form contain the same items as the questions in the first form. The difference is that this type we are dealing with overall figures that correspond to the community and their expression as a percentage of the population.

836. A third model form (Social equipment in the community) can be used to collect information for the community as a whole. Here we are referring to existing installations relating to the issues of food, education, health, security, culture, recreation, sports, and financial services. We also deal with the issues of infrastructure, electricity, communication, and the environment. And lastly, it also covers experiences in community solidarity, the existence of community leaders and support that could be obtained from outside.

837. This form can complement the information collected in the previous tables and should be filled out by the corresponding Community Planning Team using information collected through direct observation and/or by consulting public registrars and archives. In this case, the most important thing is to ensure the objectivity of the information collected. One way to do this is to set up teams of two or three people who have to come to an agreement before responding to each question.

838. At the end of this appendix, we will include a partial made up example, where we have included some figures in terms of the information we have to collect, to allow us to look more closely at the aspiration that working age residents be able to work without discrimination.

839. These model forms are only examples and have been thought up with an urban community in mind. Each community should adapt or modify them according to their circumstances and needs. For example, the age group of 5 years or less that we have used in some tables corresponds to children who have not reached the age of compulsory education, and the 5-16 years age group corresponds to those who are in compulsory education. But the exact ages may differ according to the country where the community is. The same is true for the legal retirement age, which we have set at 65.

840. Various things could be simplified in the case of a rural community or an indigenous community, although in these cases it is very likely that we would also have to introduce new questions regarding agricultural activity, size of farm, quality of land, source of water, etc., to obtain the information we want.

841. You will see that in the forms that we have provided as models, the options for answering can be exclusionary in some cases (if a family lives in a chalet, then it cannot be deemed to be a makeshift housing or apartment) and there is only room for one answer. In other cases, the options are not mutually exclusive (someone could have a landline and a mobile phone or internet and a mobile phone and a landline, etc.), meaning that when someone is filling out the form, some or all of the options can be selected. In a third case, which is the most common in our forms, we need to quantify the number of times a certain option is selected. For example, when asking about the age of residents by age groups, we have to specific how many people within the household fall within the age group. In these cases, we will often ask to break down this information by sex, and in some cases, the number of youth and children within the total figure. It is important to note that when breaking information down into men or women, we are referring to all those who identify as a certain sex, regardless of age.

842. To facilitate this work, in those questions that only allow for a single response and those that allow for multiple options, the box is placed to the left of the option and should be filled with an X. The title will indicate if we are dealing with a multiple option question. When a number is needed, the box will appear to the right of the option and will be preceded by the letters T, M, W, Y and C, which stand for total, man, woman, youth and children, respectively. The number should be placed within the box. In cases where there are more than options that those outlined, they can be written in in under Others.

Example single option:

24. Type of home

[x] single family home

[ ] apartment

[ ] makeshift house

[ ] tent

[ ] other

Example of multiple option

36. Communication

[x] landline

[ ] Internet

[x] mobile phone

[ ] none

Example of multiple option with various options

37. Commercial activities or services in home

[ ] none

[ ] shop   legal [ ] illegal [ ]

[x] workshop   legal [x] illegal [ ]

[ ] office   legal [ ] Illegal [ ]

[ ] service   legal [ ] illegal [ ]

Example with numbers

7. Those currently studying according to age group

Less than 5 years old	T [3] M [2] W [1]
5-16 years old	T [7] M [3] W [4]
17-25 years old	T [6] M [5] W [1]
+25 years old	T [1] M [0] W [1]

Example of single option combined with numbers

2. Food store   (store, bodega, etc.)

[ ] non-existent

[X] exist   T [3]

Example of Others

15. Chronic illnesses

Cancer	T [ ]
Diabetes	T [2]
AIDS	T [1]
Heart disease	T [ ]
Hepatitis	T [ ]
Leukemia	T [ ]
Epilepsy	T [ ]
Tuberculosis	T [ ]
Hypertension	T [ ]
Asthma	T [ ]
Alzheimer's disease, dementia	T [ ]
Mental illness	T [ ]
Others *Crohn's disea*.......................	T [1]

FIRST MODEL FORM FOR COLLECTING INFORMATION FOR DATABASE (RESIDENTS, THEIR HOME AND PARTICIPATION LEVELS)

Person responsible for carrying out survey...

Telephone ....Email..

....

Address of the household surveyed..

Name of the head of the family...M [   ] W [   ]

Number of people in household   [   ]

....

I. Information about residents

PERSONAL CHARACTERISTICS

1. Age

0-6	T [ ] M [ ] W [ ]
6-12	T [ ] M [ ] W [ ]
12-25	T [ ] M [ ] W [ ]
25-40	T [ ] M [ ] W [ ]
40-60	T [ ] M [ ] W [ ]
60-80	T [ ] M [ ] W [ ]
80+	T [ ] M [ ] W [ ]

2. Civil status

single	T [ ] M [ ] W [ ]
married	T [ ] M [ ] W [ ]
de facto	T [ ] M [ ] W [ ]
widow/er	T [ ] M [ ] W [ ]
divorced	T [ ] M [ ] W [ ]

3. Nationality

citizen born in the country	T [ ]
citizen born overseas	T [ ]
non-citizen	T [ ]
Undocumented foreigner	T [ ]

4. Ethnicity

Ethnic background/s

total   [ ]

Which one?..

5. Do you feel you are discriminated against due to your ethnic background

[   ] Yes

[ ] No

EDUCATION

6. Level of education

none	T [ ] M [ ] W [ ]
did not finish primary school.	T [ ] M [ ] W [ ]
finished primary school	T [ ] M [ ] W [ ]
did not finish high school	T [ ] M [ ] W [ ]
finished high school	T [ ] M [ ] W [ ]
technical college	T [ ] M [ ] W [ ]
superior technical college□	T [ ] M [ ] W [ ]
did not finish university	T [ ] M [ ] W [ ]
university	T [ ] M [ ] W [ ]
postgraduate	T [ ] M [ ] W [ ]

7. Those currently studying according to age group

Less than 5 years old	T [ ] M [ ] W [ ]
5-16 years old	T [ ] M [ ] W [ ]
17-25 years old	T [ ] M [ ] W [ ]
+25 years old	T [ ] M [ ] W [ ]

EMPLOYMENT

8. Employment situation (over 16 years age)

Permanent work	T [ ] M [ ] W [ ] Y [ ]
Temporary work	T [ ] M [ ] W [ ] Y [ ]
Unemployed with benefits	T [ ] M [ ] W [ ] Y [ ]
Unemployed without benefits	T [ ] M [ ] W [ ] Y [ ]
Retired	T [ ] M [ ] W [ ]
Not working	T [ ] M [ ] W [ ] Y [ ]

9. Is there anyone under the age of 16 working?

working	T [ ]
occasionally working	T [ ]
previously worked	T [ ]
have never worked	T [ ]

10. Occupational sector

public sector	T [ ]
private sector	T [ ]
self-employed	T [ ]
other	T [ ]

11. Occupation

electrician	T [ ] M [ ] W [ ]
mechanic	T [ ] M [ ] W [ ]
painter	T [ ] M [ ] W [ ]
bricklayer	T [ ] M [ ] W [ ]

farmer	T [ ] M [ ] W [ ]
gardener	T [ ] M [ ] W [ ]
miner	T [ ] M [ ] W [ ]
fisher	T [ ] M [ ] W [ ]
rancher	T [ ] M [ ] W [ ]
teacher	T [ ] M [ ] W [ ]
health worker	T [ ] M [ ] W [ ]
transport	T [ ] M [ ] W [ ]
retail	T [ ] M [ ] W [ ]
accountant	T [ ] M [ ] W [ ]
economist	T [ ] M [ ] W [ ]
lawyer	T [ ] M [ ] W [ ]
recreation	T [ ] M [ ] W [ ]
sports	T [ ] M [ ] W [ ]
telecommunications	T [ ] M [ ] W [ ]
artesian	T [ ] M [ ] W [ ]
arts	T [ ] M [ ] W [ ]
others	T [ ] M [ ] W [ ]

12. Organizational membership

trade union	T [ ]
business organization	T [ ]
professionals organization	T [ ]
student organization	T [ ]

13. Family income

[ ] none

[ ] less than the minimum salary

[ ] minimum salary

[ ] between 2-5 minimum salaries

[ ] more than 5 minimum salaries

[ ] more than 10 minimum salaries

[ ] more than 20 minimum salaries

14. Number of people contributing to family income

men	T [ ]
women	T [ ]
total	T [ ]

HEALTH RELATED ISSUES AND OTHERS

15. People with illnesses

cancer	T [ ]
diabetes	T [ ]
AIDS	T [ ]
heart condition	T [ ]
hepatitis	T [ ]
leukaemia	T [ ]

epilepsy	T [	]
tuberculosis	T [	]
hypertension	T [	]
asthma	T [	]
Alzheimer's, dementia	T [	]
mental illness	T [	]

other...

16. People with special capacities

Total number of persons T [ ]

17. People who need help/assistance

Total number of people   T [ ]

18. People suffering addictions

drug addiction	T [ ]
alcoholism	T [ ]
gambling	T [ ]
Total people with some kind of addiction	T [ ]

19. ¿Have there been any teenage pregnancies in the family?

currently	T [ ]
recently	T [ ]
a while ago	T [ ]

20. Girls at age of risk (11-16 years old)

Number of girls   T [ ]

SOURCES OF INFORMATION

21. Sources of information for the family (multiple options)

[   ] free-to-air television

[   ] pay-per-view television

[   ] community television

[   ] radio

[   ] community radio

[   ] newspapers

[   ] community newspapers

[   ] Internet

[   ] informational noticeboards

[   ] informational pamphlets

[   ] meetings with neighbors

[   ] none
[   ] others

II. Data regarding home

22. Floor space (m^2)   [   ]

23. Number of rooms [   ]

24. Type of home

[   ] single family home

[   ] apartment

[   ] makeshift house

[   ] tent

[   ] other

25. Form of tenancy

[   ] owner

[   ] rent

[   ] living without rent

[   ] illegal

26. State of building

[   ] good state

[   ] regular state

[   ] bad state

[   ] dangerous state

27. Bathroom or toilet

[   ] Yes, complete in the home

[   ] Yes, complete in nearby space

[   ] only toilet in home

[   ] only toilet in nearby space

[   ] latrine

[   ] none

28. Running water

[   ] Yes with meter

[   ] Yes without meter

[   ] No

29. Wastewater or sewage

[   ] public network (sewer)

[   ] septic tank

[   ] none existent

30. Electricity

[   ] public electricity network

[   ] own electrical plant

[   ] illegal connection to network

[   ] none

31. Gas

[   ] piped

[ ] bottle

[ ] none

32. Rubbish collection

[ ] collected at home

[ ] taken to a drop off point on the street

[ ] none

33. Cleanliness

[ ] clean

[ ] dirty

[ ] reasonable clean

34. Insects and rodents

[ ] present

[ ] none

35. Pets (multiple options)

[ ] for company (dogs, cats, etc)

[ ] other domestic animals (chicken, pigs etc.)

[ ] none

36. Communication (multiple options)

[ ] landline

[ ] Internet

[ ] mobile phone

[ ] none

37. Commercial activities or services in home

[ ] none

[ ] shop   legal [ ]   illegal [ ]

[ ] workshop   legal [ ]   illegal [ ]

[ ] office   legal [ ]   illegal [ ]

[ ] service   legal [ ]   illegal [ ]

38. Domestic equipment (multiple options)

[ ] wood or carbon-fired stove

[ ] gas or electric stove

[ ] oven

[ ] microwave oven

[ ] dishwasher

[ ] fridge

[ ] heater

[ ] hot water

[ ] air conditioner

[ ] computer

[ ] printer

[ ] television

[ ] satellite or cable connection[ ] DVD player

[ ] sound system

[ ] radio

3) Level of participation

39. People that participate in community organizations or activities (percentage)

	Total	Men	Women	Young	Children
community assemblies					
neighborhood association or similar organizations					
participatory budget and planning process					
elections					
sports activities and clubs					
cultural activities (choir,theater, etc,)					
excursions					
attending to the sick or elderly					
grandparents group					
health brigade					
community guard					
environmental group					
urban land committee					
volunteer work to help the community					
militia					
religious activities and groups					
political parties					
infants activities					
women's activities and organizations					
others					

40. How often do people participate in community organizations

Community organizations or activities	Always			Frequently			Occasionally			Rarely			Never		
	M	W	T	M	W	T	M	W	T	M	W	T	M	W	T
community assemblies															
neighborhood association or similar organizations															
participatory budget and planning process															
elections															
sports activities and clubs															
cultural activities (choir,theater, etc,)															
excursions															

Attending to the sick or elderly													
grandparents group													
health brigade													
community guard													
environmental group													
urban land committee													
volunteer work to help the community													
militia													
religious activities and groups													
political parties													
infants activities													
women's activities and organizations													
Others													

SECOND MODEL FORM: CONSOLIDATION IN TABLES OF INFORMATION COLLECTED FROM PREVIOUS FORM

I POPULATION. BASIC DATA

1. Population. Distribution by age group

Age	Men		Women		Total	
	No.	%	No.	%	No.	%
Less than 5						
5-16						
17-25						
26-40						
41-65						
66-80						
80+						
Total		100		100		100

2. Distribution of population above the age of 16 according to civil state

Marital status	Men		Women		Total	
	No.	%	No.	%	No.	%
Single						
Married						
De facto						
Widow/er						
Divorced						
Total, above the age of 16		100		100		100

3. Distribution of population according to nationality.

Nationality	No.	%
National citizen		
Foreign born citizen		
Foreign born permanent resident		
Illegal foreigner		
Total		100

4. Indigenous communities

Name of indigenous community	No.	%
Total, members of indigenous community		
Total, members of community		100

5. Level of discrimination (percentage of population)

	No.	%
Feel discriminated against		
Don't feel discriminated against		
Total, members of indigenous communities		100

6. Distribution of adult population (16+) according to level of education

Level of education	Men		Women		Total	
	No.	%	No.	%	No.	%
No education						
Did not complete primary school						
Completed primary school						
Did not complete high school						
Completed high school						
Did not complete technical college						
Completed technical college						
Did not complete university						
Completed university						
Completed postgraduate studies						
Total		100		100		100

7 a. Population currently studying according to age group

Age group	Men		Women		Total	
	Studying	total	Studying.	total	Studying	total
Less than 5						
5-16						
17-25						
25+						
Total, population studying						

7 b. Percentage of population studying according to age group

Age group	Men		Women		Total	
	No.	%	No.	%	No.	%
Less than 5						
5-16						
17-25						
25+						
Total population studying						

II POPULATION. EMPLOYMENT DATA.

8 a. Distribution of population above 25 years of age according to employment situation.

Age	Men		Women		Total	
	No.	%	No.	%	No.	%
Permanent work						
Temporary work						

Unemployed with benefits					
Unemployed without benefits					
Retired					
Not working					
Total		100		100		100

8 b. Employment and educational situation of youth

People 16-25 years ole	No.	%
Permanent work		
Temporary work		
Total working		
Have worked (unemployed)		
Total working or have worked		
Not working		
Studying		
Not working or studying		
Total youth		100

9 a. Child labor

Between 5-16 years of age	No.	%
Permanent work		
Temporary work		
Total minors working		
Total minors in the community		100

9 b. Extent of child labor

Homes	No.	%
Homes with minors working		
Total homes in community		100

10. Occupation, 16 years and over (as percentage of total population over the age of 16)

Occupational sector	No.	%
Public		
Private		
Self-employed		
Other		
Total number of people over 16 working		100

11. Vocation

Occupation	Men		Women		Total	
	No.	%	No.	%	No.	%
Electrician						
Mechanic						
Painter						
Bricklayer						

277

Farmer					
Gardener					
Miner					
Fisher					
Cattle rancher					
Teachers					
Health worker					
Transport worker					
Retail					
Accountant					
Economist					
Lawyer					
Recreation					
Sports					
Telecommunications					
Artisan					
Artist					
Others					
Total		100		100		100

12. Participation in employment association

Membership	No.	%
Trade union		
Business organization		
Professionals organization		
Student organization		
Total number of members		
Total population		100

13. Family income

Household income	Households	
	No.	%
Less than minimum wage		
Between 1 and 2 minimum wages		
Between 2-5 minimum wages		
Between 5-10 minimum wages		
Between 10-20 minimum wages		
20+ minimum wages		
Total number of households		100

14 a. Number of people in household contributing to family income

	Households	
	No.	%
One person		
Two people		

Three people		
Four people		
Five or more people		
Total number of households		100

14 b. People contributing to family income according to gender

	Households	
	No.	%
Only men		
More men than women		
Equal number of men and women		
More women than men		
Only women		
Total number of households		100

III POPULATION. HEALTH RELATED DATA

15 a. Incidents of chronic illness

Illness	No.	%
Cancer		
Diabetes		
AIDS		
Heart disease		
Hepatitis		
Leukemia		
Epilepsy		
Tuberculosis		
Hypertension		
Asthma		
Alzheimer's disease, dementia		
Mental illness		
others............................		
Total number of people with illnesses		
Total population		100

15 b. Households with people with chronic illnesses

Households with people with chronic illnesses	Households	
	No.	%
Cancer		
Diabetes		
AIDS		
Heart disease		
Hepatitis		
Leukemia		
Epilepsy		
Tuberculosis		
Hypertension		

Asthma		
Alzheimer's disease, dementia		
Mental illness		
others............................		
Total number of households with illnesses		
Total number of households		100

15 c. Households with chronic illnesses according to number of people with illnesses (as percentage of total household)

Number of people will chronic illnesses in household	Household	
	No.	%
None		
1 person		
2 people		
3 or more people		
Total number of households		100

16 a. People with special capacities or who need help/assistance

Population	No.	%
With special needs		
Need help/assistance		
Total population		100

16 b. Households with people with special capacities.

Number of people with special capacities in household	Households	
	No.	%
None		
1 person		
2 people		
3 or more people		
Total number of households with people with special capacities		
Total number of households		100

17. Households with people who need help/assistance.

Number of people who need help/assistance in household	Households	
	No.	%
None		
1 person		
2 people		
3 or more people		
Total number of households with people who need help/assistance		
Total number of households		100

18.a. People suffering addictions.

Population	No.	%
Drug addiction		
Alcoholism		
Gambling		
Total number of people with some kind of addiction		
Total population		100

18 b. Households with people suffering drug addiction

Number of drug addicts in household	Household	
	No.	%
None		
1 person		
2 people		
3 or more people		
Total number of households with drug addicts		
Total number of households		

18 c. Households with people suffering alcohol addiction.

Number of alcoholics in household	Households	
	No.	%
None		
1 person		
2 people		
3 or more people		
Total number of households with alcoholics		
Total number of households		

18 d. Households with people suffering gambling addiction

Number of gambling addicts in household	Households	
	No.	%
None		
1 person		
2 people		
3 or more people		
Total number of households with gambling addicts		
Total number of households		

18 e. Households with people suffering some kind of addiction

Number of addicts in household	Household	
	No.	%
None		
1 person		
2 people		
3 or more people		
Total number of households with addicts		

Total number of households		

19. Teenage pregnancy. History

History of teenage pregnancies in household	Households	
	No.	%
Currently		
Recently		
A while ago		
Never		
Total		100

20 a. Teenage pregnancy. Risk

Girls at age of risk of teenage pregnancy	Households	
	No.	%
None		
1 girl		
2 girls		
3 or more girls		
Total		100

20 b. Teenage pregnancy. Increasing risk

Girls at age of risk of teenage pregnancy in households with history of teenage pregnancy	Households	
	No.	%
None		
1 girl		
2 girls		
3 or more girls		

21. Sources of information for the family

Sources of information in the household	Household	
	No.	%
free-to-air television		
pay-per-view television		
community television		
radio		
Community radio		
newspapers		
Community newspapers		
Internet		
informational noticeboards		
informational pamphlets		
meetings with neighbors		
others		
None		
Total number of households		

IV DATA REGARDING HOUSING

22 a- Distribution of housing according to number of residents

Residents	No.	%
1 person		
2 people		
3-5 people		
5-10 people		
10+ people		
Total		

22 b. Distribution of housing according to floor space

Floor space	No.	%
Less than 20 m²		
21-60 m²		
61-100 m²		
101-140 m²		
+ 140 m²		
Total		100

23. Distribution of housing according to number of rooms

Number of rooms	No.	%
Studio		
1 room		
2 rooms		
3 rooms		
4 rooms		
4+ rooms		
Total		100

24. Distribution by type of home

Type of home	No.	%
single family home		
apartment		
makeshift house		
Tent		
Other		
Total		100

25. Distribution by form of tenancy

Tenancy	No.	%
Owner		
Rent		
Living without rent		
Illegal		

		100
Total		

26. Distribution by state of building

State of building	No.	%
Good state		
Regular state		
Bad state		
Dangerous state		
Total		100

27. Bathroom installations

Have Bathroom or toilet	No.	%
Yes, complete in the home		
Yes, complete in nearby space		
only toilet in home		
only toilet in nearby space		
latrine		
None		
Total		100

28. Running water in home

Running water	No.	%
None		
Yes, with meter		
Yes, without meter		
Total		

29. Wastewater or sewage

System	No.	%
public network (sewer)		
septic tank		
Non-existent		
Total		100

30. Electricity

System	No.	%
public electricity network		
own electrical plant		
illegal connection to network		
None		
Total		100

31. Gas

System	No.	%
Piped		

Bottle		
None		
Total		100

32. Rubbish collection

System	No.	%
collected at home		
taken to a drop off point on the street		
None		
Total		100

33. Cleanliness

State of home	No.	%
Clean		
Reasonably clean		
Dirty		
Total		100

34. Insects and rodents

Presence of insects and rodents	No.	%
Present		
None		
Total		100

35. Domestic animals

Presence of domestic animals	No.	%
Pets		
Pets and other domestic animals		
Only other domestic animals (pigs, chickens etc.)		
None		
Total		100

36. Communication

System	No.	%
Landline		
Internet		
Mobile phone		
None		
Total		100

37. Commercial activities in household (as percentage of all households).

Activity	Legal		Illegal		Total	
	No.	%	No.	%	No.	%
None						

Shop						
workshop						
Office						
Service						
Total						100

38. Domestic equipment

Equipment	No.	%
wood or carbon-fired stove		
gas or electric stove		
oven		
microwave oven		
dishwasher		
Fridge		
Washing machine		
Dryer		
Heater		
hot water		
air conditioner		
computer		
Printer		
television		
satellite or cable connection		
DVD player		
sound system		
Radio		
Total		100

V LEVELS OF PARTICIPATION

39 People that participate in community organizations or activities

Community organization or activity	Men		Women		Youth		Children		Total	
	No.	%	No.	%	No.	%	No.	%	No.	..%..
community assembly										100
Neighborhood association or similar organizations										
participatory budget and planning process										
Elections										
sports activities and clubs										
cultural activities (choir,theater, etc,)										
Excursions										
Attending to the sick or elderly										
health brigade										
community guard										
environmental group										
urban land committee										

volunteer work to help the community										
Militia										
religious activities and groups										
political parties										
women's activities and organizations										
infants activities										
Others										

40 a. Frequency of participation of men in community activities and organizations

Community activity of organization	Always		Frequently		Occasionally		Rarely		Never	
	No.	%	No.	%	No.	%	No.	%	No.	%
community assembly										
Neighborhood association or similar organizations										
participatory budget and planning process										
Elections										
sports activities and clubs										
cultural activities (choir,theater, etc,)										
Excursions										
Attending to the sick or elderly										
health brigade										
community guard										
environmental group										
urban land committee										
volunteer work to help the community										
Militia										
religious activities and groups										
political parties										
infants activities										
Others										

40 b. Frequency of participation of women in community activities and organizations

Community activity of organization	Always		Frequently		Occasionally		Rarely		Never	
	No.	%	No.	%	No.	%	No.	%	No.	%
community assembly										
Neighborhood association or similar organizations										
participatory budget and planning process										
Elections										
sports activities and clubs										
cultural activities (choir,theater, etc,)										
Excursions										
Attending to the sick or elderly										
health brigade										

community guard										
environmental group										
urban land committee										
volunteer work to help the community										
Militia										
religious activities and groups										
political parties										
women's activities and organizations										
infants activities										
Others										

40 c. Frequency of participation of people in community activities and organizations

Community activity of organization	Always		Frequently		Occasionally		Rarely		Never	
	No.	%	No.	%	No.	%	No.	%	No.	%
community assembly										
Neighborhood association or similar organizations										
participatory budget and planning process										
Elections										
sports activities and clubs										
cultural activities (choir,theater, etc,)										
Excursions										
Attending to the sick or elderly										
health brigade										
community guard										
environmental group										
urban land committee										
volunteer work to help the community										
Militia										
religious activities and groups										
political parties										
women's activities and organizations										
infants activities										
Others										

THIRD MODEL FORM: FOR SOCIAL EQUIPMENT AVAILABLE TO THE COMMUNITY

• FOOD

1. **Bakery**

[ ] non-existent

[ ] exist   T [ ]

2. Food store   (store, bodega, etc.)

[ ] non-existent

[ ] exist   T [ ]

3. Supermarket

[ ] non-existent

[ ] exist   T [ ]

4. Megamarket

[ ] in the community

[ ] in a community adjacent

[ ] in the municipality

5. Farmers or municipal market

[ ] in the community

[ ] in a community adjacent

[ ] in the municipality

• EDUCATION INSTALLATIONS

6. Pre-school

[ ] good state   T [ ]   Available places [ ]

[ ] regular state   T [ ]   Available places [ ]

[ ] bad state   T [ ]   Available places [ ]

[ ] total   T [ ]   Available places [ ]

7..Primary school

[ ] good state   T [ ]   Available places [ ]

[ ] regular state   T [ ]   Available places [ ]

[ ] bad state   T [ ]   Available places [ ]

[ ] total   T [ ]   Available places [ ]

8. High school

[ ] good state   T [ ]   Available places [ ]

[ ] regular state   T [ ]   Available places [ ]

[ ] bad state   T [ ]   Available places [ ]

[ ] total   T [ ]   Available places [ ]

9. Center for professional training

[ ] in the community   T [ ]   Available places [ ]

[ ] in a community adjacent   T [ ]   Available places [ ]

[ ] in the municipality   T [ ]   Available places [ ]

10. University

[ ] in the community

[ ] in a community adjacent

[ ] in the municipality

• **HEALTH INSTALLATIONS**

11. Health center

[ ] good state   T [ ]

[ ] regular state   T [ ]

[ ] bad state   T [ ]

[ ] non-existent

12. Emergency unit

[ ] in the community

[ ] in a community adjacent

[ ] in the municipality

13. Hospital

[ ] in the community

[ ] in a community adjacent

[ ] in the municipality

14. Pharmacy

[ ] in the community

[ ] in a community adjacent

[ ] in the municipality

• **SECURITY**

15. Dangerous areas

[ ] Yes

    Where.................

[ ] No

16. Armed groups or gang

[   ] Operate in the community

[   ] Affect the community

17. Members of the community active in armed gangs/groups

[ ] Yes, they even have a base in the community

[ ] There are a few, but they are isolated cases

[ ] No

18. Police patrol or police post

[ ] non-existent

[ ] exist

which one?

19. Neighborhood patrol

[ ] non-existent

[ ] exist

which one?

POLLUTION

20. Air pollution

[ ] None

[ ] Yes

    Where ....

21. Noise pollution

[ ] None

[ ] Yes

Where ....

22. Water pollution

[ ] None

[ ] Yes

Where ....

COMMUNICATIONS

23. Public transport

[ ] good state   T [ ]

[ ] regular state   T [ ]

[ ] bad state   T [ ]

[ ] non-existent

24. Frequency

[ ] regularly passes several times

[ ] regularly passes a few times

[ ] rarely pass by

25. State of roads

[ ] % of asphalted roads in good state

[ ] % of asphalted roads in reasonable state

[ ] % of asphalted roads in bad state

[ ] % of dirt road in good state

[ ] % of dirt road in reasonable state

[ ] % of dirt road in bad state

[ ] % only pedestrian access

26. Street lighting

good   [ ]%

regular   [ ]%

bad   [ ]%

non-existent   [ ]%

• **CULTURE AND SPORTS**

27. Cultural patrimony

[ ] No

[ ] Yes

Which one ?..

28. Cultural center

[ ] in the community

[ ] in a community adjacent

[ ] in the municipality

29. Public library

[ ] in the community

[ ] in a community adjacent

[ ] in the municipality

30. Center for elderly (grandparents' club)

[ ] in the community

[ ] in a community adjacent

[ ] in the municipality

31. Sports field

[ ] in the community

[ ] in a community adjacent

[ ] in the municipality

32. Pool

[ ] in the community

[ ] in a community adjacent

[ ] in the municipality

RECREATION

33. Plazas and gardens

[ ] No

[ ] Yes   T [ ]

   with infants' toys   Number   T [ ]

   without infants' toys   Number   T [ ]

34. Cafes

[ ] No

[ ] Yes   T [ ]

35, Restaurants

[ ] No

[ ] Yes   T [ ]

36. Cinema, Theater

[ ] in the community

[ ] in a community adjacent

[ ] in the municipality

37, Hotel
[ ] in the community

[ ] in a community adjacent

[ ] in the municipality

38 . Religious faiths with centers of worship in the community
Which ones ....

....

....

FINANCIAL SERVICES

39. Bank branches

In the community	Nº [ ]
In adjacent communities	Nº [ ]
In the municipality	Nº [ ]

40. Automatic teller machine (ATM)

[ ] None

[ ] Yes   Nº [ ]

41. Loan offices

[ ] None

[ ] Yes   Nº [ ]

ECONOMIC ACTIVITIES IN THE COMMUNITY

42. Industry companies

[ ] Large companies with   [ ] workers

[ ] Medium companies with   [ ] workers

[ ] Small companies with   [ ] workers

[ ] Workshops with   [ ] workers

43. Service companies

[ ] Large companies with   [ ] workers

[ ] Medium companies with   [ ] workers

[ ] Small companies with   [ ] workers

44. Agricultural activities

[ ] Large farms with   [ ] workers

[ ] Medium farms with   [ ] workers

[ ] Small farms with   [ ] workers

45. Fishing activities

[ ] large fishing vessel with   [ ] workers

[ ] small fishing vessel with   [ ] workers

[ ] boat with   [ ] workers

46. Extractive activities

[   ] Large companies with   [   ] workers

[   ] Medium companies with   [   ] workers

[   ] Small companies with   [   ] workers

EXTERNAL SOURCES OF EMPLOYMENT

47. Identify, if any, the external companies in the community that employ 10% or more of the local labor force.
....

SOURCES OF COMMUNITY INFORMATION.

48, Media

television network	Nº [ ]
cable television	Nº [ ]
community television	Nº [ ]
radio	Nº [ ]
community radio	Nº [ ]
newspapers	Nº [ ]
community newspapers	Nº [ ]
internet	Nº [ ]
informational panels	Nº [ ]
informational pamphlets	Nº [ ]
others	Nº [ ]

• COMMUNITY SOLIDARITY

49. Experiences involving community solidarity (multiple options)

[   ] community food halls

[   ] shelters for families or people without homes

[   ] blood donations

[   ] collection of used clothes

[   ] others

50. Natural community leaders

[   ] Exist   How many? [   ]

[   ] Do not exist

EXTERNAL SUPPORT

51. ¿Did the community receive institutional support for a particular project or initiative?..
....

52. ¿Did the community receive support from NGOs for a particular project or initiative?..
....

53. ¿Did the community receive any other type of support?...

FOURTH MODEL FORM WITH SOME USEFUL DATA FOR MORE CLOSELY INVESTIGATING THE PROBLEM OF UNEMPLOYMENT

In the form to collect information door-to-door, we could add the following questions to the more general ones listed above

I QUESTIONS REGARDING EMPLOYMENT SITUATION

A. Type of labor relations

Permanent wage	T [ ]	**M** [ ]	W [ ]
Temporary wage	T [ ]	M [ ]	W [ ]
Self-employed	T [ ]	M [ ]	W [ ]
Help from family	T [ ]	M [ ]	W [ ]
Business owner with less than 5 workers	T [ ]	M [ ]	W [ ]
Business owner with 5 or more workers	T [ ]	M [ ]	W [ ]

B. Workplace

at home	T [ ]	M [ ]	W [ ]
walking	T [ ]	M [ ]	W [ ]
in permanent establishment	T [ ]	M [ ]	W [ ]
in no permanent establishment	T [ ]	M [ ]	W [ ]

C. Transport mode to get to work

car	T [ ]	M [ ]	W [ ]
public transport	T [ ]	M [ ]	W [ ]
someone else's car	T [ ]	M [ ]	W [ ]
taxi	T [ ]	M [ ]	W [ ]
motorbike	T [ ]	M [ ]	W [ ]
bicycle	T [ ]	M [ ]	W [ ]
walk	T [ ]	M [ ]	W [ ]
others	T [ ]	M [ ]	W [ ]

D. Time taken to travel to work

less than 15 minutes	T [ ]	M [ ]	W [ ]
15-30 minutes	T [ ]	M [ ]	W [ ]
30-60 minutes	T [ ]	M [ ]	W [ ]
more than 60 minutes	T [ ]	M [ ]	W [ ]

E. Hours of work a day

less than 4 hours	T [ ]	M [ ]	W [ ]
4-6 hours	T [ ]	M [ ]	W [ ]
6-8 hours	T [ ]	M [ ]	W [ ]
8-10 hours	T [ ]	M [ ]	W [ ]
10-12 hours	T [ ]	M [ ]	W [ ]
more than 12 hours	T [ ]	M [ ]	W [ ]

F. Workdays a week

all week including public holidays	T [ ]	M [ ]	W [ ]
all week except public holiday and Sundays	T [ ]	M [ ]	W [ ]
Monday to Friday (except public holidays	T [ ]	M [ ]	W [ ]
less than 5 days a week	T [ ]	M [ ]	W [ ]

G. Income (16 years and over)

none	T [ ]	M [ ]	W [ ]
less than the minimum salary	T [ ]	M [ ]	W [ ]
minimum salary	T [ ]	M [ ]	W [ ]
between 2-5 minimum salaries	T [ ]	M [ ]	W [ ]
more than 5 minimum salaries	T [ ]	M [ ]	W [ ]
more than 10 minimum salaries	T [ ]	M [ ]	W [ ]

H. Type of income

daily	T [ ]	M [ ]	W [ ]
weekly	T [ ]	M [ ]	W [ ]
fortnightly	T [ ]	M [ ]	W [ ]
monthly	T [ ]	M [ ]	W [ ]
occasional	T [ ]	M [ ]	W [ ]
none	T [ ]	M [ ]	W [ ]

Other possible areas to investigate: media coverage, school programs dedicated to ideology of work

II. TABLES TO CONSOLIDATE INFORMATION REGARDING EMPLOYMENT SITUATION IN THE COMMUNITY AS A WHOLE

A. Type of labor relations

Type	Men		Women		Total	
	No.	%	No.	%	No.	%
Permanent wage						
Temporary wage						
Self-employed						
Help from family						
Business owner with less than 5 workers						
Business owner with 5 or more workers						
Total number of people working		100		100		100

B. Workplace

Workplace	Men		Women		Total	
	No.	%	No.	%	No.	%
home						
walking						
permanent establishment						
Non-permanent establishment						
Total number of people working		100		100		100

C. Transport mode to get to work

Transport mode	Men		Women		Total	
	No.	%	No.	%	No.	%
car						
public transport						
someone else's car						
Taxi						
motorbike						
Bicycle						
Walk						
Others						
Total number of people working outside of home						100

D. Time taken to travel to work

Time	Men		Women		Total	
	No.	%	No.	%	No.	%
less than 15 minutes						
15-30 minutes						
30-60 minutes						
more than 60 minutes						

Total number of people working outside the home		100		100		100

E. Hours of work a day

Length of workday	Men		Women		Total	
	No.	%	No.	%	No.	%
less than 4 hours						
4-6 hours						
6-8 hours						
8-10 hours						
10-12 hours						
12+ hours						
Total number of people working		100		100		100

F. Workdays

Workdays	Men		Women		Total	
	No.	%	No.	%	No.	%
all week including public holidays						
all week except public holiday and Sundays						
Monday to Friday (except public holiday)						
less than 5 days a week						
Total number of people working		100		100		100

G. Household Income (16 years and over)

Income	Men		Women		Total	
	No.	%	No.	%	No.	%
None						
less than the minimum salary						
minimum salary						
between 2-5 minimum salaries						
between 5-10 minimum salaries						
more than 10 minimum salaries						
Total number of workers 16 years or over		100		100		100

H. Type of income

Period of time	Men		Women		Total	
	No.	%	No.	%	No.	%
Daily						
weekly						
fortnightly						
monthly						
occasional						
Total number of people with an income		100		100		100

APPENDIX II
SOME MOTIVATING QUESTIONS TO FORMULATE THE ASPIRATIONS IN A COMMUNITY

a) Community organization and human relations

Do you think your community is well organized?

How does your community function?

Have the existing organizations succeeded in involving all those wanting to participate, regardless of religious or political beliefs?

Are the natural leaders of the community involved in them?

Are the committees and working groups functioning?

Was the socio-economic census carried out in a satisfactory manner?

How are the human relations in your community? Does harmony and solidarity exist among people?

Are people isolated from one another? Are they solely motivated by personal interests?

Are the elderly attended to?

Is there a sense of belonging to the territory, harmony, respect, solidarity, justice and fraternity?

What is the situation of children in the community?

b) Economy

To whom does the land in the territory belong? Is it in the hands of those who work it? Is it shared around in an equitable manner?

What do you think the lives of workers in the community should be like? Do they all have a dignified job?

Are there any artisans in your community? Do you think they should remain in the situation they are currently in or do you wish they were organized?

Could the artisans be collaborating with the rest of the community in some way?

Would it be possible and convenient to undertake some productive initiatives in your community?

Is your community very consumerist?

Is it very individualist?

Where do the people who live in your community usually buy their food? Would you like to have a better system for distributing food?

c) Culture

What are the most important cultural activities in your community? How are they organized? What problems currently exist in this regard?

Are there any cultural traditions that need to be re-established?

Do children know of these traditions and participate in them?

Are there enough spaces to develop cultural activities?

Are the necessary technological instruments available to help spread culture in the community? (Video projector, sound system, TV, DVD burner).

d) Neighborhood safety

Do you feel that your community is safe?

Does organized crime exist in the community?

Do you know of experiences in other communities that could be applied to yours to make it safer?

Is your community ready in the case of a natural disaster?

Is your community ready to defend itself were external forces to try to disturb the lives of residents?

e) Sports

Are there enough sports facilities? What condition are they currently in?

Are competitions for children and others held?

Are there any sports stars in your community? Do they play any role in the community? Do they spend time with the local children and teenagers?

Are there any sports clubs or organizations?

f) Basic services (water, street lighting, rubbish collection, public transport)

Are basic services functioning well in your community? Do all residents have access to them?

What is the state of the roads in your community?

Do the traffic lights work?

Is it easy to move from one part of the community to another, and to access basic services (schools, hospitals, etc.) from where you live?

g) Infrastructure and town planning

Are the streets and laneways pleasant to walk through in your community?

Are the streets well lit?

Can you walk without danger of tripping or falling due to cracks and potholes?

Is it easy to find an address, plaza or school?

Are there enough green spaces?

h) Health

Is yours a health community? Does it have a medical clinic?

Does the health committee function well? What could we aspire to in this regard?

Are there people in the community trained in the area of healthcare and first aid?

If someone needs an injection, where can they go? Is there a pharmacy available?

Do schools run health classes for students? Are they running campaigns against alcoholism and drugs? What it be a good idea if they did so?

Are there any means available for ensuring that ~~educational~~ health education campaigns reach every household?

Are there any mosquitos or other animals that carry diseases? Should we seek to run a good preventive health campaign?

i) Education

Do all school-aged children attend school?

Is there a primary school, kindergarten and childcare center in the community?

Do you think that residents allow themselves to be influenced by the messages carried in the media?

Does a library exist in the community?

Have any training courses been held, or are they currently being held, in the community?

Is there sufficient comprehension among residents of how important education is for the future of the younger generations?

Do you believe that the values of altruism, honesty and solidarity are practiced in your community?

Is there a strong connection between the community and the school? Are teachers given encouragement from the community? Does the community publicly recognize the achievements of the more distinguished students in anyway?

j) Housing

Does everyone in the community live in a dignified home?

Does overcrowding exist or does every family have a home?

Are the facades of houses painted in your community?

How does urban rubbish collection function? Are public places kept clean?

Do you think enough green spaces exist in your community?

APPENDIX III.

FORM TO EVALUATE A PROJECT

843. It is not enough to come up with good projects if they simply remain as ideas on paper or are not carried out correctly. That is why monitoring and evaluating projects is a fundamental step. Unfortunately, there are many more proposals for how to design a project and evaluate if they have been carried out correctly, than there are tools to evaluate its results and, in particular, evaluate the transformation of the people who participated in the project. There are even fewer tools to measure what it meant to people to actively participate in the planning process in which it was decided what projects would form part of the plan.

844. To help with this we have designed a form based on a very simple project (a plaza in a small community, which we have described previously) as an example of what we are talking about. Our idea is that each group that participates in the execution of a project carries out an evaluation of that project. For this purpose, we suggest using the form below.

845. The form will begin with a **Verification of expected results (1)**, which will allow us to determine whether the finished project coincides with the initial project or if deviations have occurred. This verification is essential when a third party (private company, public agency, etc.) has carried out the project. It can help us ensure that no voluntary or involuntary deviation has occurred that has not been authorized by the territorial entity, in terms of the initial contract and any agreed to modifications. Even in the case of directly executed projects (as is the case with our plaza) it is important to carry out this evaluation to ensure that the project has been carried out as expected.

846. In our example, we will use Table 1 from Chapter VI to evaluate the results. This table tells us which elements were to be included in the project of the plaza: streetlights, sprinklers, benches, infants' slide, sandpit, trees, grass, flowerbeds, etc. We can compare this with the final product to make sure everything has been installed. In terms of things like pathways, grass areas, flower beds, etc., we can use the draft design of the plaza used for the project to mark any changes that occurred in its final design, highlighting the reasons why these changes were made and whether previous authorization was given for the changes.

847. For more complex projects, we should use the technical specifications included in the list of conditions to determine if the finished product complies with the initial project, particularly in the case of projects that are indirectly executed.

848. Once we have finished this step, we should carry out an **Evaluation of the results (2)**. Here we should analyze whether the final product has contributed to satisfying the aspirations of the population, in this case in terms of more spaces for recreation. It is worth carrying out this evaluation at three different levels: a) *Evaluation of finished product* – that is, if it was completed correctly or if errors or defects have been detected during the planning or executing process. We are dealing here with technical errors or defects in terms of the plaza's design; b) *Level to which the project satisfies the aspiration of having spaces and forms of healthy recreation* and c) *Impact of the project on the community*.

849. Finally, we have made an effort to carry out a **Systemization of the experience (3)**, analyzing: how the team responsible for the project functioned; if it carried out its required tasks well; if residents contributed volunteer labor to the level that was hoped for; if the calculation of costs was correct; ifs the necessary inputs were obtained; and, in as exhaustive a manner as possible, how

each programmed activity was carried out. Although this point can seem somewhat excessive, we believe that it can be useful as a process for learning for future projects.

Form to evaluate a project

1. Verification of expected results

When comparing the initially projected elements with what was finally achieved, we can see that some are missing, but others were achieved.

Table comparing elements that should form part of the plaza with elements used in the project

Element	Projected amount	Actual amount
Street lights	5	4 (1 missing)
Sprinklers	2	1 (1 missing)
Benches	7	7
Infants' slide	1	1
Children's swing	3	4 (1 more than projected)
Sandpit	1	1
Trees	11	13 (2 extra ones were donated)
Hedges	20	20
Grass	50	50
Flowerbeds	20	20

2. Evaluation of results

a) Objective evaluation of finished project

Does it have the required number of pathways?

More than enough [   ] correct amount [   ] not enough [   ]

Does it have the required number of benches?

More than enough [   ] correct amount [   ] not enough [   ]

Is it sufficiently lit up?

More than enough [   ] correct amount [   ] not enough [   ]

Are there enough sprinklers?

More than enough [   ] correct amount [   ] not enough [   ]

Are there enough trees?

More than enough [   ] correct amount [   ] not enough [   ]

Is there grass on all the required areas?

More than enough [   ] correct amount [   ] not enough [   ]

Where enough flowers planted?

More than enough [   ] correct amount [   ] not enough [   ]

Are there enough children's toys?

More than enough [　] correct amount [　] not enough [　]

Other detected defects or errors ....

Suggestions to improve the plaza ....

b) Does it meet the aspiration of having spaces and equipment for healthy recreation?

Completely [　] partially [　] barely [　] no [　]

How many people will use it?

Everyone [　]　a majority of the people [　] an important number of residents [　]　only some [　]

How many children who previously played on the road today play in the plaza?

Few [　] half [　]　more than half [　] all [　]

Briefly describe the use you have observed of the plaza during the day and week
....

c) How has the project impacted on the community?

Has the project and its significance for the community been evaluated in an assembly? Yes [　] No [　]

Are people happy with having a new space for recreation?　Yes [　] No [　]

Has a billboard been placed at the entrance to the plaza to explain that it is the result of the participatory planning process? Yes [　] No [　]

Has a group or commission been created to look after the maintenance of the plaza and to water the plants? Yes [　] No [　]

How well has it been maintained?　Good [　]　regular [　] bad [　]

Are there any other ideas of how it might impact on the community?
....
....
....

—

3. Systematization of the experience

Behavior of the team responsible for the project

Very good [　]　good [　]　regular [　]　bad [　]

Score 1 = lowest, 5 = highest	1	2	3	4	5	Final score
Correctly informed the population about the project						
Asked people for their opinions about how to improve the project						
Obtained the necessary estimated funds via a collection						
Called on people to volunteer their labor at an appropriate time						
Correctly distributed tasks						
Did a good check over of the tasks carried out						
Carried out activities to encourage volunteers						

Bought or found in time the necessary inputs					
Negotiated well with higher up authorities to obtain support on certain issues					
Communicated well with the people					
Was sufficiently capable of delegating and not supplanting the work of the people					
Maintained an oversight document					

Volunteer labor

Was the amount of required labor correctly estimated? Yes [ ] No [ ]

How was the response to the call for volunteers in the case of Men [M]; Women [W]; Youth [Y]; Children [C]?

[ ] good   M [ ] W [ ] Y [ ] C [ ]

[ ] regular   M [ ] W [ ] Y [ ] C [ ]

[ ] bad   M [ ] W [ ] Y [ ] C [ ]

How efficient was it?

[ ] good   M [ ] W [ ] Y [ ] C [ ]

[ ] regular   M [ ] W [ ] Y [ ] C [ ]

[ ] bad   M [ ] W [ ] Y [ ] C [ ]

What was participation like?

[ ] good   M [ ] W [ ] Y [ ] C [ ]

[ ] regular   M [ ] W [ ] Y [ ] C [ ]

[ ] bad   M [ ] W [ ] Y [ ] C [ ]

Did lunches arrive on time? Yes [ ] No [ ]

Did the people who participated in volunteer labor receive some kind of recognition for their work? Yes [ ] No [ ]

What?...

....

Costs

Were costs correctly estimated?   Yes [ ] No [ ]

Were the necessary funds collected?   Yes [ ] No [ ]

Did the funds arrive on time? Yes [ ] No [ ]

Materials

Were the necessary materials obtained?	Yes [ ]	No [ ]
Gravel		
Cement		
Sand		
Paint		
Rocks		

Were the necessary tools obtained?	Yes [ ]	No [ ]
Shovels		
Picks		
Hoes		
Rakes		

Big hammers		
Bricklayers pallets		
Paintbrushes		

Was the necessary machinery obtained?	Yes [ ] No [ ]	
Portable cement mixer		
Truck to transport materials		

Clean up of land

How well was the clean up carried out?

good [ ]   regular [ ]   bad [ ]

Was there a container to dispose of rubbish?

no [ ]   an insufficient one [ ]   yes [ ]

How accurate was the calculation of time required for this activity?

correctly [   ]   took longer [   ]   took less time [ ]

If it took longer, why was this the case?...

Trenches and pipes

How well was the excavation of trenches and installation of pipes for water done?

good [ ] regular [ ]   bad [ ]

How accurate was the calculation of time required for this activity?

correctly [ ] took longer [ ]   took less time [ ]

If it took longer, why was this the case?...

Electricity

How well was the electricity supply installed?

good [ ] regular [ ]   bad [ ]

Were the required tools obtained?

no [ ]   an insufficient amount [ ]   yes [ ]

Did all the inputs and materials arrive?

no [ ]   an insufficient amount [ ]   yes [ ]

How accurate was the calculation of time required for this activity?

correctly [ ] took longer [ ]   took less time [ ]

If it took longer, why was this the case?...

 Pathways

How well were the pathways installed?

good [ ] regular [ ]   bad [ ]

Were the required tools obtained?

no [ ]   an insufficient amount [ ]   yes [ ]

Did all the inputs and materials arrive?

no [ ]   an insufficient amount [ ]   yes [ ]

How accurate was the calculation of time required for this activity?

correctly [ ] took longer [ ]   took less time [ ]

If it took longer, why was this the case?...

....

Planting of trees, hedges and flowers

How well was this carried out?

good [ ]   regular [ ]   bad [ ]

Installation of benches

Were the required tools obtained?

no [ ]   an insufficient amount [ ]   yes [ ]

Did all the inputs and materials arrive?

no [ ]   an insufficient amount [ ]   yes [ ]

How accurate was the calculation of time required for this activity?

correctly [ ]   took longer [ ]   took less time [ ]

If it took longer, why was this the
case?...

Sandpit and playground

How well was this carried out?

good [ ]   regular [ ]   bad [ ]

Were the required tools obtained?

no [ ]   an insufficient amount [ ]   yes [ ]

Which ones were missing?
....

Did all the inputs and materials arrive?

no [ ]   an insufficient amount [ ]   yes [ ]

Which ones were missing?
....

How accurate was the calculation of time required for this activity?

correctly [ ]   took longer [ ]   took less time [ ]

If it took longer, why was this the
case?...

To finish

Would you like to add any further comments?
....
....
....

CPSIA information can be obtained
at www.ICGtesting.com
Printed in the USA
LVHW061920120419
614002LV00016B/133/P